Practical tips for developing your staff

PRACTICAL TIPS FOR LIBRARY AND INFORMATION PROFESSIONALS

This series provides a set of practical guides for the busy professional in need of inspiration. Sourced from experienced library and information practitioners, grounded in theory, yet not overwhelmed by it, the information in these guides will tell you what you need to know to make a quick impact in a range of topical areas of professional interest.

SERIES EDITOR: HELEN BLANCHETT
Subject specialist (scholarly communications), Jisc

After qualifying and working as a librarian in her early career, Helen worked for Jisc Netskills for 13 years providing training and working on a diverse range of projects across various sectors and then as librarian in the liaison team at Newcastle University. She has a keen interest in all aspects of information and digital literacy, and in supporting staff and students in their development.

PRACTICAL TIPS FOR LIBRARY AND INFORMATION PROFESSIONALS
SERIES EDITOR: HELEN BLANCHETT

Practical tips for developing your staff

Tracey Pratchett and Gil Young
with Carol Brooks, Lisa Jeskins
and Helen Monagle

facet
publishing

Published by Facet Publishing
7 Ridgmount Street, London WC1E 7AE
www.facetpublishing.co.uk

Facet Publishing is wholly owned by CILIP: the Chartered
Institute of Library and Information Professionals.

British Library Cataloguing in Publication Data
A catalogue record for this book is available from the British Library.

ISBN 978-1-78330-018-1 (paperback)
ISBN 978-1-78330-180-5 (hardback)
ISBN 978-1-78330-181-2 (e-book)

First published 2016

Text printed on FSC accredited material.

Typeset from author's files in 10/13 pt Palatino Linotype and Myriad Pro
by Facet Publishing Production.
Printed and made in Great Britain by CPI Group (UK) Ltd, Croydon,
CR0 4YY.

Every purchase of a Facet book helps to fund CILIP's
advocacy, awareness and accreditation programmes
for information professionals.

Contents

List of figures and tables

Figures

Tables

Acknowledgements

The authors would like to thank the many people who assisted them in writing this book. Without their generous support, which ranged from sharing their knowledge and experiences to providing personal examples from their own practice and offering up ideas and time, we would never have got it done. Thanks to you all.

All royalties from this book will be donated to LIHNN (Library and Information Health Network North West) to fulfil the aim of the network in encouraging and facilitating the continuing education and training of LKS staff in the North West.

The authors

Carol Brooks: Carol has over 30 years' experience in training and development in both libraries and with the Territorial Army. She is the founder of Chrysalis Development, www.chrysalisdevelopment.co.uk. Accredited to deliver training using the Jigsaw Discovery Tool, which she uses in many of her courses, she has a passion for investigating how we can use behavioural and learning tools to enable retention of learning.

Lisa Jeskins: Lisa is a freelance training consultant (www.lisajeskinstraining. com/) who loves creating and delivering interactive, memorable learning experiences. She primarily works with information professionals. As a Chartered Librarian with experience in a wide range of library roles, both in large university libraries and as a solo librarian, she understands the challenges that all levels of information professionals face. Lisa is Chair of the LILAC (Librarians' Information Literacy Conference) Committee and is the Conference Officer for the CILIP Information Literacy Group. She is a CILIP mentor for Chartership candidates and is currently working toward Fellowship.

Helen Monagle: Helen is a serials librarian at Manchester Metropolitan University. She successfully completed Chartership in July 2015 and graduated with a master's degree in Library and Information Management from Manchester Metropolitan University. Her interests include cataloguing, UX, facilitating access to e-resources, statistics and development opportunities for new professionals. She is one of the co-founders of NLPN (https:// nlpn.wordpress.com), a network for new and aspiring library professionals.

Tracey Pratchett: Tracey has a flexible and innovative approach to developing both herself and others within her team. She has worked in the health sector for nine years as a clinical librarian, and for the past year as the Knowledge and Library Services Manager at Lancashire Teaching Hospitals. Prior to this she worked in both further education and public libraries. Many of the Tips in this book have been used by Tracey to develop her current role and to benefit her team. As the joint project lead for the MAP (Making Alignment a Priority) toolkit (https://maptoolkit.wordpress.com), and a member of the Knowledge for Healthcare Metrics Working Group, she enjoys sharing learning and developing staff through both informal and formal networks.

Gil Young: Gil has worked in the academic, health and public library sectors. She is currently employed as the NHS LKS Workforce Development Manager for the Health Care Libraries Unit North. She is a CILIP Fellow and an associate member of the CIPD. She is also a CILIP mentor and was the first winner of the CILIP mentor of the year award.

List of abbreviations

ACAS	Advisory, Conciliation and Arbitration Service.
ALA	American Library Association, www.ala.org.
BIALL	British and Irish Association of Law Librarians, www.biall.org.uk.
CILIP	Chartered Institute of Library and Information Professionals, www.cilip.org.uk.
CIPD	Chartered Institute of Personnel and Development, www.cipd.co.uk.
CoP	Communities of practice.
CPD	Continuing professional development.
FIL	Forum for Interlending and Information Delivery, www.forumforinterlending.org.uk.
HCLU	Health Care Libraries Unit – North, www.lihnn.nhs.uk/index.php/hclu-top.
HEE	Health Education England, https://hee.nhs.uk.
HLG	CILIP Health Libraries Group, www.cilip.org.uk/about/special-interest-groups/health-libraries-group.
HR	Human resources.
IFLA	International Federation of Library Associations and Institutions, www.ifla.org.
IL group	CILIP Information Literacy Group, www.cilip.org.uk/about/special-interest-groups/information-literacy-group.
KM	Knowledge management.
LIHNN	Library and Information Health Network North West, www.lihnn.nhs.uk.

LILAC   Librarians' Information Literacy Conference,
              www.lilacconference.com.
LKS   Library and knowledge services.
LLAMA   Library Leadership and Management Association,
              www.ala.org/llama.
LSE   London School of Economics, www.lse.ac.uk/home.aspx.
MAP   Making Alignment a Priority Toolkit,
              https://maptoolkit.wordpress.com.
MMU   Manchester Metropolitan University, www2.mmu.ac.uk.
MOOC   Massive online open course.
NHS   National Health Service.
NISO   National Information Standards Organization, www.niso.org.
NLPN   New Library Professionals Network,
              https://nlpn.wordpress.com.
PDP   Personal development plan.
PID   Project implementation document.
PKSB   CILIP Professional Knowledge and Skills Base,
              www.cilip.org.uk/jobs-careers/professional-knowledge-skills-
              base.
SLA   School Library Association, www.sla.org.uk.
SWOT   Strengths, weaknesses, opportunities, threats.
UKSG   United Kingdom Serials Group, www.uksg.org.

Series Editor's introduction

Helen Blanchett, Jisc, UK

This series provides a set of practical guides for the busy professional in need of inspiration. Sourced from experienced library and information practitioners, grounded in theory, yet not overwhelmed by it, the information in these guides will tell you what you need to know to make a quick impact in a range of topical areas of professional interest.

Each book takes a tips-based approach to introduce best-practice ideas and encourage adaptation and innovation.

The series is aimed at experienced library and information professionals looking for new ideas and inspiration, as well as new professionals wanting to tap into the experience of others and students and educators interested in how theory is put into practice.

Practical tips for developing your staff

Staff costs in any organization usually account for a large proportion of its budget: people are indeed our most valuable resource, not just in financial terms. Ensuring staff are supported to develop the skills, knowledge and experience to perform effectively is a key challenge for any organization.

In a profession affected by constant change, staff must be equipped to develop and thrive. Change, however, is only one driver of staff development. Encouraging staff to challenge themselves to gain new skills in order to progress their careers is also important.

Effective staff development should improve organizational and individual performance, but also have wider benefits in terms of staff morale and motivation. Finding effective methods of engaging and developing staff can be a challenge, especially in times of increasingly constrained training and development budgets.

The authors bring the benefit of their wide knowledge and varied experiences together in this book, to provide a range of practical suggestions as to how to develop staff. The tips go beyond the knee-jerk 'run a training course' response, and cover a range of creative approaches.

I am very grateful to Gil and Tracey for their hard work on leading this book and to Carol, Lisa and Helen for their contributions. I hope you will find it useful and inspiring.

Introduction

About this book

Continuous professional development (CPD) is a key component of a successful and satisfying career. This practical book offers a wide range of ideas and methods for all library and knowledge service (LKS) professionals to manage the development of those who work for and with them. It will also be a valuable guide for individuals wishing to manage their own CPD.

As part of the *Practical Tips* series, it offers innovative Tips and tried-and-tested best practice to enable LKS workers to take control of their professional development regardless of the budget and time available to them. You will find flexible tips and implementation advice on topics including:

- enabling others to plan, reflect on and evaluate their personal development
- appraisals and goal setting: linking personal objectives to organizational objectives
- performance management
- sourcing funding to attend and run events
- planning formal development activities such as courses and conferences
- accessing informal activities
- using social media as a development tool
- role of professional bodies and networks
- mentoring, buddying and coaching
- networking.

The Tips have been written by a wide range of LKS professionals working across different sectors and at different stages in their careers.

Section summaries

The Tips are divided into three sections:

1 **Theories:** This section of the book outlines some of the main theories around how people behave, learn and develop. Having an understanding of how individuals learn and behave is important for line managers if they are to provide meaningful development opportunities.
2 **Infrastructure:** An overview of the basic structures which need to be in place within an organization to enable learning and development to take place. This section includes information on recruitment, managing performance and exit procedures.
3 **Activities and tools:** This section covers a wide range of activities and tools which can be used to assist individuals in all aspects of their development. Many of the activities in this section will form part of an individual's day-to-day working life, including attending meetings, delivering training sessions and writing reports. The purpose of including these is to demonstrate that development can be something which happens continuously and does not necessarily require dedicated time, although that does have a role.

Using this book

This book is not intended to be read in a linear fashion. Instead it has been designed to be dipped into as and when required. Each Tip or activity comes with an overview and detail, guidance on timing and some issues to think about for when trying out the techniques. The important More sections provide the reader with further suggestions and ideas to extend each Tip. We hope these ideas will prompt you to think about ways you can adapt the Tips to your own situation and that you will find this book an invaluable support for your professional practice.

Tracey Pratchett and Gil Young

Theories

Tips 1–10

1. Understanding how people behave, learn and develop

AS A MANAGER you want your staff to enjoy their work and fulfil their potential whilst actively contributing to the aims of the team, the service and the organization. The first step in achieving this is to understand how and why the individuals that make up your team behave in the ways they do and the implications this has for how they like to learn and how they interact with others. As a line manager it is important that you have an understanding of how your own preferences will influence your management style and how to modify your natural preferences to manage those who might be very different from you. To enable you to develop this understanding this section of the book outlines some of the main theories around how people behave, learn and develop.

There are many theories about how we learn, develop and behave, with a great deal of overlap between them. Without a doubt everyone has one or more 'preferred' style(s) which influence the way they think, behave and learn. It would be easy to say that our backgrounds and experiences influence the way we develop but the latest neuroscience research makes it very clear that our minds have a high level of plasticity, which means that whatever has been our preferred style can be changed. Indeed, we know that as we grow and develop we change but we often don't realize how much we can influence that change for ourselves.

Many of the personality/behavioural type analyses are developed from the original work of Carl Gustav Jung (1875–1961), whose model, 'Psychological Types', developed in 1921, was based on the theory that each person has an innate urge to grow. Part of that growing process is to learn how we operate individually, develop the parts of us that we need to learn more about and learn about the people around us. His model works on the theory that the brain has three axes:

- Feeling–Thinking
- Intuition–Sensing
- Introversion–Extraversion.

From these we can find out which are our dominant thought processes and styles. Jung identified eight 'types', from which many others have developed more detailed theories and a range of methods of assessing primary styles. This has led to a number of 'quadrant' tools which identify and relate to the four areas of the brain and our preferences as to which area we tend to use most. Interestingly, these all use colour references but confusingly they use them in different quadrants. Below is a comparison (Table 1.1) of the ones we have covered in more detail in this book and a couple of others which are so similar that we haven't gone into detail on them:

Table 1.1 *Comparison of 'quadrant' tools*				
Tool	**Characteristics**			
	Dominance/ Leadership	**Order and structures**	**People and relationships**	**Creatives**
Jigsaw	Red (Eva Reddy)	Blue (Mr Huey Blue)	Green (Carey and the Harmonisers)	Yellow (Ray O'Sunshine)
DiSC	Green (Dominance)	Yellow (Conscientiousness)	Blue (Steadiness)	Pink/Red (Influence)
Benziger	Front left Logic and results	Basal (rear) left Process and routine	Basal (rear) right Intuition and empathy	Front right Vision and creativity
*Insight	Fiery Red	Cool Blue	Earth Green	Sunshine Yellow
*Bolton and Bolton Social Styles	Drivers	Analyticals	Amiables	Expressives
*Not covered in this book				

There are also a range of tools which focus on our learning styles or preferences that are useful both to understand ourselves but also, and perhaps more importantly, to give us indications about the best way to work with colleagues and help them to assimilate learning most effectively. Two of these are also quadrant models and although some indicators closely align to the 'behaviour styles' above they do not correlate exactly.

The Chartered Institute of Personnel and Development (CIPD) state that

Learning styles might at a basic level be considered to consist of three inter-related elements:

- Information processing – habitual modes of perceiving, storing and organising information (for example, pictorially or verbally)
- Instructional preferences – predispositions towards learning in a certain way (for example, collaboratively or independently) or in a certain setting (such as a particular environment or time of day)
- Learning strategies – adaptive responses to learning specific subject matter in a particular context.

CIPD, 2014

Rather than representing a single concept, 'learning styles' is thus an umbrella term covering a spectrum of modalities, preferences and strategies. What we therefore see when we look at models of learning styles are the efforts of individuals to bring together the concepts and processes within those three elements.

Finally, there is the issue of evaluating the development activity to gain an understanding of what an individual has learned and how this has impacted upon themselves, the team and the organization. There are many models for evaluation but we look at Kirkpatrick's four levels of evaluation model, which is by far the best known and most used. Evaluation is vital – without it we cannot know if the learning and development which we spend good money on has produced any valid improvements or results. Kirkpatrick offers us a range of ways of seeing how learning and development has impacted upon our initial feelings, and the longer-term impacts on ourselves, our team and our organization. Whilst it was designed for organizational use it is also a useful model to reflect personally on the values of our own CPD (continuous professional development).

In the following Tips we will illustrate a few of the many tools which can be used to look at how we think and learn. The most important point is to know that you and your team members are not 'labelled' or 'bound' by whatever you find out – these are tools to help you find a starting point to successfully develop your staff.

👍 Best for

- Generating an understanding of how your own preferences for the ways you like to behave, learn and develop will influence your management style.
- A means of beginning to think about how the individuals that make up your team like to behave, learn and develop which can enable you to provide meaningful development opportunities.

⚠ To think about

- Don't box yourself into believing you or others can only learn or behave in one style. We all have the capability to use all of the styles even though we might have a preference for one or another.
- There is no secure evidential base to support any one particular theory of behavioural or learning preference.

References

CIPD (2014) Learning Styles and the Psychology of Learning, www.cipd.co.uk/hr-resources/factsheets/psychology-neuroscience-learning.aspx. [Accessed 24 September 2016]

Further reading

Fordham, F. (1991) *An Introduction to Jung's Psychology*, 3rd edn, Penguin, London.
Stevens, A. (2001) *Jung: a very short introduction*, rev. edn, OUP, Oxford.

2. Kolb learning cycle and styles

DAVID **K**OLB**'S** **LEARNING** styles model and experiential learning theory (ELT) model was published in 1984. Kolb's theory is that ideally (but not always) this process represents a cycle where the learner 'touches all the bases', so they take part in experiencing, reflecting, thinking and acting. Experiences lead to observations and reflections which are then assimilated (absorbed and translated) into abstract concepts with implications for action, which the individual can actively test and experiment with, which in turn enable the creation of new experiences.

Working with Roger Fry, Kolb argues that the cycle of learning can begin at any one of the four points and that it should be approached as a continuous cycle. However, it is suggested that it often begins with an individual carrying out a particular action and then seeing the effect of the action.

The second action would then be to look at the first action and reflect on it in relation to its situation, so that if the action was taken again in the same circumstances it would be possible to anticipate what would follow on from the action.

The third step is to understand the general principle under which the particular instance falls so that you can identify what might be different in other circumstances. This idea of 'generalization' allows individuals to see the connection between actions and effects over a range of circumstances and is closely linked with the final stage of planning for future actions and trying them out.

Kolb's model (Figure 2.1), therefore, works on two levels – the first is a four-stage cycle of actions or abilities.

1 Concrete experience – (CE)
2 Reflective observation – (RO)
3 Abstract conceptualization – (AC)
4 Active experimentation – (AE).

Kolb and Fry argued that few of us reach the ideal of working around this cycle in perfect order and most of us have a strength or orientation to one of the stages. So some individuals are more prone to focusing on the action,

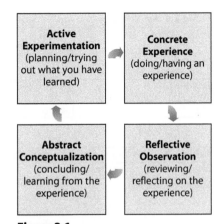

Figure 2.1
Kolb's experiential learning cycle, adapted from McLeod (2013)

others on the reflection, and so on; because of this they went on to develop a learning styles inventory, placing people somewhere on one of two continuums:

• concrete experience and abstract conceptualization
• active experimentation and reflective observation.

What Kolb is suggesting here is that the two ends of each continuum are actually conflicts and whilst we might want to do both at the same time, that actually creates conflict, which means that we resolve that conflict through choice when confronted with new learning situations.

This second dimension led to a four-type definition of learning styles (each representing the combination of two preferred styles, rather like a two-by-two matrix of the four-stage cycle styles, as illustrated in Table 2.1), for which Kolb used the terms:

1 Diverging (CE/RO)
2 Converging (AC/AE)
3 Assimilating (AC/RO)
4 Accommodating (CE/AE).

The four styles' attributes are described in Table 2.2.

It is essential to ensure that you don't reduce anyone's potential to learn to one single style but instead recognize that there are strengths and weaknesses associated with each style and 'locking' yourself or others into one style will put you all at a serious disadvantage.

Table 2.1 *Kolb's two-by-two matrix of the four-stage cycle, adapted from Chapman (2016)*

	DOING (Active Experimentation – AE)	WATCHING (Reflective Observation – RO)
FEELING (Concrete Experience – CE)	Accommodating (CE/AE)	Diverging (CE/RO)
THINKING (Abstract Conceptualization – AC)	Converging (AC/AE)	Assimilating (AC/RO)

Table 2.2 *Kolb's four styles' attributes, adapted from Smith (2010)*

Learning Style	Description
Converger (AC/AE)	• Strong in practical application of ideas • Use learning to solve specific problems • Like technical tasks • Unemotional • Make decisions by finding solutions to questions and problems • Have technical abilities • Less concerned with people • Like to work with practical applications • Has narrow interests
Diverger (CE/RO)	• Prefer to watch rather than do • Strong in imagination • Like to gather information • Good at generating ideas • Look at things from different perspectives • Interested in people • Broad cultural interests • Emotional • Like to work in groups
Assimilator (AC/RO)	• Strong ability to create theoretical models • Prefer concise, logical approach • Ideas and concepts more important than people • Like clear explanations • Less inclined to 'do' • Able to take on board a wide range of information • Good at organizing information into clear, logical format • Excel in inductive reasoning • Concerned with abstract concepts rather than people • Like time to think things through
Accommodator (CE/AE)	• Greatest strength is doing things • Rely on intuition rather than logic to solve problems • More of a risk taker • Love new challenges • Perform well when required to react to immediate circumstances • Good at carrying out plans • Like practical, experiential approach • Good at setting targets • Good at finding alternative solutions to achieving outcome

Other issues you need to recognize are that:

• This model only relates to 'experiential' learning and there are other forms of learning, such as memorization and information assimilation.

- Boud, Cohen and Walker (1993) would argue that it fails to help people uncover the elements of reflection.
- As a model it is firmly based in western, especially American, culture and the way learning is approached may be affected by environment.
- The reality of thinking does not always follow neatly in stages or steps, making this model seem a little too neat and simplistic.
- There is little real empirical research to test the model.

Nevertheless, in terms of our non-academic lives, Kolb's learning cycle and styles are helpful in giving a structure to consider how you and your team can make the best of learning from experience. In Tip 3 (p. 8) you will also see the words Reflectors, Activists, Pragmatists and Theorists. These are from the development of the Kolb styles by Honey and Mumford.

🖒 Best for

■ Reviewing the learning cycle, assessing your learning style and considering the learning styles of colleagues and team members.

▶ More

■ There are other learning style models such as VAK, VARK and Belbin team roles (although it could be argued this is more of a personality/behavioural style tool) and Honey and Mumford's Learning Styles is a further developed style model.

■ At least some aspects of learning styles and strategies can be taught, regardless of natural inclination.

References

Boud, D., Cohen, R. and Walker, D. (1993) Using Experience for Learning, Open University Press, London.

Chapman, A. (2016) Kolb Learning Styles, www.businessballs.com/kolblearningstyles.htm. [Accessed 7 February 2016]

McLeod, S. (2013) Kolb – Learning Styles, www.simplypsychology.org/learning-kolb.html. [Accessed 21 February 2016]

Smith, M. K. (2010) 'David Kolb on Experiential Learning', Infed, the encyclopedia of informal education, http://infed.org/mob/david-a-kolb-on-experiential-learning. [Accessed 7 February 2016]

Further reading

CIPD (2012) *From Steady State to Ready State: a need for fresh thinking in learning and talent development?*, CIPD, London.

CIPD (2014) *Learning Styles and the Psychology of Learning*, www.cipd.co.uk/hr-resources/factsheets/psychology-neuroscience-learning.aspx. [Accessed 24 September 2016]

Kolb, D. A. (2014) *Experiential Learning: experience as the source of learning and development*, Pearson FT Press, London.

Mobbs, R. (2003) *How to be an e-tutor*, www.le.ac.uk/users/rjm1/etutor/resources/learningtheories/honeymumford.html. [Accessed 7 February 2016]

3. Honey and Mumford – learning styles

PETER HONEY AND Alan Mumford developed their learning styles system as a variation on the Kolb model in the 1970s. They devised a questionnaire that identifies an individual's primary style for learning, which they characterized as Activist, Reflector, Pragmatist and Theorist. The relationship between each of these styles is outlined in Figure 3.1.

Honey and Mumford say of their system:

> Our description of the stages in the learning cycle originated from the work of David Kolb. Kolb uses different words to describe the stages of the learning cycle and four learning styles . . ..

and

> The similarities between his model and ours are greater than the differences . . .
>
> Honey and Mumford, 1992, 4

However, the essence of the tool is helping individuals to identify why they often step into a learning opportunity at a specific stage – for instance, the pragmatist leaping into opening the package and building the new toy without stopping to read

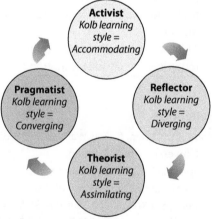

Figure 3.1
Honey and Mumford's learning styles, adapted from Chapman (2016)

the instructions! Once you understand your preferred method of learning and those of your staff, you can identify when you and they need to develop and use the other styles appropriately. Tables 3.1 to 3.4 summarize the four keys stage and styles. They include the corresponding Kolb learning styles.

Table 3.1 *Honey and Mumford's Activist, adapted from Honey and Mumford (1992)*

Activist
Kolb learning style = Accommodating
'Having an Experience' (stage 1), and Activists (style 1): 'here and now', gregarious, seek challenge and immediate experience, open-minded, bored with implementation.

• learn by doing • 'hands-on' preference • tend to launch in – unlikely to read instructions • open-minded approach to learning • enter new experiences without bias • enjoy the here and now • enthusiastic about anything new	• philosophy: 'I'll try anything once' • tend to act first and consider the consequences afterwards • days are filled with activity • thrive on the challenge of new experiences • get bored with implementation and longer term consolidation • gregarious • like to be centre of activity

Table 3.2 *Honey and Mumford's Reflector, adapted from Honey and Mumford (1992)*

Reflector
Kolb learning style = Diverging
'Reviewing the Experience' (stage 2) and Reflectors (style 2): 'stand back', gather data, ponder and analyse, delay reaching conclusions, listen before speaking, thoughtful.

• learn by observing and thinking about what happened • like to stand back to ponder experiences • observe situations from many different perspectives • collect data, both first hand and from others • prefer to think about it thoroughly before coming to a conclusion • collection and analysis of data is vital • tend to postpone reaching definitive conclusions for as long as possible • philosophy is to be cautious • thoughtful, like to consider all possible angles and implications	• prefer to take a back seat in meetings and discussions • enjoy observing other people in action • listen to others and get the drift of the discussion before making their own points • tend to adopt a low profile • have a slightly distant, tolerant, unruffled air about them • when they act it is part of a wide picture which includes the past as well as the present and others' observations as well as their own • avoid leaping in and prefer to watch from the sidelines • prefer to stand back and view experiences from a number of different perspectives, collecting data and taking the time to work towards an appropriate conclusion

Table 3.3 *Honey and Mumford's Theorist, adapted from Honey and Mumford (1992)*

Theorist
Kolb learning style = Assimilating
'Concluding from the Experience' (stage 3) and Theorists (style 3): think things through in logical steps, assimilate disparate facts into coherent theories, rationally objective, reject subjectivity and flippancy.

• like to understand the theory behind the actions • need models, concepts and facts in order to engage in the learning process • prefer to analyse and draw new information into a logical 'theory' • think problems through in a step-by-step logical way • tend to be perfectionists • keen on basic assumptions, principles, theories models and systems thinking	• philosophy: 'If it's logical it's good' • frequently ask questions: 'Does it make sense?' 'How does this fit with that?' 'What are the basic assumptions?' • tend to be detached, analytical • approach to problems is consistently logical • prefer to maximize certainty • feel uncomfortable with subjective judgements, lateral thinking and anything flippant

Table 3.4 *Honey and Mumford's Pragmatist, adapted from Honey and Mumford (1992)*

Pragmatist

Kolb learning style = Converging

'Planning the next steps' (stage 4) and Pragmatists (style 4): seek and try out new ideas, practical, down-to-earth, enjoy problem solving and decision making, quickly bored by long discussions.

• need to be able to see how to put the learning into practice in the real world • see abstract concepts and games as being of limited use • keen on trying out ideas, theories and techniques to see if they work in practice • positively search out new ideas • return from courses brimming with new ideas that they want to try out • like to get on with things and act quickly and confidently on ideas that attract them	• tend to be impatient with ruminating and open-ended discussions • essentially practical and down to earth • like making practical decisions and solving problems • respond to problems and opportunities 'as a challenge' • philosophy: 'There is always a better way' and 'Good enough is enough.'

The important thing to note with this, as with Kolb, is that you must avoid 'boxing' yourself or others into one style. What the questionnaire will highlight is an individual's natural preference but everyone will at one time or another need to cultivate the other styles. In their *Manual of Learning Styles*, Honey and Mumford (1992) provide a range of exercises you can do to develop your lower preferences and those of your staff.

👍 Best for

■ Assessing your own learning style and considering the learning styles of the individuals that make up your team.

References

Chapman, A. (2016) *Kolb Learning Styles*, www.businessballs.com/kolblearningstyles.htm. [Accessed 7 February 2016]

Honey, P. and Mumford, A. (1992) *Manual of Learning Styles*, 3rd edn, Peter Honey Publications, Oxford.

Further reading

Honey, P. (2003) *101 Ways to Develop Your People, Without Really Trying: a manager's guide to work based learning*, 2nd edn, Peter Honey Publications, Oxford.

Honey, P. (2008) *Strengthen your Strengths – A Guide to Enhancing your Self-Management Skills*, Peter Honey Publications, Oxford.

Honey, P. and Mumford, A. (2006) *The Learning Styles Helper's Guide*, rev edn, Peter Honey Publications, Oxford.

Honey, P. and Mumford, A. (2016) *Honey and Mumford: learning style questionnaire*, https://www.talentlens.co.uk/devlop/pter-honey-learning-styles-series. [Accessed

10 February 2016]

Mumford, A. (1999) *Effective Learning (Management Shapers)*, CIPD, London.

4. VAK learning styles

ORIGINALLY DEVELOPED BY psychologists in the 1920s, the Visual-Auditory-Kinaesthetic learning styles model or inventory is usually abbreviated to VAK. It provides a simple way to explain and understand your learning style and those of others. As the title suggests it identifies three preferences for learning: visual, auditory and kinaesthetic (see Table 4.1)

Table 4.1 *Visual-Auditory-Kinaesthetic learning styles preferences, adapted from About Health (2015) and Chapman (2015)*

Preference	Style Indicators
Visual Has a preference for seen or observed things, including pictures, diagrams, displays, handouts, flip-charts, etc. They will use phrases like, 'show me', 'let's have a look at' and will best be able to perform a new task after reading the instructions or watching someone else do it first. These people will work best from lists or written instructions.	• You pay close attention to body language. • Art, beauty and aesthetics are important to you. • Visualizing information in your mind helps you remember it better.
Auditory (or Aural) Has a preference for the transfer of learning through listening to the spoken word, of self or others, of sounds or noises. They will use phrases such as, 'tell me', 'let's talk it over' and will be best able to perform a new task after listening to instructions from an expert. These people are happy being given spoken instructions and can remember all the words to the songs they hear!	• You prefer to listen to class lectures rather than reading from the textbook. • Reading out loud helps you remember information better. • You prefer to listen to a recording of your class lectures or a podcast rather than going over your class notes. • You create songs to help remember information.
Kinaesthetic Has a preference for physical experience – touching, feeling, holding, doing, practical hands-on experiences. They will use phrases such as 'let me try', 'how do you feel' and will best perform a task by going ahead and trying it out and learning as they go. These are people who like to experiment, hands-on, and never look at the instructions first!	• You enjoy performing tasks that involve directly manipulating objects and materials. • It is difficult for you to sit still for long periods of time. • You are good at applied activities, such as painting, cooking, mechanics, sports and woodworking. • You have to actually practise doing something in order to learn it.

There is some controversy, coupled with a lack of research to confirm or disprove, whether identifying styles does provide support in helping individuals to learn and develop. Nevertheless, for many, they do aid an understanding of preferences which could allow you to access information about the ways in which you and your team like to learn, which will enable you to provide meaningful and relevant development opportunities. Assessment is available through licensed facilitators or online and there are many very simple tools online to get you and your team started.

🖒 Best for

- Helping people raise their awareness of their own and other people's visual, auditory or kinaesthetic styles.

▶ More

- There are some alternative models such as VARK, developed by Neil Fleming, which adds 'Reading and writing', and VAKT, which adds 'Tactile', as a fourth dimension.

References

About Health (2015) *VARK Learning Styles*,
   http://psychology.about.com/od/educationalpsychology/a/vark-learning-styles.htm. [Accessed 16 February 2016]
Chapman, A. (2015) *Free Vak Learning Styles Test*, www.businessballs.com/vaklearningstylestest.htm. [Accessed 10 November 2016]

Further reading

CIPD (2014) *Learning Styles and the Psychology of Learning*, www.cipd.co.uk/hr-resources/factsheets/psychology-neuroscience-learning.aspx. [Accessed 24 September 2016]
Walsh, B. E. and Willard, R. (2011) *Vak Self-Audit: visual, auditory, and kinesthetic communication and learning styles: exploring patterns of how you interact and learn*, Walsh Seminars, Canada.

5. MBTI® – Myers Briggs® Type Indicator

DEVELOPED IN **1942** by Isabel Briggs Myers and her mother Katharine Briggs, the Myers Briggs® Type Indicator (MBTI®) is a well known system for understanding and interpreting personality. It uses the three dimensions from Carl Jung's 'Psychological Types' ideas with an added, fourth dimension of Judging–Perceiving which explains how individuals handle the information they obtain. MBTI® identifies 16 personality types, each made up of four letters, called the Psychological Scales. To see how this works in practice and to learn more about the personality types follow the links in the Further Reading section below (p. 14).

The assessment is done by use of a questionnaire which is carried out by registered practitioners. This is usually undertaken through group sessions, though there is an online version which can be completed. Each of the 16 different types is developed from the side of the scale which is dominant and a certain set of characteristics is associated with each combination to describe what the individual is like. For example an ISTJ is dominant in Introversion, Sensing, Thinking and Feeling which translates as that individual usually being quite serious, practical, quiet and dependable. They will be responsible and determined and will provide accurate work, coping well with high-stress situations. However, they can be impatient and appear to be unappreciative of the efforts of others.

Whilst individuals tend to have a preference for one or the other side of the four scales we all contain both areas within our brains. The measurements show our more innate preference, but we can, and do, develop the opposite where and when we need it. Even if we are more dominantly focused on a particular side of a scale it does not stop us from using the opposite side – so, for instance, just because you rely on your feelings a lot does not mean that you cannot use objective data to make a decision. The same applies to all the individuals that make up your team.

It is important to be aware that there is no 'right' or 'wrong' combination. Each type will indicate different skills and every individual will bring different gifts to the table. Even if you manage a team of individuals with the same combination they will each be different, due to a variety of other influences on their lives and the actual placement they scored on the scale. However, they would also have a great deal in common. You should be aware that the circumstances of you and your team members when you take the assessment can impact upon the results, especially if you or others are quite evenly balanced between each end of a particular scale.

The insight you gain through undertaking this, and other personality type exercises, can assist you in understanding your own behaviours and reactions and those of your team. You, and they, can learn how to adapt and work differently with others by developing an understanding of the preferences and behaviours of others, even if their specific typology is not known. The quote below is from an individual who has recently undertaken an MBTI assessment and demonstrates the potential value of using this tool in practice:

> It cast a lot of light on the way me and my boss's different styles interact with one another and how I could handle this better. It also gave me a lot of self-knowledge about the way I approach situations in and outside work.
>
> Feedback from Knowing Me, Knowing You course, 11 June 2015

👍 Best for

■ Understanding and interpreting both your personality and those of your team members.

▶ **More**

■ If you can't access a registered practitioner then try the online assessment at www.cpp.com/en/index.aspx.

Further reading

Briggs Myers, I., McCaulley, M.H., Quenk, N.L. and Hammer, A.L. (1998) *MBTI Manual: a guide to the development and use of the Myers-Briggs Type Indicator®*, 3rd edn, CPP, Sunnyvale.

Briggs Myers, I. and Myers, P. B. (1995) *Gifts Differing: understanding personality type*, 2nd rev. edn, Davies-Black Publishing, Sunnyvale.

Chapman, A. (2014) *Personality Types and Tests*, www.businessballs.com/personalitystylesmodels.htm. [Accessed 10 February 2016]

Myers and Briggs Foundation (2016a) MBTI® Basics, www.myersbriggs.org/my-mbti-personalitytype/mbti-basics/. [Accessed 10 February 2016]

Myers and Briggs Foundation (2016b) *My MBTI® Personality Type*, www.myersbriggs.org/my-mbti-personality-type. [Accessed 10 February 2016]

Acknowledgement

Many thanks to Claire Bradshaw (https://clairembradshaw.wordpress.com) for permission to reproduce part of the feedback from her course, Knowing Me, Knowing You.

6. Jigsaw Discovery Tool©

THE JIGSAW DISCOVERY Tool© was developed by Michelle McArthur and Keith Nicholson of Jigsaw@Work, because they were tired of the complexity of other assessments. They wanted to develop something simple and memorable which would help individuals to understand their 'preferred' style and understand the role of the brain in determining behaviour. It has been developed over a number of years by bringing together the work and research of some of the world's greatest psychologists and leading neuroscientists. It aims to demystify the complex terminology in neuroscience to make it as accessible and practical as possible for everyone.

Participants develop their own behavioural map by selecting 16 words, from 64 jigsaw pieces, which best describe them. They then identify the colourful characters which reflect the four areas of the brain to see the characteristics of their preferred style(s). The tool recognizes the importance of the interconnectedness of the different areas of the brain and has a whole-brain approach which is an integral part of the behavioural framework illustrated by the behavioural maps the participants create.

Behavioural maps will illustrate the preferred style(s)/behaviour(s) of the individual and breaks them down into four coloured characters (Table 6.1). The tool can be used to help you and members of your team identify preferred styles for communication, work patterns, learning, behaviour and how you can all best work together. There is no 'right' or 'wrong' behavioural map and none is better than another. Each individual is encouraged to use the tool to understand themselves and others, identifying when they might want to develop or strengthen other styles.

Table 6.1 *Jigsaw Discovery Tool© characters and their learning preferences, adapted from McArthur (2015)*

	Eva Reddy (RED)			Ray O'Sunshine (YELLOW)	
Key Drivers	• Achievement • Success • Speed • Efficiency		Key Drivers	• Enjoyment • Freedom • Innovation • Likes to be different	
Learning Preferences	Like to understand the theory behind ideas and be able to put it into context of the high-level concept (big picture). They also like to be left alone to get on with it and implement/apply their learning to their world.		Learning Preferences	Like to be told what is ultimately needed and then be allowed to trial-and-error their ideas and learn from what doesn't work.	
	Carey and the Harmonisers (GREEN)			Mr Huey Blue (BLUE)	
Key Drivers	• Supporting • Helping • Pleasing • Caring for others • Fairness • Equality		Key Drivers	• Correctness • Attention to detail • Maintaining order • Strives for perfection	
Learning Preferences	Like coaching. They prefer working as part of a group and benefit from collective learning. They also like things to be demonstrated to them.		Learning Preferences	Like to learn from hard evidence and proof. They need validation of ideas and particularly want all the detailed (small picture) information. They require answers to all of the 'what if?' situations. They learn by implementation, once information has been validated and they have step-by-step instructions of what to do.	

It is simple and highly memorable. Developing the behavioural map is a fun exercise which engages people at all levels. The tool is available through Jigsaw@Work and their Licensed Associates who can use the tool as part of courses on various subjects, because it is so flexible and fits into a wide range of development. The quotes below are from library assistants who have recently undertaken a Jigsaw assessment and outline what they found most useful about this exercise:

Being able to recognise other team members 'colour' and communicate more effectively.

Offered new insights into how to approach different interactions, and reaffirmed things that I already do.

Learning how different people can be, in so many different ways.

Finding out my communication styles so I am more aware of how I come across and how I can alter that.

Feedback from 'Can you hear me?
Improving your skills for communicating effectively', Summer 2015

👍 Best for

- Enhancing your and your team members' understanding of each other in an interactive and fun way. Its use gives individuals real 'ah-ha' moments and it works brilliantly in a team environment where it can instantly help understanding and collaboration.

References

McArthur, M. (2015) *The Jigsaw Discovery Tool, a 21st Century Behavioural Planning Tool*, Jigsaw@work, Wakefield.

Further reading

Jigsaw@work (2001) *Jigsaw@work – People Developers*, www.jigsawatwork.com. [Accessed 10 February 2016]

Acknowledgement

Many thanks to Carol Brooks (www.chrysalisdevelopment.co.uk) for permission to reproduce part of the feedback from her course, 'Can you hear me? Improving your skills for communicating effectively'.

7. The DiSC® model

THE DiSC® MODEL owned by the US Inscape Publishing company is used with the intention of enabling individuals to:

Gain the insight they need to be more successful, productive, and fulfilled at work . . . DiSC® instruments are based on a simple idea – that the foundation of personal and professional success lies in knowing yourself, understanding others, and realising the impact of your actions and attitudes on other people.

Whamond, 2011

The DiSC® model is attributed to Dr William Moulton Marston, a psychologist, whose book *Emotions of Normal People* (1923) first explained the model using the DiSC® terminology. In this work he also provided the descriptive words on which the commonly used DiSC® personality assessment systems were built. Using two scales: Task versus People and Fast-Paced versus Moderate-Paced, the dimensions of behaviour and situation feature strongly in Marston's ideas. Using these two axes, four types – Dominance, Influence, Conscientiousness and Steadiness – are developed (Figure 7.1).

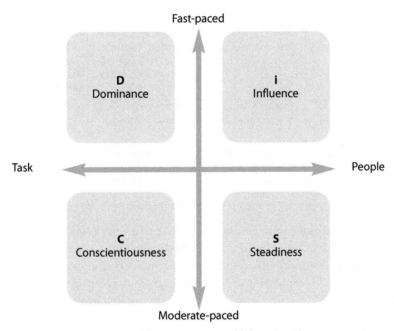

Figure 7.1 *DiSC® model, adapted from US Inscape Publishing (2016)*

The analysis breaks down the four types into three areas of influence: their behaviours, what they want from other individuals and what they want from their roles. The descriptors relate to those whose score is high in the quadrant and it is important to note that just because you or members of your team sit in the quadrant does not mean you or they will display these behaviours exclusively or that in all circumstances those behaviours are either good or bad. Given that this model also has its basis in Jung, the links to the Jung axes of introversion and extraversion are shown in Table 7.1.

Table 7.1 *Links between the DiSC® model and the Jung axes of introversion and extroversion, adapted from Chapman (2014) and US Inscape Publishing (2016)*

D	i	S	C
Dominance	**Influence**	**Steadiness**	**Conscientiousness**
Green	Red	Blue	Yellow
Generally proactive and extrovert.	Generally proactive and extrovert.	Generally reactive and introvert.	Generally reactive and introvert.
Direct, decisive, dominant/strong-willed, demanding, driven, and determined, self-assured, forceful, task/results-oriented, instigates, leads and directs, firm, fast-paced, and self-confident.	Motivates others via influence and persuasion, outgoing, optimistic, convincing, magnetic, enthusiastic, warm, trusting, good communication skills, high-spirited, friendly, affable, inspires others, intuitive, lively, friendly.	Reliable, dependable, process-oriented, listener, friendly, trustworthy, solid, ethical, patient, humble, accommodating, methodical, even-tempered, calm, predictable, deliberate, stable and consistent.	Analytical, reserved, painstaking, investigative, precise, curious, decides using facts and figures, correct, checker, detailed, private, systematic, careful, cautious, diplomatic, accurate and tactful.
Things	People	People	Things
Motivated by winning, competition and success.	Motivated by recognition, personal approval, group activities and relationships.	Motivated by time, space, co-operation, opportunities to help, sincere appreciation and continuity to do things properly.	Motivated by truth, attention to detail, perfection, opportunities to gain knowledge, showing their expertise, and quality work.
Strong focus on task and forceful style can upset people.	Emphasis on image can neglect substance.	Dependence on process can become resistance.	Need for perfection can delay or obstruct.
Fears failure and loss of power, being seen as vulnerable, being taken advantage of.	Fears rejection and loss of reputaion and influence, disapproval and being ignored.	Fears insecurity, loss of stability and offending others and change.	Fears inaccuracy, unpredictability, criticism and being wrong.

Dr Marston did not make an analytical tool from his research but various other people have done so. Inscape Publishing are the company who have developed it most and there are other assessments on the internet. Although often delivered by an accredited trainer as part of group sessions, you can undertake the DiSC® profile online without being in a group context.

👍 Best for

- Assessing your own behavioural style and considering the learning styles of your team members.

References

Chapman, A. (2014) *Personality Types and Tests*, www.businessballs.com/personalitystylesmodels.htm. [Accessed 21 October 2015]

Moulton Marston, W. (1923) *Emotions of Normal People*, Ulan Press, Stroud.

US Inscape Publishing (2016) *DiSC®*, www.discassessment.co.uk. [Viewed 10 February 2016]

Whamond, C. (2011) *DISC* (sic), www.whamond.net/learnings/disc. [Viewed 27 May 2016]

8. Benziger Thinking Styles Assessment (BTSA)

KATHERINE BENZIGER IS unusual compared to many other personality thinkers because she places greatest emphasis on 'wellness' and the need to help individuals avoid 'falsifying' their true type. Whilst this theory was originally developed by Carl Jung, no one else has really focused on it or identified the extent 'falsifying type' has on people's wellbeing.

Benziger identifies that very many individuals 'falsify type' to fit into a role or career path that might not be right for them, which in turn has a negative impact on health, happiness and personal effectiveness. She went on to develop the theories about how this then impacts on whole organizations and their output.

Whilst Benziger drew great inspiration from Carl Jung and from the work of Myers Briggs and Hans Eysenck, her work has also been influenced and supported by developments into brain imaging, using modern scanning technologies to actually determine which parts of the brain are being used for various functions and types of thinking. Put simply, her theory expresses personality in terms of four quadrants of the brain (Table 8.1):

Table 8.1 *Benziger's four brain quadrants, adapted from Chapman (2014)*

Basal (Rear) Right – intuition and empathy	Basal (Rear) Left – process and routine
Frontal Right – vision and creativity	Frontal Left – logic and results

These modes of thinking relate to Jung's Four Functions (Thinking, Feeling, Sensing, Intuition) and the theory provides many people with an immensely helpful way to make sense of what Jung said and advocated. Importantly, although Benziger acknowledges and uses the Jungian introversion and extroversion dimension, she does not represent it within the four-quadrant model of the four functional types. The BTSA model uses the representation of the brain (viewed from above, top is front) and the summary definitions shown in

Mode 4 Frontal left	Mode 3 Frontal right
Mode 1 Basal left	Mode 2 Basal right

Figure 8.1 *Four brain modes, adapted from Benziger (2016)*

Figure 8.1. The brain has four specialized areas, each being responsible for different brain functions (which imply strengths, behaviour and thinking style). Within Benziger's model the specialized areas are called 'modes'.

According to Benziger each of us possesses natural strengths in only one of these specialized areas, which causes us to favour and use a certain style ahead of others. Outside that one style, we may have strengths and weaknesses which are based on what competencies we have been exposed to, or have developed, and indeed which competencies we have not been exposed to. Katherine Benziger refers to the natural specialized area as the 'behavioural mode'.

In terms of wellbeing, the BTSA helps us to identify the area of our brain which is truly efficient. The theory is that if we can identify which is our natural thinking style we can also identify the suitability of the work we do and adopt strategies to improve abilities elsewhere. Where we have developed into using another mode in either work or home life we have adopted 'Falsification of Type', which means that we are likely to suffer stress, low self-esteem and fatigue.

BTSA does two things:

1 It unveils and gives coping tools for dealing with Falsification of Type.
2 It reveals the inherent strength in the area of your brain's natural giftedness.

The Benziger model shows that if you could primarily use that part of the brain you were born to use and learn the coping strategies to help you deal with those less efficient parts of your brain you would experience the positive flow of thoughts, feelings and mental activities that would make you personally confident and highly effective in business situations.

Dr Benziger's key book, *The Art of Using Your Whole Brain* (2000), was first published in 1989, revised as *Thriving in Mind* in 2000. The BTSA is accessed through a simple personality assessment in her books.

↺ Best for

■ If you or team members feel continually stressed and are heading for burn-out, this tool can help individuals to identify if they have developed a strategy of using a behavioural mode which is not their natural preference.

References

Benziger, K. (2000) *Thriving in Mind: the art and science of using your whole brain*, rev. edn, KBA LLC, Carbondale.

Benziger, K. (2016) *Benziger Thinking Styles Assessment (BTSA)*, www.benziger.org. [Accessed 10 February 2016]

Chapman, A. (2014) *Personality Theories, Types and Tests – in Summary*, www.businessballs.com/personalitystylesmodels.htm. [Accessed 10 February 2016]

9. SDI – Strength Deployment Inventory®

SDI **WAS DEVELOPED** by Elias H. Porter. It is the primary inventory of a suite of inventories based on his Relationship Awareness Theory (RAT), which is a group of ideas that help individuals to build productive relationships and manage conflict by providing a window into the motivation that drives our behaviour. Table 9.1 shows the definitions used in SDI.

Table 9.1 *SDI definitions, adapted from Personal Strengths (UK) Ltd (2015)* *Reproduced with the permission of Personal Strengths Publishing, Inc., Carlsbad, CA, USA*
Strength
SDI helps individuals identify their personal strengths in relating to others under two conditions: 1. When everything is going well.   2. When they are faced with conflict.
Deployment
Means to move strategically or to take a position for effective action.   The SDI suggests ways that one's personal strengths may be used to improve relationships with others.
Inventory
SDI is not a test where judgments are 'right' or 'wrong' and answers are graded. It is an inventory for taking stock of motivational values (the basis for how you feel and act in different situations).

SDI is a self-assessment tool that helps individuals understand what gives them a sense of self-worth and what's important to them when relating to others. It can help you to understand how other people see things, thus helping you to develop effective relationships with your team members. The tool is available through licensed facilitators at www.personalstrengthsuk.com. It is helpful if you are seeking to:

- improve teamwork
- develop leaders
- support change management
- drive up sales
- improve customer service
- improve relationships
- improve conflict management.

Using the SDI increases relationship effectiveness and seeks to reduce the underlying conflicts that diminish relationships. The power of SDI is in how quickly and easily it gets individuals connecting and really talking to each other. SDI facilitates strong relationships through:

- the insights individuals gain
- the acceptance it encourages

- the conversations it informs
- the trust it increases
- the conflict it reduces.

There are a number of patterns of motivation where an individual's score might take them (Table 9.2).

A conflict sequence is also calculated which allows individuals to show how their motivation and related behaviour change when faced with conflict and opposition. The applications of SDI are endless and have one common theme; better human interactions lead to better outcomes. Table 9.3 outlines why SDI works.

Relationship Awareness Theory® and SDI can be invaluable in any environment where positive, effective relationship skills will enhance productivity and satisfaction. Some of the areas in which SDI can be applied include:

- team development
- conflict management
- leadership and management
- change
- customer service
- coaching
- projects
- culture and values.

Table 9.2 *Patterns of motivation*
Reproduced with the permission of Personal Strengths Publishing, Inc., Carlsbad, CA, USA

Blue		Altruistic–Nurturing
Red		Assertive–Directing
Green		Analytical–Autonomizing
Hub		Flexible–Cohering
Red	Blue	Assertive–Nurturing
Red	Green	Judicious–Competing
Blue	Green	Cautious–Supporting

Table 9.3 *Why SDI works, adapted from Personal Strengths (UK) Ltd (2015)*
Reproduced with the permission of Personal Strengths Publishing, Inc., Carlsbad, CA, USA

SDI depersonalizes conflict	It's a unique non-threatening method for conflict management – it helps people to understand how to reduce the potential for interpersonal conflict.
SDI is memorable	It's an experiential tool promoting common sense concepts in a highly visual manner.
SDI recognizes our differences	It's an inventory of the unique way we each value and prioritize different strengths, how we take different approaches and interpret the actions of others.
SDI illuminates the reason for our actions	It's a snapshot of who we are — going beyond behaviour to reveal our driving motivational values.
SDI is life-focused	It takes a whole of life perspective rather than only focusing on work or specific roles.
SDI is easy to use and apply	It's relevant to all levels across an organization, making it an ideal communication foundation to increase a culture of connectedness.

👍 Best for

- The conflict element of this tool is useful for understanding how you and members of your team can alter your behaviour when faced with conflict.

References

Personal Strengths (UK) Ltd (2015) *totalsdi*, http://totalsdi.uk. [Accessed 4 August 2016]

Acknowledgements

All copyrights and trademarks are used with the permission of Personal Strengths Publishing, Inc., Carlsbad, CA, USA.

10. Kirkpatrick's four levels of evaluation model

As A MANAGER you need to be clear about what an individual is aiming to achieve by undertaking a development activity and the impact that this will have on the team as a whole and ultimately on the organization. Part of this involves your being able to produce evidence that development activities are making a difference. The Kirkpatrick Model (Kirkpatrick and Kirkpatrick, 2016), defined in Table 10.1, states that evaluation of training and development interventions needs to take place at four different levels to provide real evidence about their value and impact.

The Kirkpatrick levels are clear and easy to follow, though they do require you to be fully involved in the evaluation of the training and development your team members undertake. The best way to do this is to have a set process

Table 10.1 *The Kirkpatrick Model, adapted from Kirkpatrick and Kirkpatrick (2016)*

Evaluation level and type	Definition	Examples of evaluation tools and methods	Relevance and practicability
1. REACTION	The degree to which participants find the training favourable, engaging and relevant to their jobs.	'Happy sheets', feedback forms/Post-its. Verbal reaction, post-training surveys or questionnaires.	Quick and very easy to obtain. Not expensive to gather or to analyse.
2. LEARNING	The degree to which participants acquire the intended knowledge, skills, attitude, confidence and commitment based on their participation in the training.	Typically assessments or tests before and after the training. Interview or observation can also be used. Demonstrations, presentations, teach-backs. Any activity or interaction during training could be used to evaluate learning.	Relatively simple to set up; clear-cut for quantifiable skills. Less easy for complex learning.
3. BEHAVIOUR	The degree to which participants apply what they learned during training when they are back on the job.	Observation and interview over time are required to assess change, relevance of change and sustainability of change. Checklists, job-aids and self-assessments help training graduates to self-monitor.	Measurement of behaviour change typically requires co-operation and skill of line managers.
4. RESULTS	The degree to which targeted outcomes occur as a result of the training and the support and accountability package.	Identified metrics can be tracked and reported in dashboards, and through the organization's existing reports and systems.	Measures are already in place via normal management systems and reporting – the challenge is to relate to the trainee.

which you follow to ensure that development activities are having the desired outcome and to embed this process in other management activities such as appraisals and your regular one-to-ones.

Prior to an individual undertaking a development activity you will need to discuss and agree with them what they are trying to accomplish (Level 4), what they need to do to accomplish their goals (Level 3) and what knowledge and skills they need to develop and practise to be successful (Level 2). Once the intervention has taken place you will need to work with the individual to embed the learning and agree how you will collect evidence that the intervention has made the required difference. Table 10.2 suggests some of the ways you can collect this information.

Table 10.2 *Ways to collect data, adapted from Kirkpatrick and Kirkpatrick (2016)*
© 2010-2016, Kirkpatrick Partners, LLC. All rights reserved. Used with permission.

METHODS	EVALUATION LEVELS			
	1 Reaction	2 Learning	3 Behaviour	4 Results
Survey, questionnaire, individual or group interview	✔	✔	✔	✔
Action plan monitoring, action learning		✔	✔	✔
Work review, skill observation, behaviour observation, action learning			✔	✔
Case study, knowledge test, knowledge check, presentation, teach back		✔		
Request for validation			✔	✔
Key business and HR metrics				✔

🖒 Best for

■ Ensuring that learning and development is delivering measurable results which you can evidence.

▶ More

■ Many other tools are available, including Jack Phillips' Five Level ROI model, Kaufman's Five Levels of Evaluation and Atkins' UCLA Model.
■ See also Tip 84, 'Training courses – attending', p. 220.

References

Kirkpatrick, J.D. and Kirkpatrick, W.K. (2016) *Kirkpatrick's Four Levels of Training Evaluation*, ATD Press: Alexandria, VA.

Further reading

Kirkpatrick, J. D. and Kirkpatrick, W. K. (2010) *Training on Trial: how workplace learning must reinvent itself to remain relevant*, Amacom, New York.

SECTION 2

Infrastructure

Tips 11–33

11. Why develop staff?

THIS BOOK IS about developing staff but the question that then arises is, why do it? Why should we, as individuals and managers, want to develop ourselves and our staff members? Why should managers and organizations support and enable us in doing so? What is in it for the individual, the service and the organization?

Development v. training

The first point to consider is the word 'develop' as opposed to 'train'. Training is generally perceived as something quite basic. It is about people learning how to carry out a particular task in order to do a job. It has its place in developing staff, particularly in terms of meeting legal requirements such as health and safety considerations, but it is not the only aspect to consider. Development is much broader. It is about developing the whole person:

> . . . enable[ing] learning and personal development, with all that this implies . . .
> focusing on enabling learning and development for people as individuals –
> which extends the range of development way outside traditional work skills and
> knowledge, and creates far more exciting, liberating, motivational opportunities
> – for people and for employers.
>
> Chapman, 2014

The value of continued professional development

The Chartered Institute of Personnel and Development (CIPD) has conducted extensive research on the value of continued professional development (CPD) to the individual and to the organization. Their conclusions are shown in Tables 11.1 and 11.2 (from CIPD, 2015).

Table 11.1 *How CPD benefits you (CIPD, 2015)*
Reproduced with the permission of the publisher, the Chartered Institute of Personnel and Development, London (www.cipd.co.uk)
• Build confidence and credibility; you can see your progression by tracking your learning. • Earn more by showcasing your achievements. A handy tool for appraisals. • Achieve your career goals by focusing on your training and development. • Cope positively with change by constantly updating your skill set. • Be more productive and efficient by reflecting on your learning and highlighting gaps in your knowledge and experience.

Table 11.2 *How CPD benefits your organization (CIPD, 2015)*
• Helps maximize staff potential by linking learning to actions and theory to practice. • Helps HR professionals to set SMART (specific, measurable, achievable, realistic and time-bound) objectives, for training activity to be more closely linked to business needs. • Promotes staff development. This leads to better staff morale and a motivated workforce and helps give a positive image/brand to organizations. • Adds value; reflecting it will help staff to consciously apply learning to their role and the organization's development. • Linking to appraisals. This is a good tool to help employees focus their achievements throughout the year.

Developing staff is therefore something which is good for the individual and the organization. Ultimately the purpose is to develop and move the organization forward as a whole whilst maintaining the engagement and commitment of individual staff members. In order to develop staff who contribute to the aims of the service and the organization you need to start in the right place.

Skills, knowledge, behaviour and experience

The range of skills, knowledge, behaviour and experience required by those working in LKS will vary from service to service and is often dependent upon the service model (Brophy, 2005). The rapid advances in technology mean that 'what is learnt today will soon be superseded, so the requirement is really about developing the ability and willingness to learn new tools and techniques continually, rather than developing technical expertise' (Corrall, 2004, 32). Organizations need to employ individuals who are willing and able to meet the challenge of continually updating their skills and knowledge. Increasingly jobs will change and evolve over a much shorter time period than they did in the past. Many of the jobs which are advertised now, and the skills and knowledge required to do them, did not exist a few years ago.

Employing people costs money. To employ them but not to invest in their development is counterproductive and can be damaging at both the individual and the organizational level. Development at all levels, including that of the team and the individual, 'is not an optional extra' (McFarlane, 2015, 11) and is central to raising the profile of LKS profession.

Research by the CIPD and Penna (2008) claims that workers in their late 20s, 30s and early 40s picture their career as a 'scramble net' as opposed to the steady progression up the career ladder of former generations. Such workers are used to uncertainty and change. In order to survive and prosper they recognize, amongst other things, the importance of building wide networks, utilizing new technology and making themselves visible both within and outside their profession. The emphasis is on developing generic and specialist skills which can be transferred between teams, organizations and sectors. Career development and progression is determined by skills and knowledge as opposed to age. If organizations do not support the development of such staff then they will not keep them.

'Willingness to undertake training and development' is a standard criterion on many person specifications and job descriptions but how seriously, as managers and individuals, do we take this? The purpose of the second section of this book is to lay the foundations of a relationship between the individual and the service/organization which is conducive to development. Creating an environment and a relationship where development will happen to the benefit of everyone starts at the point that an organization perceives a need to employ someone to fulfil a role.

👍 Best for

- All staff, teams, services and organizations.

▶ More

- Development should be aligned to the organization's strategic objectives. In larger organizations there may be a learning and development strategy which should be used as a starting point in developing a strategy for a team or an individual.
- Consider working towards the Investors in People standard or Customer Service Excellence as a way of demonstrating your commitment to the principals of developing staff.

⚠ To think about

- Development is not all about sending people on expensive training programmes. These do have their place but there are many inexpensive and imaginative ways of developing people which do not involve large financial investment, although they will involve a commitment in terms of time and application.

References

Brophy, P. (2005) *The Academic Library*, 2nd edn, Facet Publishing, London.
Chapman, A. (2014) *Training and Learning Development*, www.businessballs.com/traindev.htm. [Accessed 11 February 2016]
CIPD (2015) *Benefits of CPD*, www.cipd.co.uk/cpd/benefits.aspx. [Accessed 11 February 2016]
CIPD and Penna (2008) *Gen Up: how the four generations work*, www.talentglue.co.uk/blog/box/gen-up-how-the-four-generations-works. [Accessed 24 September 2016]
Corrall, S. (2004) Rethinking Professional Competence for the Networked Environment. In Oldroyd, M. (ed.) *Developing Academic Library Staff for Future Success*, Facet Publishing, London.
McFarlane, K. (2015) Information Management Leaders – We Have Work To Do, *CILIP Update*, March, 11.

Further reading

Cabinet Office (2015) *Customer Service Excellence*, www.customerserviceexcellence.uk.com. [Accessed 11 February 2016]
CIPD (2015) *Learning and Development Strategy*, www.cipd.co.uk/hr-resources/factsheets/learning-talent-development-strategy.aspx. [Accessed 11 February 2016]
Investors in People (2015) *The Standard for People Management*, www.investorsinpeople.com/resources/publications/standard. [Accessed 24 September 2016]

12. Workforce planning

WORKFORCE PLANNING IS about having the right staff in the right place at the right time in order to achieve the aims and objectives of the organization or department. At an organizational level it can involve many processes. Listed below are those activities which the Chartered Institute of Personnel and Development (CIPD) has identified as being part of the workforce planning process (CIPD, 2015):

- succession planning

- flexible working
- labour demand and supply forecasting
- recruitment and retention planning
- skills audit gap analysis
- talent management
- multi-skilling
- job design
- risk management
- outsourcing
- career planning
- scenario planning.

Within the context of this book workforce planning is about ensuring that staff have the skills, knowledge, behaviours and levels of experience to do their jobs. It is not about ensuring that every member of staff is able to do everything but more about using your knowledge of your service to ensure that it is as future-proofed as you can make it. It is about understanding your workforce so that you can work together to achieve the aims and objectives of your service.

Activities which will assist you in accomplishing this, many of which are outlined in further detail in the following tips, include:

- identifying the skills, knowledge, behaviours and levels of experience that are essential in ensuring the work gets done at the level required.
- ensuring that more than one team member can demonstrate these if required.
- putting in place a developmental plan to rectify any gaps you identify.
- ensuring that all essential processes are documented to enable team members to carry out each other's roles if someone is absent at short notice or leaves and is not immediately replaced.
- horizon scanning to identify future skills, knowledge, behaviours and level of experience which will become essential in the near future.
- identifying members of your team who demonstrate potential as future managers or leaders and enabling them to develop the skills, knowledge, behaviours and levels of experience which will allow them to progress.
- understanding why people move on from the team and the types of roles they go to.

Workforce planning is closely linked with service development. At the time of writing CILIP is undertaking a mapping project which aims to produce an accurate picture of the current library, archive, records, information and knowledge workforce. CILIP believe that understanding the workforce is crucial to enabling the development of 'better and targeted services' (CILIP, 2015).

This principle is true regardless of the size of the workforce. Services cannot move forward if those who work within them are not continually developing their skills, knowledge and behaviours. The Knowledge for Healthcare Framework has identified that in order to meet future challenges within the NHS 'the healthcare library and knowledge workforce requires enhanced skills, including synthesising information, knowledge management, marketing, website design and usability testing' (HEE, 2014, 16).

⚐ Best for

- Ensuring that the workforce has the skills to deliver individual, team, department and organizational objectives.

▶ More

- Using analytical tools such as PESTLE (political, economic, sociological, technological, legal, environmental) and SWOT (strengths, weaknesses, opportunities, threats) (Tip 81, p. 211) can be a useful starting point for this process. This can be done individually by managers but is often more usefully achieved as a team exercise.

⚠ To think about

- Don't over-complicate the process. The important thing is to employ individuals who are flexible and keen to develop.

References

CILIP (2015) *Workforce Mapping Project*, www.cilip.org.uk/about/projects-reviews/workforce-mapping. [Accessed 24 September 2016]

CIPD (2015) *Workforce Planning*, www.cipd.co.uk/hr-resources/factsheets/workforce-planning.aspx. [Accessed 7 February 2016]

HEE (2014) *Knowledge for Healthcare Framework*, https://hee.nhs.uk/sites/default/files/documents/Knowledge%20for%20healthcare%20-%20a%20development%20framework.pdf. [Accessed 24 September 2016]

Further reading

CIPD (2015) *PESTLE Analysis*, www.cipd.co.uk/hr-resources/factsheets/pestle-analysis.aspx. [Accessed 7 February 2016]

13. Job descriptions

THE JOB DESCRIPTION outlines the main tasks and responsibilities of a role. It should provide you with a clear outline of the role you wish to recruit to and give potential candidates a good understanding of what would be expected of them if they were successful in the recruitment process. It is an important document, as it forms part of the contract of employment with the successful applicant.

If you have a human resources (HR) department they will usually help you with this. Very often they will have a procedure for you to follow and there might be a standard layout which you will be expected to use. The job description forms the basis for the person specification which is outlined in the next Tip (p. 34). The job description should make clear the following (the headings may vary depending on the organization):

- the job title
- the name of the employing organization
- the department or division in which the job is based
- the title of the person the role is accountable to
- the title(s) of the roles the person is responsible for
- the main purpose of the role
- the main duties and responsibilities associated with the role
- information about the legal requirements of the role, such as responsibilities around health and safety, risk management, confidentiality, data protection and freedom of information.

🖒 Best for

- Clarifying for both the applicant and the employer the main tasks and responsibilities of the role.

▶ More

- In addition to forming part of the legal contract between the employer and employee the job description is one of the building blocks for the psychological contract which will be formed between the successful applicant and the employing organization. The psychological contract is the 'expectations of an employee or workforce towards the employer' (Chapman, 2014).
- Once you have written the job description, and the accompanying person specification, it will usually have to be approved by HR or, in some cases, a panel. It is often at this stage that a salary and/or grade is attached to the post. It is important that the description makes it clear at what level each of

the tasks should be performed to assist in this process. For example, if you are anticipating that the post holder will manage or lead in some or all aspects of the role then make sure this is explicit in the job description.

⚠ To think about

■ It is impossible to cover every single aspect of a role in the job description, particularly as many roles will be subject to rapid change. Most descriptions now include a statement to cover this. This usually states that the job description outlines the current main duties of the post which may be subject to review and that the post holder will be expected to undertake any other duties commensurate with the level of the post or the requirements of the service/organization.

References

Chapman, A. (2014) *The Psychological Contract*, www.businessballs.com/psychological-contracts-theory.htm. [Accessed 11 February 2016]

Further reading

Advisory, Conciliation and Arbitration Service (2014) *Recruitment and Induction*, ACAS, London.
CIPD (2016) *The Psychological Contract*, www.cipd.co.uk/hr-resources/factsheets/psychological-contract.aspx. [Accessed 11 February 2016]

14. Person specifications

THE **PERSON SPECIFICATION** should be drawn up after you have undertaken the role analysis and put together the job description. In some organizations you will be required to base this upon an agreed competency framework. This might be one put together internally or a nationally agreed framework such as Agenda for Change (NHS Employers, 2014) or the Higher Education Role Analysis (ECC, 2014). Your HR department will be able to advise you on this.

The person specification should clearly list the qualifications, skills, knowledge and experience which an individual should possess in order to be successful in a role. The specification is usually broken down into those attributes which are considered to be essential to the role and those which are desirable. Most organizations indicate how the candidate will be expected to demonstrate that they are the right person for the role, the most common being an application form or CV followed by an interview which is often supplemented by a presentation or practical test.

👍 Best for

- Clarifying the competencies required by an individual to undertake the job.
- Enabling those short listing and interviewing for a post to assess a candidate's suitability and ability to carry out a specified role.
- Providing a framework to feedback to applicants and candidates why they were unsuccessful or successful.

▶ More

- The person specification can be used as a framework for developing the person once they are in a role. The successful candidate can use it, in discussion with their line manager, to identify those areas where they require further development.
- If you are drawing up a person specification for a new role then do ask managers in other roles and organizations if you can see examples.

⚠ To think about

- Be realistic. Only classify an attribute as essential if it really is. Strictly speaking you should not be making a job offer to someone who has not demonstrated that they possess an ability which you declared was essential to the role.
- A person specification must be accurate and should only include those aspects of the role which a person could be reasonably asked to provide evidence of. If you cannot think of a way for a person to demonstrate an attribute, for example by providing certificates for qualifications or being able to tell you at interview about something they have done, then you should not include it.

References

ECC (2014) *ECC: a history*, www.ecc.ac.uk/about-us/ecc-a-history. [Accessed 11 February 2016]

NHS Employers (2014) *How Agenda for Change Works*, www.nhsemployers.org/your-workforce/pay-and-reward/pay/agenda-for-change-pay/how-agenda-for-change-works. [Accessed 11 February 2016]

Further reading

CIPD (2015) *Competence and Competency Frameworks,* www.cipd.co.uk/hr-resources/factsheets/competence-competency-frameworks.aspx. [Accessed 11 February 2016]

Acknowledgement

Many thanks to Linda Ferguson, Deputy Director of the Northern Health Care Libraries Unit (www.lihnn.nhs.uk/index.php/hclu) for her help in writing this section.

15. Advertisements

JOB ADVERTISEMENTS CAN often be the first impression that a potential member of staff gets of your service and the organization it serves. They are an essential part of your marketing. In some organizations you might have very little say about how advertisements are worded with reference to the organizational image but you should have a say about the service and role information. As with all communications you need to be clear about the message you want to get across. Following the AIDA (Mind Tools, 2016) formula will assist you with this:

> **AIDA**
> Attract **ATTENTION**
> Build **INTEREST**
> Create **DESIRE**
> Call to **ACTION**

Alan Chapman clarifies this on the BusinessBalls website as follows:

> This means that good job advertisements must first attract attention (from appropriate jobseekers); attract relevant interest (by establishing relevance in the minds of the ideal candidates); create desire (to pursue what looks like a great opportunity), and finally provide a clear instruction for the next action or response.
>
> Chapman, 2006

🖒 Best for

- All vacancies. The advertisement gives you an opportunity to sell the post and your organization. Even if a role is not right for someone at this stage in their career the advertisement could flag you up as an employer they would be interested in working for in the future.

▶ More

- It is good practice to include a contact number or e-mail address so that potential candidates can contact you for an informal chat.
- Think about where to place your advertisement. If it is for a specialist or senior role then advertise as widely as possible.
- Do not underestimate the power of social media. Tweet links to the job advertisement and make use of e-mail lists.
- Enlist the help of your HR team and, if you have one, your communications or marketing team.

⚠ To think about

- Do not oversell the organization or the role. Honesty is important.
- Do not forget the basics such as whether the job is full- or part-time, permanent or temporary, salary range and closing date for applications.

References

Chapman, A. (2006) *Job Adverts: how to design and write effective job advertisements – tips and techniques*, www.businessballs.com/jobadvertswriting.htm. [Accessed 11 February 2016]

Mind Tools (2016) *AIDA: Attention-Interest-Desire-Action*, https://www.mindtools.com/pages/article/AIDA.htm. [Accessed 23 February 2016]

16. Shortlisting

SHORTLISTING MUST BE a systematic and transparent process which is generally, but not always, carried out by those who are going to interview. The most common way of shortlisting is to score the application, using a grid system, against the person specification. At the most basic level the scores are added up at the end and the people who score the highest are invited for interview.

The simplest scoring system to use is:

- fully demonstrates that they meet the criterion = 2 points
- partially demonstrates that they meet the criterion = 1 point
- does not meet the criterion = 0 points.

It is generally recommended that criteria are divided up into essential and desirable and essential criteria should be scored first. Those scoring highest on essential criteria are then scored against desirable criteria and the ones with the highest overall scores are invited to interview.

You should ensure that shortlisting is completed by a minimum of two people. Each person must review the candidates' applications alone before meeting the rest of the shortlisting team in order to avoid bias. The shortlisting team will then meet and compare their notes to decide which candidates they will invite for interview. If a decision cannot be made, ask an appropriate colleague or obtain advice from HR to assist with the process.

Shortlisting should take place as soon as possible after the closing date. It is important to inform candidates in plenty of time if they have an interview. Depending on the number of applicants it is not always practical to inform them all that they haven't been selected for interview but do so if you can and offer feedback. It is important to remember that at this stage an external candidate will still be forming their impression of what the organization will be like to work for. For internal candidates they need to know as soon as possible if their application is to be taken forward as this could have an impact on their future commitment to the organization.

👍 Best for

- Narrowing down the field of applicants to people who will be invited for interview. The aim is to get the best candidates through to the next stage of the process. The ones who, on paper, can do the job.

▶ More

- Involving team members in this process is a good development activity. It helps them understand the process, which can be helpful when they are applying for roles in the future, particularly internal ones. It will also give them a clear understanding of the role you are recruiting to, especially if there have been changes to the job description or if it is a new post.
- If there are a large number of internal candidates for a role or the post is a very senior one it is a good idea to involve someone external to your service or organization to ensure impartiality.
- Generally speaking, libraries don't get hundreds of applications for posts but if a post has attracted a large number of applicants use the essential criteria firstly to narrow down the field, followed by the desirable criteria. If you are still left with too many candidates to interview then look again at the criteria and decide if there are particular ones which are absolutely key to the post. These can then be weighted and the applications re-scored accordingly.

⚠ To think about

- If internal candidates are not offered an interview then inform them in person and offer feedback. It is important that the individual understands why they have not been successful this time. This conversation needs handling sensitively and should be supported by opportunities for them to develop in those areas where they were judged not to meet the standard required.

■ Some organizations have set principles to which you must adhere. For example if a person with a disability or an internal candidate meets all the essential criteria then they must be offered an interview. Make sure you check with your HR department if this is the case for your organization before you begin the shortlisting process.

Further reading

CIPD (2015) *Recruitment: an overview*, www.cipd.co.uk/hr-resources/factsheets/recruitment-overview.aspx. [Viewed 11 February 2016]

CIPD (2015) *Selection Methods*, www.cipd.co.uk/hr-resources/factsheets/selection-methods.aspx. [Viewed 11 February 2016]

17. Interviews

THE PURPOSE OF the interview is to select the best candidate from those shortlisted for the job on offer. For many organizations the interview is the only method used at this stage. Others combine it with tasks such as presentations or tests.

Preparation

Good interviews require in-depth preparation from those who will be conducting them. It is good practice to include the proposed interview date on the job advertisement if possible. Prior to the interview the candidates need to be informed of the following:

• the date, time and venue of the interview
• where they should report to on arrival and who they should ask for
• the names and positions of the people conducting the interview
• if required, details of any presentation or other task they will be expected to undertake
• what paperwork, e.g. certificates, proof of identity, they need to bring with them
• information about how to claim for expenses, if these are paid.

Format

The format of the interview needs to be decided well in advance. There are different types of interviews. The most commonly used in the LKS sector are individual competency interviews conducted by a panel, which this Tip focuses on. Many organizations will have a set interview procedure. It is important to consult with your HR department, if you have one, to ensure that you are following the approved format.

Interviewers

The composition of the interview panel should be decided as early as possible to ensure availability. It is advisable to have at least two people interviewing and, whilst this can vary depending on the role on offer, the proposed line manager should always be involved. Other possible individuals to consider for the panel include:

- the line manager's line manager
- the head of service
- a service stakeholder or user
- an HR member
- another team member
- external interviewer.

Questions

The most important part of the interview preparation is setting and agreeing the questions. These should be linked to the person specification and should build on the information the candidate has provided in their application. Table 17.1 outlines different types of question which are useful to consider when planning the interview.

The majority of set questions in an interview should be open with probing and funnelling techniques used to elicit further information. Generally speaking, closed questions should be used sparingly in this situation. The purpose of the questions is to provide candidates with the opportunity to demonstrate the skills and knowledge they can bring to the role.

The interviewers need to agree who will be asking which questions. If HR does not have a set system for recording and scoring answers then this needs to be agreed in advance. The interviewers need to decide if any weighting system is to be used in the interview for essential skills or knowledge. Finally they need to agree who will be responsible for informing candidates of the panel's decision, providing feedback to individuals and, if required, informing HR of the offered appointment and dealing with any paperwork.

Table 17.1 *Interview question types, adapted from Mind Tools (2015)*

Useful types of question for interviews		
Question type		**Useful for**
Closed	A closed question usually receives a single word or very short, factual answer.	• testing your understanding, or the other person's • concluding a discussion or making a decision • frame setting.
Open	Open questions elicit longer answers. They usually begin with what, why, how. An open question asks the respondent for his or her knowledge, opinion or feelings. 'Tell me' and 'describe' can also be used in the same way as open questions.	• developing an open conversation • finding out more detail • finding out the other person's opinion or issues.
Probing	Asking probing questions is another strategy for finding out more detail. Sometimes it's as simple as asking your respondent for an example, to help you understand a statement they have made. At other times, you need additional information for clarification or to investigate whether there is proof for what has been said.	• gaining clarification to ensure you have the whole story and that you understand it thoroughly • drawing information out of people who are trying to avoid telling you something.
Funnelling	This technique involves starting with general questions, and then homing in on a point in each answer, and asking for more and more detail at each level.	• finding out more detail about a specific point • gaining the interest or increasing the confidence of the person you're speaking with.

The interview

On the day of the interview the room should be prepared well in advance. Ensure that all the equipment is working, if any is required, and that the panel members have copies of the questions with space to make notes for each candidate's responses, copies of the application forms and plenty of spare pens/pencils. Try to make the room as comfortable as possible in terms of temperature – slightly too cool is generally better than too warm – and provide water for the candidates and the panel. Make sure that you will not be disturbed during the interview by people entering the room and check that no fire alarms are scheduled for when you are interviewing. If they are then make sure you inform the relevant candidate that a fire alarm test will be taking place.

When the candidate enters the room the Chair of the panel should introduce him/herself and everyone else present and explain their roles. Inform the candidate that you will be making notes of their answers. If you are going straight to interview with no presentation to the panel first then make sure the candidate is comfortable and then begin asking the questions as agreed. It is important to remember that whilst interviewing is a two-way process it is the interviewee who should be doing most of the talking.

Once the panel has asked all their questions the candidate should be given the opportunity to ask their own questions. At the end of the interview tell the candidate when you expect to make a decision and how they will be informed. Bear in mind that if it is not possible to make a decision on the day it is better to tell candidates you will be notifying them of the decision in a couple of days as opposed to promising to inform them sooner and then not being in a position to do so. It is a good idea to check contact details at this point to ensure you have the correct information to reach them.

Try to schedule plenty of time between interviews. Panel members should score each candidate individually and then discuss the candidate just seen but aim not to compare candidates at this stage. Discussing each candidate following their interview helps fix them in your head in preparation for the final decision at the end of the process.

Selection and feedback

Once you have seen all the candidates the panel should each spend some time individually reviewing each candidate before coming together for a group discussion. If the candidates have given a presentation, been shown around the workplace by a member of the team or done some sort of test which involved other people those people's feedback should be sought at this point.

Once the decision has been made the panel should agree on the feedback which is to be given to the candidates. Feedback should be offered to all candidates, those who have been successful and those who have not. The panel need to decide at this stage what process they should follow if the successful candidate declines the job offer. It is good practice to contact the successful candidate first in case they do decline the offer or request time to think it over.

If the panel cannot agree on their preferred candidate or the successful candidate declines the offer and there isn't a suitable second choice they have a number of options. If the issue is that it has been agreed that none of the candidates are suitable for the role then the panel can either review application forms which were previously discarded or even decide to begin the process again. If the panel can't decide between candidates then having a break from the process and coming back to it the following day can often be beneficial. If a decision still cannot be reached then a second interview with the preferred candidates might be required. The second interview should focus on any gaps in the candidate's skills and knowledge which the panel perceived in the first interview. These options all add to the cost of the recruitment process but are cheaper in the long run than making an unsatisfactory appointment.

🖒 Best for

- Finding out more about the individual candidate's experience, skills and knowledge to enable you to select the person who is the best possible fit for the role you have on offer.

▶ More

- Other ways to involve team members in the process include getting them to show the candidates around the organization, asking the candidates to present to the whole team or having a team member oversee the test, if one has been set. Remember to get feedback from the team if you ask them to participate in this way.
- External interviewers are a good way of getting an outsider's perspective on the candidates. They can be particularly useful when internal candidates are being interviewed, as they will not have prior knowledge of their skills and working methods and so will be helpful in providing an impartial viewpoint which will assist in ensuring the process is perceived to be fair and transparent.

⚠ To think about

- Make notes but be sensitive to the candidate. Don't let note taking take priority over listening to what the person being interviewed is saying. It is very offputting for a candidate to sit in silence when the panel are furiously scribbling away. The notes the panel take should be reminders or memory prompts. If it is important to your organization to have verbatim notes of an interview then include a note-taker on the panel. Do remember that written interview notes might be seen by the candidate so be sensitive as to what you put in writing. Notes should focus on facts and what the candidate actually says, not personal opinions or interpretations.

References

Mind Tools (2015) *Questioning Techniques: asking questions effectively*, www.mindtools.com/pages/article/newTMC_88.htm. [Accessed 11 February 2016]

Further reading

CIPD (2015) *Recruitment: an overview*, www.cipd.co.uk/hr-resources/factsheets/recruitment-overview.aspx. [Viewed 11 February 2016]

CIPD (2015) *Selection Methods*, www.cipd.co.uk/hr-resources/factsheets/selection-methods.aspx. [Viewed 11 February 2016]

18. Interviews – presentations and tests

PRESENTATIONS AND/OR TESTS can be a useful part of the selection process. The same principles used in setting interview questions are applicable when deciding on a test or asking candidates to deliver a presentation. The test or presentation needs to be appropriate to the level of the job and the skills or knowledge being tested should be taken from the person specification.

There are various types of test which candidates can be asked to undertake. Some of the most frequently used in the LKS Sector are:

- preparing and delivering a presentation
- preparing and delivering a mini training session
- undertaking a literature search
- preparing a business case
- shelving
- preparing a strategy
- preparing a marketing plan
- planning a promotional campaign
- producing examples of tailored resources.

Presentations are one of the most common additional activities for candidates. In some cases the candidates will present only to the interview panel. In other cases, particularly for higher-level posts, the presentation will take place in front of the whole team, who will be asked to provide feedback.

Generally presentation titles are sent to candidates in advance but in some cases it might be appropriate to give the candidates the title on the day. They would then be given time to prepare and present on their given topic.

The main task for those assessing a presentation should be deciding if the candidate has covered the topic they were asked to present on in a way that is relevant and meaningful to the post they are being interviewed for. The checklist in Table 18.1 can be helpful in assisting the assessors in scoring the presentation as part of the overall selection process.

Table 18.1 *Presentation scoring checklist*	
• Did the individual clearly introduce themselves and their topic?	
• Was the presentation well structured?	
• Did they keep to time?	
• What was the quality of their visual aids and any other supporting materials?	
• Did the presentation have a clear beginning, middle and end?	
• Did they use a variety of methods likely to appeal to all intelligences?	
• Did they engage with the audience?	
• Did they speak clearly and make eye contact?	

Not all tests have to be carried out on the day of the interview. They can take place beforehand as a means of narrowing down those invited to interview or the candidates can be asked to do the tasks in their own time and either submit them in advance or bring them with them on the day. This approach is particularly useful when asking candidates to produce examples of plans or resources. They can then be asked to explain their rationale for the approach they have taken. This can be a useful way of starting an interview as it gives the candidate the opportunity to talk about something tangible which they have thought about in advance and will, hopefully, encourage them to relax to enable them to perform well.

🖒 Best for

■ Further probing individual candidate's skills, knowledge and experience to ascertain their suitability for the role on offer.

▲ To think about

■ It is important to keep all types of tests relevant to the role on offer and manageable within the constraints of the interview. If you are including a presentation, for example, you will need to schedule extra time into the interview and presenting should be something which the candidate will be expected to do as part of the role.

Further reading

CIPD (2015) *Selection Methods*, www.cipd.co.uk/hr-resources/factsheets/selection-methods.aspx. [Viewed 11 February 2016]

19. Interviews – feedback

PROVIDING FEEDBACK IS an important part of the selection process. It should be offered, as a matter of course, to both successful and unsuccessful candidates. In the case of the successful candidate this is best done face to face as part of the induction process. With unsuccessful candidates it is generally more practical to deliver feedback via a phone call or, if this is not possible, e-mail. This should take place as soon as possible after the selection process has ended.

Giving constructive feedback to unsuccessful candidates is important from the organizational perspective as it confirms that the organization has taken the whole selection process seriously. Providing feedback is a means of acknowledging that individuals have put time and effort into the process even though they have not been successful. It means that unsuccessful candidates will be able to learn from the process they have just participated in and will, hopefully, have a better chance of securing the next role they interview for.

As stated in Tip 17 (p. 39), the panel should agree in advance who will inform the candidates of the outcome of the process and decide how feedback will be provided. It is suggested that unsuccessful candidates are informed of the outcome and then asked if they would like feedback. If they say yes a time should be agreed when the person delivering the feedback can contact them to provide this.

The feedback needs to be related back to the person specification and describe how the individual fared with regard to each of the criteria. It should focus on the individual, include specific examples and, if appropriate, include suggestions as to how the candidate could improve future performance. It should not take the form of a comparison with the successful candidate. Verbal feedback is generally a better option as it gives the candidate the opportunity to seek clarification of the points being made and to express their opinion of the process. Verbal feedback can be followed up with a written statement of the main points made if the candidate requests it. The CIPD (2012) have produced a useful model of delivering effective feedback to unsuccessful candidates which is reproduced in Figure 19.1.

🖒 Best for

- For the successful candidate, receiving feedback from their line manager is the starting point for building their ongoing relationship. Using their performance in the selection process can be a means of identifying individual strengths and areas which require future development.
- For unsuccessful candidates receiving feedback is the last step in the process they have just participated in. Done well it should leave the individuals concerned with a good impression of the organization as a whole and a better understanding of their individual strengths and development needs.

▶ More

- In some cases a candidate might have only just missed out on the role on offer and would be someone the organization would be interested in employing if the opportunity arose in the future. Providing constructive feedback to such candidates and telling them that you would welcome applications from them in the future is a way of leaving the door open to an individual who would be a good fit for your team and organization.
- Occasionally the situation might arise where another position arises very soon after the interview which is suitable for this candidate. Some organizations

have policies whereby if this occurs, and a suitable candidate has been interviewed within a set period, the role can be offered to them without advertising it more widely or re-interviewing the individual. If the candidate had a good experience with the organization which included receiving constructive feedback then, depending on their circumstances, they are more likely to accept such an offer, which will save the employing organization time and money.

Set the scene
- Check it is a good time for them to talk
- Thank them for submitting an application or attending an interview
- Explain who you are and what you role was in the shortlisting/intereviewing process
- Start with something positive

Invite self-assessment
- Ask the person how they think the interview went
- Ask what they are hoping to get out of the feedback session
- Provide the context – provide the number of applications received and the number of applicants shortlisted and/or appointed

Give your feedback
- Pull out 2-3 key points to focus on
- Prepare – know what you want to say
- Confine your feedback to the selection criteria/competencies measured
- Talk about facts

End
- Give the individual a chance to respond
- Check that they understand what you have said
- End on a positive note

Figure 19.1 *Four steps to providing effective feedback, adapted from CIPD (2012) Reproduced with permission of the publisher, the Chartered Institute of Personnel and Development, London (www.cipd.co.uk)*

⚠ To think about

- Generally speaking it is not helpful to tell a candidate that they were second in the selection process. This is particularly unhelpful when an internal applicant is rejected, but will be line managed by the successful candidate. Sharing this information could cause resentment and get the relationship between the individuals off to a bad start which could be difficult to recover from.

References

CIPD (2012) *Giving Feedback to Candidates,*
www.cipd.co.uk/toolclicks/interpersonalskills/training-tools/interviewing-skills/giving-feedback/support-material.aspx. [Accessed 11 February 2016]

20. Inductions

A **GOOD INDUCTION** is crucial to building a relationship between the new member of staff, their immediate team and the employing organization. Many larger organizations will have formal induction events, often lasting one or two days, which it is compulsory for all new staff to attend. However, a proper induction into an organization and team needs to consist of more than this and should last longer.

All staff have a need to understand the basics of how their organization works. This includes when and how they are paid, car parking, the aims and objective of the organization and health and safety considerations, including fire procedures and personal safety. If this information is not covered at organizational level then it is essential that it be dealt with by the line manager or a designated person. It might be useful to put together a checklist to ensure that all the basics have been covered. If you have an HR department they should be able to assist with this. CIPD and ACAS both provide useful guidance on what an induction needs to cover (see Further Reading, p. 50).

Induction at a local level needs to cover much more than the essentials. If the new post holder will not have the opportunity to spend time with the outgoing post holder the first step to a successful induction will be the exit interview with the person who is moving on (Tip 32, p. 74). At this interview try and ascertain what the outgoing post holder wishes they had been told when they started, what they would like to share with their successor and any useful contacts. If it can be arranged for them to spend time with the new person then do this. If the post is a new one then the line manager needs to think about these questions and prepare answers for the incoming staff member. Induction will vary from post to post and from organization to organization. The following list covers some of the topics, conversation points and activities which you might want to consider, including in an induction plan for a new post holder:

- Organizational objectives.
- Service strategy and other important documents, e.g. marketing plan.
- What are the key tasks of the role?
- What are the individual's expectations of the post?
- How often will the individual and their line manager meet in the first few weeks?
- What are their training/development needs? How will these be addressed?
- What committees/departmental meetings should the post holder attend? Who is the key contact for these? Where are the minutes and other relevant documents stored?
- Would the post holder benefit from having a buddy or a mentor?
- Visits to other departments and organizations can be useful.

👍 Best for

- ■ Building a relationship between an individual and their team, line manager and organization.
- ■ Enabling a new post holder to settle in and build their confidence.

▶ More

- ■ A well planned induction is a necessity not just for those new to an organization. Although it may not need to be as all-encompassing as for a totally new member of staff, thought should be given to inductions for staff who have been promoted or have been absent from the workplace for a prolonged period of time due to family reasons or illness or those who have taken a sabbatical.

⚠ To think about

- ■ Do not stint on an induction. Rushing this and thereby overwhelming an individual with information, missing things out or making assumptions about what someone knows or understands can cause long-term damage to the relationship between an individual and their team/organization.
- ■ One-to-ones between the line manager and the new member of staff are a crucial part of induction and should be prioritized.

Further reading

ACAS (2014) *Recruitment and Induction,* www.acas.org.uk/index.aspx?articleid=1461.
[Accessed 11 February 2016]
CIPD (2014) *Induction,* www.cipd.co.uk/hr-resources/factsheets/induction.aspx.
[Accessed 11 February 2016]

21. Managing performance

AT ITS MOST basic level the purpose of management is to ensure that the work gets done. To achieve this aim managers need to create an environment in which staff can perform their roles to the agreed standard. In turn staff members need to develop the skills, knowledge, experience and behaviours to enable them to do this. Managing staff performance, in a positive and pro-active way, is the key to achieving this purpose.

In some organizations there will be a clear performance management framework which managers will be expected to adhere to. In others there may be arrangements for some aspects of performance management, such as recruitment and appraisals, whilst in others there may be nothing formal. In all of these instances managers will be able to introduce some performance management activities. Where there is a formal system it is best to work within it, as otherwise you are making work for yourself. It is recommended that whatever the structure of your organization you discuss any concerns you have about setting up a performance management framework with your HR department, if you have one, or with other managers.

Performance management begins before an individual has started with an organization. The steps described prior to this Tip are instrumental in starting to build the relationship between the individual and their manager, team and organization. The job description and the person specification are the basic framework documents which outline what is expected of the individual in their role. The individual's experience of the selection process and their induction will have started to build their impressions of the organization, which will form part of their emotional or psychological contract.

Communication is the key to creating a culture which enables good performance. Day-to-day performance management is made up of a number of activities which are covered in the Tips following this one, which include appraisals (p. 54 and p. 56), one-to-ones (p. 61) and team meetings (p. 68).

Individuals need to understand what their manager means by good performance. They need to be clear about what is deemed an acceptable level of performance and how the work that they do contributes to the work of the team and the overall success of their organization.

Managers need to develop clear methods of communication with the individuals and teams that they are responsible for. They need to know the areas that their individual staff are competent in and understand where they need support to develop. Managing performance using the tools outlined in the following Tips should provide the benefits set out in Table 21.1.

Table 21.1 *Benefits of managing performance*	
For the individual	**For the manager**
• A clear understanding of what is expected of them in terms of their day-to-day tasks and their longer-term projects. • The opportunity to contribute to decisions about the work of the team and the direction in which it should progress. • A means of sharing their development needs and long-term aspirations in a supportive environment. • Protected time to discuss any concerns or ideas.	• An opportunity to get to know their direct reports and to understand what is important to them in terms of work. • Assurance that all team members are clear about what is an acceptable level of performance. • A means to ensure that staff receive regular and individual feedback on their progress and performance. • A way of addressing any concerns about performance before it becomes an issue.

🖒 Best for

■ Ensuring that the work gets done to an acceptable standard in a way that benefits the individual, the team and the organization.

■ Building a pro-active, respectful and two-way relationship between an individual and their line manager.

▶ More

■ For some organizations managing performance has become associated with dealing with problems or unsatisfactory behaviour, which is a negative way of approaching performance management. All performance needs to be managed. It should be a day-to-day part of the manager's role which ensures issues are dealt with before they become problematic.

■ If you are a manager who is inheriting a team which has never been performance managed before then proceed slowly. Introducing one-to-ones and team meetings is a good way to start. The one-to-ones will enable you to get to know the individuals who make up your team and the team meetings will provide you with an opportunity to see how they interact with each other.

▲ To think about

■ Performance management is not about micro-managing individuals. Rather it is about creating an environment in which staff feel motivated to do their job well and wish to further develop themselves. It is a two-way process which enables the individual to comment on how their role develops and the work they do.

Further reading

CIPD (2015) *Performance Management: an overview*, www.cipd.co.uk/hr-resources/factsheets/performance-management-overview.aspx. [Accessed 10 January 2016]

Harrison, R. (2009) *Learning and Development*, 5th edn, CIPD, London.

22. Team development plans

A **KEY COMPONENT** of successful performance management is to ensure that individuals are equipped with the skills, knowledge, experience and behaviours to do the job in hand. As a manager you will need to understand clearly those areas where individual team members and the team as a whole are competent and any areas which require further development. You will then need to draw up a plan to address any development needs you have identified. This plan should take into account the aspirations of individual members of the team.

The first step in drawing up an effective development plan is gaining an understanding of what the development needs are in terms of the individual, the team and the organization. This needs to take into account a number of factors, including:

- the requirements of the task/job/project
- the current skills, experience and knowledge level of the individual
- the current skills, experience and knowledge level of the team as a whole
- how individual team members like to learn.

As a line manager you will have numerous sources of information from which to gather this information. These include, but are not limited to:

- your own observations of the skills, knowledge and experience of individual team members and the team as a whole
- information obtained through more formal avenues such as personal development plans, one-to-ones and appraisals
- your knowledge of the tasks individuals and the team are currently expected to perform
- your knowledge of forthcoming projects
- horizon scanning, both internally and externally, to identify future trends and developments which may have an impact on your service.

In addition to this information you might have access to organizational information, such as a training needs analysis conducted by HR or, if your team is part of a larger LKS team, an analysis carried out for the service as a whole. The CILIP Professional Skills and Knowledge Base (CILIP, 2013) can be a useful tool in helping to identify individual development needs.

Armed with this knowledge you can begin to put together a development plan. The priority is to get the current work done, followed by work coming up and then look at the longer-term needs of the individual, team and organization. In some organizations there might be some mandatory training requirements which you will need to take account of and ensure that team members are given the time to complete these.

The plan will need to include proposed ways of developing the skills each team member requires. This does not have to be a course or include time spent away from the workplace, although these methods will have their place. Many of the tips in the third section of this book (p. 81) focus on activities which occur naturally in the workplace and demonstrate how they can be used for development.

The plan will need to include deadlines for planned development. This can sometimes be difficult if the identified need is not an immediate one. If training takes place too early then individuals can forget what they have learned. Leave it too late and they can feel stressed and unprepared to take on new tasks or areas of work.

The final factor to consider is how you will know development has taken place. You will need to consider how you will check the level of understanding and expertise that the individual has achieved as a result of the development activity.

A basic example of a team development plan is provided in Table 22.1 and you can find lots more on the internet. It is best to keep it as simple as possible. The purpose is not designing or updating complicated plans but to spend time ensuring that staff develop and the work gets done.

👍 Best for

- Understanding the development needs of the individuals who make up your team to ensure that the job gets done to the required level.
- Planning development activities which meet the requirements of the individual, the team and the organization.

References

CILIP (2013) *Your Professional Knowledge and Skills Base: identify gaps and maximise opportunities along your career path*, CILIP, London.

Table 22.1 *Example of a team development plan*

Name	Development need	How need will be met	Resources	Deadline	Progress
A	Becoming more confident in presenting to large groups.	Arrange for A to shadow a more confident team member. Ask A to peer-review the colleague's session and ask them to peer-review theirs. Provide opportunities for A to present in a safe environment, such as team meetings.	No additional resources required.	Sept – in prep for delivering inductions to new starters.	Sept – A reports that they feel more confident in delivering presentations. This is reflected in the peer reviews carried out by colleagues and by the evaluation forms completed by attendees at the inductions.
	Become a Chartered member of CILIP	Get A to look into course on assembling a portfolio. Assist A in finding a mentor outside this sector.	Provide time for A to undertake activities as required, including mentor meetings.	Dec	Sept – A is currently in the process of putting together their portfolio and still aims to submit by December
B	Improve confidence in literature searching skills	Arrange for B to buddy up with a more confident colleague in another team who will check their searches for them and provide feedback.	No additional resources required.	Sept–Mar	Sept – Have identified buddy and a meeting has taken place to agree how this will work.
Whole team	Improve customer service skills	Commission a trainer to run a course on the principles of good customer service. Work with team to write customer charter which outlines our responsibilities to the customer.	Cost of hiring trainer. Training room in library can be used as venue.	Sept	Sept – course took place in July. Feedback from team members was positive and they have worked together to produce a customer charter. Success will be measured by customer feedback and survey over the next 3 months.

Further reading

CIPD (2015) *Identifying Learning and Development Needs*, www.cipd.co.uk/hr-resources/factsheets/identifying-learning-talent-development-needs.aspx. [Accessed 23 January 2016]

23. Appraisals – preparing

CIPD (2015) DESCRIBES performance appraisals (or performance reviews) as an opportunity for an employee and their line manager to discuss their performance, future goals, development needs and to identify any resources or training which they need. Typically, the appraisal is an annual event, although some organizations may undertake these more regularly. It usually ends with both parties agreeing a number of personal objectives for the coming year which are linked to both departmental and organizational core objectives. The appraisal provides an opportunity to bring together organizational, LKS and individual aims into one place and the meeting should be a two-way conversation between the employee and their line manager.

To ensure that both parties get the most out of an appraisal meeting, it is essential that both the individual employee and their line manager prepare in advance. Here are a number of tips which can help your meeting to run smoothly:

- Agree a date and a time that is mutually beneficial allowing enough time to prepare.
- Book a room that is comfortable and suitable for both of you. Your office may be the easiest place to meet, but may be intimidating for the appraisee. You could meet in a coffee shop or somewhere more informal, but ensure that you can maintain confidentiality.
- Ensure that the individual understands the process and that they have a copy of last year's appraisal and the new documentation.
- Read last year's appraisal documentation and complete the documentation for the coming year:
  — how do you rate their performance?
  — have they fulfilled last year's objectives?
  — if not, do you know why?
- Review the job description. Are they fulfilling the requirements of their job description and does it still represent their role?
- Ensure that you have a good understanding of your organizational mission, values and goals so that you can link these to the appraisal process.
- Prior to the meeting identify those key objectives which are clearly linked to your LKS's overall plan. These may change during the meeting, but it is good to have a clear idea beforehand of what you would like the team member to achieve in the coming year.
- Review their sickness and training records to identify any trends or training needs which may need to be addressed.
- Familiarize yourself with courses, mandatory training requirements and other opportunities which may help the individual to fulfil their role.

Usually your organization will provide standard paperwork that both parties should review and complete in advance of the meeting. However, in addition to more formal paperwork, you can start planning for your employee appraisals a year in advance. Keeping a structured or unstructured diary listing their key achievements and challenges throughout the year will ensure that you have all the information you need to hand for a really successful meeting (University of California Human Resources, 2015).

🖒 Best for

■ Ensuring that the appraisal meeting runs smoothly, covers the right topics and finishes on time.

▶ More

■ Although the appraisal is the formal documentation of a team member's aims, when used alongside regular one-to-one meetings it should not present any surprises for either the line manager or the individual.

⚠ To think about

■ If you do not prepare adequately for the meeting this can send a message to the employee that they are not important. This can damage morale, especially if they have put a lot of effort into preparing for the appraisal.

References

CIPD (2015) *Performance Appraisal*,
   www.cipd.co.uk/hr-resources/factsheets/performance-appraisal.aspx.
   [Accessed 24 September 2016]
University of California Human Resources (2015) *Supervisor's Guide to Performance Appraisals*, http://hr.ucr.edu/docs/performance/supervisorsguide.pdf. [Accessed 5 October 2015]

24. Appraisals – conducting

HAVING PREPARED ALL the paperwork in advance of the appraisal meeting both you and your employee should arrive with a clear idea of what will happen. CIPD (2015) indicates that a performance appraisal meeting should include:

• measurement against clearly defined objectives and values
• an opportunity to give feedback to the individual about their progress and performance
• an opportunity for positive reinforcement
• facilitation of an honest and open discussion in which the employee can raise concerns or issues

- ending by defining SMART goals (see Tip 25, p. 59) and objectives for the coming year which both parties agree.

The appraisal meeting should provide space for the employee to discuss their career objectives, identify their personal training needs and highlight their plans for the coming year. Whilst the appraisal is often focused on service and organizational objectives and how the employee can contribute to these, it also provides space for you to find out more about the individual and their aspirations.

Role of the manager

As the line manager or supervisor, your role is to manage the process and keep things on track. The meeting should have a clear structure and be focused on the individual, but it should be sensitively handled and allow for an honest and open discussion. Having a working relationship which is based on trust is integral to being able to give and receive honest feedback and you should both agree the next steps.

You need to ensure that you do not dominate the discussion and that you both have the opportunity to speak and be heard. You are not dictating what should happen or controlling the discussion, even if there are both positive and negative issues that you wish to discuss. The appraisal is about assessing an individual's performance, identifying training needs and setting goals for improvement. If not handled well it can be demotivating for the employee and can result in disengagement.

Facilitating an effective appraisal meeting requires you to have well developed skills in a number of areas and the following list provides some techniques which can improve the appraisal meeting.

- use coaching techniques for a solution-focused approach
- use mentoring techniques to provide guidance and to make suggestions
- develop feedback skills to ensure clarity of purpose
- employ active listening techniques to ensure you hear what they say
- ask the right questions in a non-threatening way to help you learn what is important to the employee
- learn how to have difficult conversations so that you can address issues with performance.

Complete the relevant paperwork as soon as possible after the meeting and send it to the appraisee for feedback. The paperwork should include an overview of the previous year's performance, both positive and negative, including objectives which link to LKS and organizational objectives, whilst also supporting the individual's personal career goals. This performance appraisal should be signed off by both of you and should underpin any one-to-ones that you have with the team member during the year.

Ongoing process

The appraisal is part of an ongoing process and regular meetings should occur throughout the year to ensure that performance is to the standard agreed in the appraisal. Regular meetings will help ensure that objectives are on track and will enable you both to identify problems and develop solutions along the way. There should be no surprises for either you or your employee in the annual performance appraisal meeting, as any ongoing issues with performance or any new training needs should be addressed throughout the year.

👍 Best for

- Providing space for the employee to discuss any challenges or performance issues, to identify any training needs and to highlight their aspirations.
- The performance appraisal enables you as the line manager to review the previous year's objectives and assess completion. It also provides a space for you to offer feedback to the team member about good performance and also to follow up any areas where performance is below standard.
- Coming to an agreement about priorities for the coming year which you are both signed up to.

▶ More

- The meeting is not just about looking backwards over the past year, but should focus on developing the individual in their role for the coming year.
- Ensure that you are well informed before the meeting and have all your paperwork to hand and examples of work that you would like to discuss. Feedback from colleagues and service users will also help you to have a well rounded discussion.

⚠ To think about

- Ensure that you are honest about what went well over the past year and what can be improved upon. You need to be clear in your feedback, even if it is not all positive, and be prepared to have challenging conversations.
- It is human nature to remember the bad things that happened, but do not allow these to become the main focus of the meeting. Refer to your diary and

highlight the positives as well as the negatives, otherwise the whole experience will become demotivating for the individual. The worst thing that you can do is save up any performance issues until appraisal day and deal with them all then; ensure that the individual is supported throughout the year.

■ Switch off your computer and your telephone and give the employee your full attention. Even better, find somewhere private away from the office which might provide a more relaxed and informal space to have a confidential discussion.

References

CIPD (2015) *Performance Appraisal*, www.cipd.co.uk/hr-resources/factsheets/ performance-appraisal.aspx. [Accessed 5 October 2016]

Further reading

University of California Human Resources (2015) *Supervisor's Guide to Performance Appraisals*, http://hr.ucr.edu/docs/performance/supervisorsguide.pdf. [Accessed 5 October 2016]

25. Setting objectives

MANAGERS AND TEAM leaders will be required to set objectives for individuals and teams within the LKS environment. If outcomes are not agreed and clearly defined from the outset, this can jeopardize the success of any project, whether large or small.

At the beginning of the project, even before any objectives are set, discuss with your team what the desired outcome will look like. This could be the development and delivery of a new training course, updating the LKS website or a reclassification project. Being really clear from the outset is integral to the success of any project.

I want all pages on the library website to be revamped with the new logo and the content to be updated.

I want you to develop a literature search training course for junior library staff and to deliver it on 12th April.

During the summer holidays we need to reclassify the business section of the library.

It is a good strategy to ask team members to articulate the outcome in their own words. This ensures that everyone has the same goal in mind.

Once you are all agreed on the outcome of a project, you can start to work with the team to allocate personal objectives. All objectives should be SMART (see Table 25.1).

Table 25.1 *SMART objectives, adapted from Chapman (2014)*	
Specific	Avoid unclear or ambiguous objectives and ensure they are clearly described, e.g. 'increase usage statistics'.
Measurable	Decide how you will measure success and what the desired outcome will be, e.g. '10% increase in usage'.
Agreed	Everyone who is involved should be able to describe the objectives and outcomes and should be involved in development.
Realistic	Ensure that the objectives can be achieved within existing resources, e.g. staff, time, equipment, etc.
Timebound	Set clear timescales for regular monitoring and completion.

Some simple tips for good objective setting:

- Make sure that you select the right person for the job.
- Ensure they are supported and given additional training as needed.
- Discuss what resources are needed to ensure successful delivery.
- Agree deadlines and ensure that they are realistic.
- Monitor progress and provide support and feedback on an ongoing basis.
- If you cannot determine whether the objective is being achieved, revisit and redefine if necessary, as it may not be SMART.

👍 Best for

- Ensuring that individuals within the team know exactly what they are expected to do and what the outcomes of their work will look like.
- Ensuring successful completion of both large- and small-scale projects.

▶ More

- Ensuring that all team members can clearly articulate their objectives and have the right resources and skills to be able to implement them. By telling you what they think the expected outcome will be, you can ensure that everyone is working towards the same goal.
- Apply the SMART mnemonic to all objectives to ensure success.

⚠ To think about

- Objectives which are not SMART are difficult to achieve and difficult to measure. Put some time into clearly defining objectives.
- Projects often fail when one or more team members do not have a clear understanding of the expected outcome.

References

Chapman, A. (2014) *Acronyms and Abbreviations: SMART,* www.businessballs.com/acronyms.htm#SMART-acronym. [Accessed 11 February 2016]

26. One-to-ones

REGULAR ONE-TO-ONE MEETINGS with your direct reports are essential to improving communication and establishing good relationships. Meetings can be monthly or weekly, dependent on time constraints or your LKS's needs. Meetings should remain confidential, be open, honest and provide an opportunity for two-way communication. Adair (2007) suggests that the one-to-one can help to create a supportive relationship, ensure clear direction and identify ongoing development needs. Meetings can be informal, used as a way to keep in touch with team members, or can be part of a formal performance management, appraisal or development process.

Well conducted meetings should be organized to give the individual time to discuss any problems, raise any issues and make suggestions for improving services. You should encourage the individual to use this time to ask you whether they can attend training courses or events which may help them to fulfil the requirements of their job. As a manager it is your role to listen, take suggestions on board, coach staff to find solutions, work with the individual to resolve any issues and essentially follow through on any actions.

Whilst the one-to-one meeting should provide a safe space for the individual to talk to you, it is also an opportunity for you to address any issues with performance, keep track of projects and objectives and find out what is really important to your team members. Ensure that you give constructive feedback. Crucially you should not dominate the meeting, but you must ensure that you have set time aside to address any issues that you want to discuss. The meeting should not be confrontational and you need to be aware of the power balance in play.

A well organized meeting will be rewarding, with each participant having a clear understanding of the purpose. An agenda set prior to the meeting ensures that the individual can prepare and it is important that you both review the notes of the previous meeting. A basic template can help to maintain focus for the meeting and could include the following points:

- meeting date
- areas for discussion – individual
- areas for discussion – manager
- follow-up actions.

Hedges (2013) makes a number of suggestions for successful one-to-ones: having a clear schedule, sharing the air, being present (no phone or e-mail), following up on actions and having a clear structure.

Example from practice: Victoria Treadway (2015) – LKS manager (NHS)

Victoria used one-to-one meetings to reconnect with her team when transferring to her new role as a library manager and after returning from a 10-month period of maternity leave.

'The benefits to me as a manager are clear, and the service benefits are beginning to emerge. My next step is to ask for feedback from the team; that's something I hope to do over the next few weeks. I'd love to continue the regular, scheduled one-to-ones on a permanent basis, and I hope that they'll continue to be as productive and valuable as they have been so far.'

⭐ Best for

- Maintaining relationships with individuals in the team and identifying issues before they become entrenched and problematic. You can coach the individual to find a solution or act as a mentor and offer suggestions.
- Identifying problems or issues early, tracking performance against individual and team objectives and providing an opportunity to set clear objectives and keep projects on track.
- If you take just one Tip from this book, then make it this one. One-to-ones are the most effective method of getting to know the individual members of your team and understanding what is important to them.

▶ More

- Good for building trust and rapport and making you accessible to your team.

⚠ To think about

- Ensure that you follow up any actions and make a note of anything which is agreed at the meeting. A quick e-mail or notes are really useful to ensure that you both know what you agreed to do and to clarify actions.

■ Do not cancel meetings or frequently postpone them. If this becomes a regular occurrence, you are in danger of sending the message that a meeting with the individual is less important than other things. This can be damaging to relationships and really impact negatively on morale.

References

Adair, J. (2007) 100 *Greatest Ideas for Effective Leadership and Management,* Capstone Publishing, Chichester.

Hedges, K. (2013) *The Secret to Effective One-on-one Meetings with Direct Reports,* Forbes blog, www.forbes.com/sites/work-in-progress/2013/11/11/the-secret-to-effective-one-on-one-meetings-with-direct-reports. [Accessed 21 February 2016]

Treadway, V. (2015) *Don't Underestimate the Power of the One-to-one!,* LIHNN Clinical Librarians Blog, https://lihnnclinicallibs.wordpress.com/2015/01/21/case-study-dont-underestimate-the-power-of-the-one-to-one-by-victoria-treadway. [Accessed 21 February 2016]

27. Feedback – general

PROVIDING STAFF WITH feedback on their performance as individuals and as a team is an important part of performance management. It enables individuals to be clear about what is expected of them and assists them in identifying areas they need to develop.

If you hold regular one-to-ones with your staff you will have plenty of opportunities to provide feedback. It should be a way of enabling two-way communication between yourself and the individuals you line manage. It is not about telling people what to do, rather it is a means of encouraging them to think about and reflect upon their own performance. Done well, providing regular feedback should enhance an individual's confidence and improve their overall performance.

The principle behind feedback is that it is about the individual and their performance. It should not be about things they cannot change and it should be relevant to their role. There are numerous models of proving feedback. A quick search on the internet for 'feedback models' will provide you with lots of examples for you to select one which suits your style of management and which you feel comfortable with.

If you are new to providing feedback you might need to prepare in advance what you are going to say. Points to reflect on in preparation for providing feedback include the following:

- Think about what you want the outcome of the feedback to be. What is the skill, knowledge or behaviour that you want changed or encouraged?
- Can you provide a clear example of what you are providing feedback on? It is not good practice to provide feedback on something that you have not witnessed yourself or that you do not have clear evidence of.
- Consider the questions you might want to ask the individual to encourage them to reflect on the situation under discussion. What do they think happened? What do they think went well? What would they do differently in future? What support do they need to make any changes? The idea is for the individual to take ownership of their own performance and work to improve or maintain it.
- Think about the language you want to use. You need to use positive language and ask open questions. This is about working together, not about one individual judging another. You need to keep the discussion factual and allow the individual the opportunity to put their point of view across.
- If the feedback is around encouraging a change in the individual how might you deal with the situation if they do not perceive it as something which needs to change? This is why it is important that you have observed the situation under discussion or have concrete evidence of what has happened.

One of the simplest feedback models to put the above into practice is the EEC model, which is outlined in Table 27.1.

Table 27.1 *EEC model, adapted from KnowHow NonProfit (2014)*	
Evidence	This is where you give an example of what the individual has actually done. This should be something you have witnessed yourself or that you can clearly evidence.
Effect	Explain to the individual the effect of their actions. Do not be judgemental or emotional. Stick to the facts.
Change	Work with the individual to identify what changes they need to make. This is about guiding them as opposed to telling them what to do.

👍 Best for

- Providing an individual with information about their ongoing performance in a supportive way which encourages them to develop and take responsibility for their development.

► More

- Feedback is not just about bringing about change. In many cases it will be appropriate to provide feedback to let an individual know that they are performing well. As it is good practice to manage all performance then part of this is remembering to provide feedback when something has gone well or better than expected.

- If an individual requires more detailed feedback on their performance, 360 degree feedback could be something to consider. This is where a number of people who work with the individual but have different relationships with them, such as line manager, fellow team member, someone they line-manage, colleagues in other teams and maybe even service users or customers, complete a questionnaire about the performance of the individual. See the Further Reading section below for a link to further information on this process.

⚠ To think about

- It is not practical to provide detailed feedback on every aspect of performance all the time. As a manager you will need to decide when feedback is needed and when it is not.
- Generally speaking it is best to provide feedback as close to the incident under discussion as possible. This is one of the reasons that regular one-to-ones are so important.

References

KnowHow NonProfit (2014) *Giving and Receiving Feedback*, https://knowhownonprofit.org/people/your-development/working-with-people/feedback. [Accessed 27 January 2016]

Further reading

CIPD (2015) *Feedback – 360 Degree*, www.cipd.co.uk/hr-resources/factsheets/360-degree-feedback.aspx. [Accessed 28 January 2016]

28. Team building

A **LARGE PROPORTION** of the work carried out in LKS is carried out by teams. Teams are important because they can achieve more than individuals working alone and can allow those individuals to play to their strengths. Being a member of a high-performing team allows individuals to develop, provides motivation and can make work more satisfying and fun.

What makes a team?

Teams can be made up of different numbers of individuals. In some organizations the team may be as small as two people, in others it will be much larger. In many places people can be a member of more than one team. Teams can have clearly defined roles such as working on a specific project or function, for example managing stock or running information literacy training. Alternatively they can have a broader remit, particularly where there are only a small number of individuals employed to undertake this type of work and be responsible for all the tasks carried out in respect of LKS. Increasingly individuals may work in geographically dispersed teams where the only communication is digital or they may be working on specific projects with people employed by other organizations.

Effective team working

If you are in the position of bringing a team together then it is important for you to think about what is the objective of the team and the skills, knowledge and experience you require from the individual team members to fulfil it. More often you will be inheriting a team from someone else or you might be promoted to lead a team of which you were previously a member. Whatever the circumstances, as a manager of a team you have a responsibility to ensure the individuals work together in an effective and efficient manner. For teams to work effectively, individual members need to have a clear understanding of what they are expected to contribute and what the roles of the other members are. Team leaders need to understand the individual strengths and development needs of the team members whilst offering guidance and direction to ensure that the task in hand is completed to a satisfactory level. Communication from and to the manager and amongst team members is crucial to success. How this is facilitated should be agreed early on and then should be subject to regular review.

The Tuckman model

Tuckman (Chapman, 2016) has identified five stages in developing successful teams and the role of the line manager at each stage. Using this model can assist you in assessing the stage your team is at and help you to determine your own role. The first four stages of this model are outlined in Figure 28.1.

The fifth stage which Tuckman identified is Adjourning. This occurs when the team breaks up. This can be because the particular project they were bought together to work on has come to an end but could also be because someone is leaving the team. When someone leaves a high-performing team and is either replaced or the work redistributed then the team will have to

Figure 28.1 *Tuckman's model developing a successful team, adapted from Chapman (2016)*

repeat the process outlined above. They might move through the stages more quickly than they did the first time round but the process will still take place. It is important for the line manager to acknowledge that this is happening and to accept that they may have to provide more guidance and support than they had previously been required to supply.

The above model can be useful in helping to understand conflict within teams. As the leader of a team you need to decide when to step in to deal with conflict and when to leave team members to sort it out amongst themselves. Generally speaking, it is best to try and let the team sort itself out. Conflict within a team is not always a sign that the team is not working. It can be a demonstration that the individual members are comfortable in expressing their own views and ideas which can lead to increased motivation and a higher standard of work. You will need to step in if the situation starts to cause distress to individuals or gets in the way of the work. Having regular one-to-ones with individual team members should mean that you are aware if the team's way of working is causing problems and be in a position to deal with it before it gets out of hand.

👍 Best for

■ Getting the work done in the most efficient and effective way.

▶ **More**

- Dr Meredith Belbin has written extensively on the different roles which individuals demonstrate in teams. Undertaking a Belbin assessment can be a useful exercise in understanding how the individuals that make up your team like to work within a group situation and could explain any areas of conflict. See the Further Reading section below for more information.
- Team meetings are an important part of team building. In some organizations such meetings, along with away days, might be the only time the team get together. These meetings should occur frequently, although if you have part-time members of the team, either because they are also assigned to other teams or because they work part-time, then it is important to rotate when the meetings take place to ensure that everyone gets to attend at least some of the meetings. If the team is geographically dispersed then meeting digitally is an option. Team meetings do not necessarily require a formal record of what has taken place but it can be useful to take some notes to remind members of what has been discussed and any resulting actions.
- Away days can be a good way of building and consolidating team relationships. They can be used for numerous purposes, including planning a project, problem solving or simply as a means for individuals to get to know each other better away from the pressures and interruptions of the main workplace. They do require planning in advance and should have a clear purpose to ensure they are a worthwhile use of time and money. They have a particular purpose for teams which work remotely, as this may be the only opportunity they have to physically get together.

References

Chapman, A. (2016) *Tuckman Forming Storming Norming Performing Model*, www.businessballs.com/tuckmanformingstormingnormingperforming.htm. [Accessed 29 January 2016]

Further reading

Belbin, M. (2016) *Belbin Team Roles*, www.belbin.com/about/belbin-team-roles. [Accessed 28 January 2016]

29. Team meetings

AS MANAGERS OR supervisors of LKS teams you will be regularly involved in formal, scheduled meetings as part of the day-to-day running of the service. These could be meetings with other LKS staff or alternatively with stakeholders or users of your service, examples of which are management meetings, user group meetings or health and safety meetings (ILM, 2007). This Tip focuses on group meetings (one-to-one meetings are discussed in Tip 26, p. 61) and we will consider how you can make the most of these meetings by organizing them and facilitating them effectively.

Love them or not, meetings are an essential part of managing your teams and provide the opportunity for you to communicate with them to track progress against organizational objectives, complete and allocate work, address any issues or deliver information to the group. ILM (2007) suggest that team meetings have a range of purposes, including communicating information, management control, decision making and solving problems.

For a meeting to be successful it is essential that attendees understand the purpose of the meeting and a good way of doing this is to agree these beforehand and record them in the terms of reference. Terms of reference provide clarity about the purpose of the meeting, how it will run, where it will take place, who needs to attend and frequency. Establishing a clear purpose at the outset provides a shared vision and identity for the team. A well conducted meeting will be well prepared and people should know what they need to bring and whether they will have any specific roles, e.g. Chair, minute taker or participant. An agenda which includes timings for the meeting, minutes of the previous meeting, an action log and any additional reading should be distributed in advance and any questions for discussion will ensure that attendees can adequately prepare and contribute (ILM, 2007).

Meetings should be linked to LKS plans, be regularly monitored and should be collaborative and participative. Mind Tools (2016) indicate that a successful meeting will leave people feeling energized, as the meeting objective was accomplished, it was not too long and a clear process was followed. Friedmann (2003) outlines a number of common problems which can impact negatively on the effectiveness of a meeting; going over time, allowing one person to dominate, a one-way dialogue, failure to complete actions, lack of focus, discussing things which are not relevant and inviting too many people. A smaller number of participants is beneficial for decision making but a larger number of participants can allow for a broader input and wider discussion. A good Chair can ensure that the meeting stays on task and a secretary should be assigned to ensure that an accurate record of the discussion is maintained and that actions are completed, projects are monitored and decisions are captured (ILM, 2007).

🖒 Best for

■ Providing the opportunity to communicate with members of your team, for them to be involved in decision making and to ensure that actions are completed.

▶ More

- After the meeting, reflect on what went well and what may be improved next time. Continual monitoring will ensure that your meetings are productive and an effective use of attendees' time.

⚠ To think about

- A poorly run meeting will disengage members of your team and feel like a waste of their time. Good organization is key.

References

Friedmann, S. (2003) *Meeting and Event Planning for Dummies*, Wiley Publishing, Hoboken.

ILM (2007) *Effective Meetings for Managers*, 5th edn, Institute of Leadership and Management, London.

Mind Tools (2016) *Running Effective Meetings*, https://www.mindtools.com/CommSkll/RunningMeetings.htm. [Accessed 17 January 2016]

30. Sharing learning with the team

ONE OF THE best ways to learn is to know the subject well enough to share it with others. Often the biggest loss in the workplace is that we send one person to a training event but the learning stays with them and is not shared with the rest of the team. There might be some chat about it but there is nothing structured which helps people to really take hold of the new ideas and think about how they might use or implement them into their workplace. The products of learning not only make teams more effective, the process of learning can be team-building. Teams capture, formalize and capitalize expertise on behalf of the organization and by doing so knowledge becomes shared and less dependent on individuals who may leave the organization.

Managers have a fundamental role in ensuring that any learning gained by team members should be shared with the team. There are a number of steps which help this process:

- Before the event discuss what is expected, both in terms of what the participant expects to gain from the event, but also in terms of how they will share it on return to the team.
- After the event discuss how it went. What were the main learning points? What did they feel might be useful to the workplace or team? What ideas do they have about how the learning might be implemented?

- Set up a means by which the learning can be shared. Is it appropriate to cascade the learning or elements of it as 'mini' events? Is it something which should be shared in a team meeting? How will it best be structured?
- Set a period of time during which the individual can assimilate the learning and agree how and when they will be ready to share it.

If this process becomes part of the culture of the team, everyone knows what will be expected of them if they were the one lucky enough to be selected to attend. Even if it is just through team meetings, the sharing and discussion which follows can be invaluable. Perhaps have 'learning events attended' as a standing item on your agenda so no events get missed. One suggested structure for a report to the team might include the following:

- What was the main essence of the event?
- What were the main learning points drawn out?
- What might be implementable within the team/workplace?
- What recommendations are you making?

The discussion which follows should be about enthusing the rest of the team and identifying ways forward. Do you need a small working party to clarify what needs doing and how it might be done most effectively, when and where? Is it something which can really have a decision made on it right now and an action planned? Is it something which needs holding on file to be considered in your next round of development plans?

Whatever the outcome, the structured discussion will add immense value to your team. Members will start to see attending learning events not just as something personal but as a valuable contribution to the development of the whole team. You will also raise the perceived value of training as a whole and you will have started to develop critical reflection about the workplace and how it can develop.

Another really valuable way of people sharing their learning is through the development of a team blog. Such a blog requires everyone to participate, not just as authors but in adding comments. A blog doesn't need to just concentrate on learning 'events' but can include identifying learning through reading or action. Reflection requires that we consider what we learned from what happened – both negative and positive. A team can learn a lot together by sharing this reflection and considering different views on each situation. How valuable it will be if the team start to see 'learning' in everything they do and working on ways to continually grow and develop.

👍 Best for

- Ensuring you gain the maximum value from people attending training events. It helps to keep staff motivated, engaged and enthused in their workplace and valuing development.

▶ More

- Writing up development and learning for professional journals or professional blogs can raise both the profile of the individual and the organization.

⚠ To think about

- Initially, for some, the fear of sharing might put them off attending events. Be sure to reassure them of your support and give them a structure to help them identify what needs to be shared most.
- Keep it as a regular item so that nothing slips through the net. Once it is embedded everyone will find it easier to participate.
- Keep the 'negative – we've tried it before' voices out of discussions. There is no such thing as a 'new' idea – just a refashioned one! Even old ideas might work now in a different time, with different people and a different culture.

Further reading

Britton, B. and Serrat, O. (2013) *Learning in Teams,*
   www.slideshare.net/Celcius233/learning-in-teams-27627653. [Accessed 12 February 2016]

31. Writing references

AS A MANAGER, colleague or friend you will most likely be approached for a reference at some point in your life. The most usual scenario is that a current or past employee will ask you for a reference to support their application for a new job, but you could be asked for a personal or character reference in relation to an application to rent a property, an academic placement or a nomination for an award. If you are asked to provide a character reference or personal reference you can do this in your own right but these should not be offered on organizational headed paper.

If you are providing a written reference for an individual on behalf of the organization in your role as their manager or supervisor, you should check your organizational policy for writing references, such as the one provided for staff working at the University of Manchester (University of Manchester, 2015) to clarify the process. If your organization does not have such a policy, your HR department should be able to advise whether you have the appropriate level of authority to proceed.

Commonly, when you receive a request to provide a reference, the applying organization will send you a number of questions that they require answers to, or a general statement to guide you. If this is not the case and you are asked to write a general account or letter, there are a number of templates that you can access on the BusinessBalls website to get you started (Chapman, 2016). Some of the things that you should consider when writing references are summarized below (University of Manchester, 2015; Chapman, 2016; Sakrouge, 2015):

- Include only the facts; do not speculate or provide opinion.
- If you provide a reference you have a duty of care.
- It must be factual, accurate, fair, balanced and not libellous.
- It must not be discriminatory.
- It must comply with the Data Protection Act.
- Do not get personal in a reference, ensure that you remain objective.
- Try to provide positive statements.
- Information about disciplinary proceedings should be backed up with dates and figures.

Sakrouge (2015) states that although there is no legal obligation for an employer to provide a reference for a current or former employee, it is unusual for a request to be denied. If you are considering rejecting a request for a reference, you need to ensure that you are not being discriminatory. Deciding not to provide a reference, for whatever reason, will reflect poorly on the candidate, as most employers now offer new positions subject to suitable references being received (University of Manchester, 2015).

If you do provide a reference on behalf of your organization it should be 'true, accurate and fair. It [the employer] can also be sued for defamation or malicious falsehood in respect of damaging comments which it knew, or should have known, were untrue' (Sakrouge, 2015). When you write a reference for someone, imagine that they will be reading it. Whilst you as an individual, due to an exemption in the Data Protection Act 1998, may not have to disclose the existence of a reference that you have written, an individual can make a subject access request to the receiving individual or organization to see a copy (Information Commissioner's Office, 2005).

🖒 Best for

- ■ Giving a clear picture of the employee and outlining their strengths and what they can offer to a different organization.

► **More**

- As it is about them, employees can ask to see a copy of the reference, so remember this when you are writing it.
- You could always allow the employee to read the reference before it is submitted. They have asked you for the reference, so there is no reason for you not to show it to them or ask them whether there is anything they would like you to include.

⚠ To think about

- Do not get personal or use this as an opportunity to say things which should have been said to the employee whilst they worked for you. Stick to the facts and ensure that they are correct.
- If you provide information in a reference which is deemed to be untrue you could be sued for defamation, so ensure that you fulfil your duty of care.

References

Chapman, A. (2016) *Businessballs: references letters*, www.businessballs.com/referencesletterssamples.htm. [Accessed 7 February 2016]

Information Commissioner's Office (2005) *Data Protection Good Practice Note: subject access and employment references*, https://ico.org.uk/media/for-organisations/documents/2775/references_v1_final.pdf. [Accessed 7 February 2016]

Sakrouge, A. (2015) *References*, www.cipd.co.uk/hr-inform/employment-law/ termination/references/default.aspx. [Accessed 7 February 2016]

University of Manchester (2015) *Policy on Providing Employment References for Employees/Former Employees*, http://documents.manchester.ac.uk/display.aspx?DocID=15719. [Accessed 7 February 2016]

32. Exit interviews

A N EXIT INTERVIEW occurs when an employee has handed in their notice. It is an opportunity for you to formally obtain structured feedback from them about your performance as a manager, their working environment and any other issues which may have contributed to their reasons for leaving (Schachter, 2005).

It is good practice to offer all employees who leave your service the opportunity to have an exit interview before their final day; ideally this should be arranged as soon as they hand in their notice. Most organizations will have a procedure or policy to guide you through the process (Schachter, 2005), so in the first instance contact your HR or Personnel department to find the relevant documentation. If your organization does not provide guidance, use the following tips and resources to develop your own process.

The exit interview provides the employee with the opportunity to feed back to you retrospectively about:

- their experience of working in the LKS
- their reasons for leaving the job
- their experiences of the working environment
- their perceptions of leadership
- any 'tacit' knowledge or information which they hold which is valuable to your service
- any issues or problems that they have encountered whilst working within the service.

As an employer, you can use this information to:

- learn lessons about why people are leaving
- ensure that any issues identified, which are within your control, are included in your LKS plan
- improve the recruitment process for new staff
- make changes which will benefit the remaining team
- reduce high turnover of staff and loss of talent from your service
- log and retain 'tacit' knowledge of outgoing staff to ensure effective handover and service delivery
- reduce the costs of recruitment for the organization (CIPD, 2006)
- demonstrate to your team that you are interested in them and prepared to make improvements (Schachter, 2005).

Reder (2013) indicates that in order for a successful exit strategy to be incorporated into your LKS a number of factors should be considered. The exit interview is a voluntary option but you should encourage outgoing employees to attend. As with any interview or meeting, it is important to arrange a time and place which suits the employee and ensures they are comfortable, to allow an honest and open discussion. The interviewer should be skilled and sensitive to the individual's needs if they want to identify any trends and all information gathered should be analysed (Armstrong, 2006). Reder (2013) suggests that the interview should include a series of open questions which should address:

- their main reasons for leaving

- any changes which would have encouraged them to stay
- their thoughts about morale within the team/organization
- what they liked and what they would change
- whether they felt valued
- whether they were offered the right training and/or development opportunities
- an understanding of their role
- whether they received regular feedback about their performance.

Best for

- The exit interview can provide valuable information and insights which can help you to make changes to your service. It can highlight any issues which are impacting on staff morale and provide a structure for you to capture valuable knowledge.
- Understanding why people are leaving your service can help you to retain staff and attract new talent. Tackling the reasons for high turnover will also reduce recruitment costs for your organization.

▶ More

- The exit interview cannot stop the outgoing employee from leaving, but can provide information to improve the working environment for remaining staff.
- If an individual does not accept the offer of an interview, you could provide a printed questionnaire or survey for them to complete after they have left, although they may not return it (CIPD, 2006).

▲ To think about

- If you are an individual's direct report, they may not find it easy to be honest with you about their real reasons for leaving or to raise any issues that they have encountered. You can arrange for the interview to be carried out by someone else to ensure that the information received is constructive, valuable and can be used to inform future recruitment.
- It is essential that you act to resolve or improve any problems which are identified, otherwise the interview is just a tick-box exercise. Any information obtained should be fed into your team action plans in order to have any value.
- Often people do not take up the offer of an exit interview, as they have already made the decision to leave due to dissatisfaction with their current working arrangements. If you do not know why they have resigned, you will have to accept that you will never know.

■ By the time the employee has handed in their notice, the exit interview is too late to encourage them to stay. Use regular one-to-one discussions and performance reviews to identify and act upon issues as they arise and keep valuable talent within your team.

References

Armstrong, M. (2006) *A Handbook of Human Resource Management Practice*, 10th edn, Kogan Page, London.

CIPD (2006) *Exit Strategy*, www.cipd.co.uk/pm/peoplemanagement/b/weblog/archive/2013/01/29/exitstrategy-2006-01.aspx. [Accessed 6 January 2016]

Reder, S. (2013) Why Exactly Are You Leaving?, *Canadian HR Reporter*, **26** (11), 10.

Schachter, D. (2005) Exit Interviews Can Provide Valuable Feedback, *Information Outlook*, **9** (7), 9–10.

33. Effective handover

WHEN AN EMPLOYEE leaves your service a good handover is an essential part of the process. By applying an effective handover process you can ensure that the outgoing employee does not leave with crucial knowledge which is critical to the continued smooth running of your service (Agarwal and Islam, 2015). In an ideal scenario, when an employee has handed in their notice a replacement will commence employment as soon as possible.

Ideally the new employee should have the opportunity to 'shadow' the outgoing employee for a week or so to learn the ropes. This takes the pressure off the new employee and can help them to settle in. It will also mean that they will understand the requirements of the role and become a more productive part of the team more quickly.

Unfortunately, lengthy recruitment processes and delays can often mean that the outgoing employee has left your service weeks or even months before a replacement is appointed. However, as a manager or supervisor there are still a number of things that you can do to ensure that an effective handover process can still take place when the new employee begins. Arranging for someone within the existing team to shadow the outgoing employee before they leave and be trained in crucial elements of the role is the second-best thing to having the outgoing employee train their replacement. You may need to redistribute other work within the team to ensure that the person picking up extra work does not become overloaded, but you will have someone who can fill the role of the outgoing employee and keep important elements of the service running.

Finally, a good collection of written documentation about the post and its duties should be produced by the outgoing employee and saved in a shared drive or digital repository. Often job roles change over time, and when an employee leaves this is a good opportunity to review the requirements of the post. Involve the outgoing employee in writing the job description for their replacement, to ensure that it accurately represents the role that they are leaving.

Ask the outgoing employee to update all relevant procedures and protocols and to leave detailed notes which can be used by existing staff and the new employee. Ask them to compile a list of regular tasks outlining routine daily, weekly, monthly and annual activities which should be handed over. Any ongoing projects should have clear action plans and project documentation and any other reports or documents should also be filed in the central, shared location. Finally, ask the outgoing employee to write a list of key contacts including their e-mail, telephone number and what they can help with.

Example from practice: Emma Cragg (2013) – The Digitalist

Emma Cragg wrote a popular blog post about writing effective handover notes before she moved to her new role as web content officer at Newcastle University. When she started writing her handover notes, Emma realized that there was little information out there, so these are her top tips:

■ **Start immediately!**

For specific pieces of work leave:

■ brief description
■ list of actions and timeframes
■ links to files, e-mails or any useful information
■ the status of the work
■ details of who else knows about it or has input into it
■ any deadlines or milestones.

General information to be recorded:

■ key contacts
■ upcoming meetings or events
■ information sources, e.g. websites, blogs, social media accounts
■ usernames and passwords for relevant accounts.

If you implement a structured approach to handover, you will ensure the transfer of tacit knowledge from the outgoing employee, ensuring that you and your team have access to their information and knowledge (Agarwal and

Islam, 2015). Some of this information could be gathered in the face-to-face exit interview, but ideally the process of handover should begin as soon as you receive notice from the employee. On a practical note, ensure that the outgoing employee leaves an out-of-office message on their e-mail outlining who should be contacted now that they have left the organization, and arrange for any e-mails to be redirected elsewhere. This structured process will ensure that valuable knowledge is retained and will ensure minimum disruption to the delivery of services.

👍 Best for

- Ensuring that your service is not disrupted and that the new employee has all the information to hand so that they can become productive as soon as possible.

▶ More

- Create a checklist of the things that you need for the outgoing employee and discuss this in a face-to-face meeting as soon after they give notice. They may be able to suggest additional items to be handed over, as they have detailed knowledge of the role.

⚠ To think about

- If you do not undertake an effective handover you will compromise the standard of service delivery, which could impact on your service's reputation.

References

Agarwal, N. K. and Islam, M. A. (2015) Knowledge Retention and Transfer: how libraries manage employees leaving and joining, *VINE*, **45** (2), 150–71.
Cragg, E. (2013) *The Art of Writing Handover Notes*, www.digitalist.info/2013/12/10/the-art-of-writing-handover-notes. [Accessed 24 January 2016]

Further reading

HCLU /LIHNN (2014) *Support for New Managers*, www.lihnn.nhs.uk/index.php/hclu/training-and-development/library-managers/15-hclu/training-and-development#SNM. [Accessed 24 September 2016]

SECTION 3

Activities and tools

Tips 34–101

34. Action learning sets

AN ACTION LEARNING set is made up of a group of individuals who meet together to discuss a real-life work problem or issue. The focus is on working together to resolve the issue and then reflecting on the outcome. The concept was developed in the 1940s by Reg Revans (Action Learning Associates, 2015) as a means for individuals to learn from each other and share best practice. Revan's original method focused on learning achieved through applying existing knowledge and asking questions. This was updated by Marquardt in 2009 to include a reflective element (Jisc, 2014) as shown in Table 34.1.

Table 34.1 *Comparison of action learning, adapted from Jisc (2014)*	
Revans (1940s)	$L = P + Q$ Where L = learning; P = programming (knowledge already established) and Q = questioning to create insight into what people see, hear or feel.
Marquardt (2009)	$L = P + Q + R$ Where R = reflection.

Action learning sets are widely used by organizations such as the NHS as a means of utilizing individual expertise and enabling learning from experiences. The NHS Clinical Leaders Network defines action learning sets as:

. . . a method for individual and organisation development based on small groups of colleagues meeting over time to tackle real problems. Its roots are in adult learning and organisational development, ensuring that individuals can continue to be supported in their roles and learn from colleagues.

It is underpinned by a belief in individual potential: a way of learning from our actions and from what happens to us, and around us, by taking the time to question, understand and reflect, to gain insights and consider how to act in the future.

NHS Clinical Leaders Network, 2016

Action learning sets are designed to enable participants to solve work-related problems within a supportive and open environment. The groups are usually small, around four to ten at most. Action learning sets can be self-facilitating but in practice many groups find that using a facilitator, at least for the first few meetings, is an effective means of moving the work forward. The National Library for Health identified three approaches which can be undertaken by action learning sets, shown in Table 34.2.

Table 34.2 *Action learning approaches, adapted from March (2007)*	
Session type	**Approach**
OPEN	Individual members bid to discuss issues of concern to them. The members agree at the start of each meeting which bids will be successful and therefore will be discussed. The focus is on using questioning from other members to help the individual understand the issue and to identify an action plan for handling it, rather than providing direct advice or sharing experiences.
PLANNED	Where the topic is agreed in advance. This model may be helpful where a learning set is supporting members who are all developing the same set of skills at the same time, and where members will benefit from brainstorming and sharing experiences of implementing new skills. Common focuses for discussion may include 'what worked for me and what didn't – and what would I do differently next time'.
COMBINED	Allowing both the structure of a planned approach with the opportunity for individuals to raise issues of current concern as well.

Whichever session type is appropriate, the purpose of an action learning set is, as defined by the name, to take action and then learn from the actions through a shared approach to problem solving. The basic procedure and principles for running a set are taken from Action Learning Sets (2014):

- Agree some ground rules about how you will work together.
- Share out the time, so that everyone gets a turn.
- Each member 'presents', i.e. briefly describes, a problem they would like to work on.

- The set helps that person to explore the problem.
- Open questions are usually most helpful.
- Avoid giving advice.
- Ensure that the presenter has an action plan.
- Spend time after each person's turn and at the end of the meeting to discuss what has been learned.

Participation in an action learning set is an effective means of real-life problem solving which enables individuals to develop a number of different skills, including active listening, questioning skills, empathy and reflection. It is essential that members are open-minded and willing to learn from each other. Individuals need to be prepared to share their failures as well as their successes and to reflect upon the whole experience. The value of participating is demonstrated by the example from practice shown here.

Example from practice: Alison Day – LKS manager (NHS)

My action learning set of six people provides a supportive environment to work through personal development or work-based issues, helping to increase understanding and develop solutions. We have a commitment to meet four times a year (but it would be beneficial if this was more frequent). Each time we meet we have the option of raising an issue we would like addressed. Each individual then takes it in turn to share their concern in more detail whilst the rest of the group listen and ask questions to encourage the individual to understand and resolve their issue. The session ends with a commitment to take action which is very powerful as you know you will be reporting back to your action learning set on progress next time you meet.

   The set I am in at the moment is very structured, with a facilitator, which helps us all to stay on track and keep to the agreed rules of action learning sets – to ask questions and not give advice. The temptation to solve someone's issue for them is strong but the actions are more powerful if the individual finds their own solution.

Groups can be made of up of participants from the same organization or sector or from individuals belonging to different organizations or sectors depending on the issue under discussion. Active participation can assist the individual in developing their networking and influencing skills whilst at the same time solving problems or issues which they would have found difficult to resolve on their own. A successful set will demonstrate the characteristics displayed in Figure 34.1.

Figure 34.1 *Characteristics of action learning sets (NHS Clinical Leaders Network, 2016)*

👍 Best for

■ Utilizing an individual's experience to solve work-related problems within a supportive and open environment which enables them to learn from each other.

▶ More

■ Action learning sets do not have to meet physically. Virtual action learning sets using LinkedIn have demonstrated considerable success (Hale, 2012).

⚠ To think about

■ Action learning sets are not about individuals giving advice to each other. They are about listening to each other and providing an environment for members to actively work towards solving their own issues and problems.
■ Even if the set does not meet physically, action learning sets do require individuals to commit to attending and to completing their agreed actions. It is important to make best use of the time allocated and this is where appointing a facilitator can prove invaluable to ensure that the set achieves its purpose.

References

Action Learning Associates (2015) *Reg Revans: Action Learning pioneer*, www.actionlearningassociates.co.uk/action-learning/reg-revans. [Accessed 14 February 2016]

Action Learning Sets (2014) *About Action Learning*, www.actionlearningsets.com/php/news.php?id=4. [Accessed 14 February 2016]

Hale, R. (2012) Action Learning in the Cloud, *Training Journal*, September, 19–22.

Jisc (2014) *Action Learning*, www.jisc.ac.uk/guides/change-management/action-learning. [Accessed 14 February 2016]

March, L. J. (2007) *Skills for Success: the Health Library Staff Development Framework*, www.libraryservices.nhs.uk/document_uploads/Staff_Development/nlh_sdg_int roducing_learning_sets_200808.pdf. [Accessed 14 February 2016]

NHS Clinical Leaders Network (2016) *Action Learning*, www.cln.nhs.uk/aboutcln/action-learning.html. [Accessed 14 February 2016]

35. Apprentices, graduate trainees and work placements

THIS TIP IS not about the technicalities of setting up apprenticeships, graduate trainee schemes or placements. It focuses on the quality of the experience which participants in these schemes should expect during their time working within your team. If you are involved in setting up one of these schemes then you should be following the Tips laid out in Section 2 (p. 27) of this book to ensure that the relationship between the individual and the service/ organization is beneficial to all interested parties. Additional information on apprentices, graduate trainee schemes and work placements are available by following the links in the Further Reading section below (p. 88).

Work experience

The principle behind apprenticeships, graduate trainee schemes and work placements is to provide real work experience for individuals, most of whom will either be studying for further qualifications or using the experience as a basis to apply for further study. Generally speaking, apprentices and graduate trainees will be paid an agreed salary during their time with your organization. Individuals on work placements might or might not receive payment. Either way, the onus is on the employer to ensure that the experience for individuals is meaningful and a valuable use of their time.

Advantages

Advantages to individuals of such schemes include the opportunity to develop practical skills, knowledge and behaviours through real-life experience. From an employer's perspective they are contributing to ensuring that the future workforce is trained in the skills, knowledge and behaviours that will ensure that their organizations can meet future challenges and take advantage of opportunities that will enable them to grow and prosper. The example below shows how the experience of undertaking a graduate traineeship led to a successful start to a career in the profession.

Example from practice: Catherine McManamon – LKS professional (academic) and former graduate trainee

My graduate traineeship was based in one of Manchester Metropolitan University's site libraries. The trainee programme aimed to provide a broad introduction to the different aspects of HE library services as well as practical experience of supporting the staff and students of the university in a front line capacity, prior to embarking on a Master level LIS qualification.

Specifically, I gained varied customer service experience as the first point of contact for library users on the enquiry desk. The nature of the customer-facing responsibilities quickly developed my communication skills and my ability to work as part of a team. The first semester of the traineeship involved lots of new information, unfamiliar IT and library management systems and a busy library service. This meant that learning from and listening to the more experienced members of the team was essential.

The graduate traineeship also enabled me to begin to develop library support for teaching and research – facilitating user education and providing detailed support to students in their use of the library collections. This enhanced my own information literacy skills. Alongside this practical experience, I developed my professional awareness through the training sessions, presentations and library visits that were a central part of the traineeship.

Responsibilities and expectations

If you have responsibility for an individual on any of these schemes it is important that you are both clear about what is expected of that individual and what your responsibilities as a line manager are. In some cases you might be responsible for the person for the whole of their time as an apprentice, graduate trainee or placement student. In other cases you might only have responsibility for them for a proportion of their time with the organization. Either way, you and the individual on the scheme need to ensure that you each understand the expectations that the other has of your time working together. The induction process is particularly important for individuals undertaking these types of schemes in building the relationship between themselves, the team and the organization.

As a line manager you will need to understand what the individual is aiming to get from the experience. You will need to be clear about what skills, knowledge and behaviours they are aiming to develop. Linked into this is an understanding of what they hope the experience will lead to. This might be a specific job or qualification or it might be a more general experience. Understanding the motivation and expectations of the individual will lay the foundations of your relationship with them which will enable you to make the experience as productive as possible for both parties.

You will need to be clear about your expectations of the individual. This might be as basic as expecting them to be at work for a certain time to taking responsibility for specific areas of work. Many of these schemes will require the individual to undertake a project or have time off to attend further training or study. As the person responsible for them you will need to be aware of these requirements and ensure that they are able to meet them. Most work placements will be organized in partnership with the college or university that the individual is attending and there will usually be a named contact based at the home institution for the employer to liaise with.

Many of the schemes covered by this Tip will have a formal process for laying out these expectations. You will need a copy of this and should discuss it with the individual at the earliest opportunity. If this doesn't exist then it is a good idea to draw one up at the start of the relationship to clarify:

- how long the relationship will last
- working conditions including hours and place of work, holiday and absence procedures and any other contractual obligations such as health and safety requirements. You can refer them to HR for these if appropriate.
- the training they will receive and the specific outcomes expected from the training
- any qualifications they are working towards or any specific work or projects they are expected to undertake
- the names of any external contacts such as tutors or placement co-ordinators. You will also need to know if the individual will be visited by any of these people during their time with you and what the purpose of the visit will be.

⚐ Best for

- Providing participants with the opportunity to gain work experience and develop their individual skills, knowledge and behaviours, which will ultimately benefit themselves and the organization by contributing to the development of a skilled and flexible workforce.

▶ More

■ Most schemes of this type will require the individual to complete a placement diary or learning log. If for some reason the individual concerned has not been asked to complete something of this type it is good practice to ask them to do so. This will enable you and the individual to map their progress and give a basis for discussing any issues as they arise.

⚠ To think about

■ These schemes should never be used as a source of cheap labour and it is important that managers are clear about the amount of time and energy it will take to run them. A badly run apprenticeship, graduate trainee scheme or placement will damage the reputation of the organization and could seriously undermine the confidence of the individual.

Further reading

CILIP (2016) *Graduate Training*, www.lisjobnet.com/graduate-training. [Accessed 3 April 2016]

Department for Business, Innovation and Skills (2015) *Employ an Apprentice*, https://www.gov.uk/take-on-an-apprentice. [Accessed 3 April 2016]

Prospects (2016) *Work Experience and Internships*, www.prospects.ac.uk/jobs-and-work-experience/work-experience-and-internships. [Accessed 3 April 2016]

36. Awards

> Recognition makes employees feel valued and appreciated, it contributes to higher employee morale, increases organizational productivity, and can aid in recruitment and retention. Recognition is a powerful motivator. It serves to reinforce the enthusiasm, commitment, and social conscience of employees and is a great vehicle for conveying the agency mission and goals.
>
> University Library University of Illinois at Urbana-Champaign, 2012

EMPLOYEE RECOGNITION CAN result in increased motivation, improved performance and a more productive workforce; nominating members of your team for awards is one way to do this. Research shows that different rewards, both tangible and intangible, can influence an individual's behaviour (CIPD, 2015). There are many opportunities open to you as a manager to nominate individuals and teams from within your LKS for awards.

Awards may be local; for example, you could run an Employee of the Month scheme within your library to recognize the good work that individuals are doing on a day-to-day basis or introduce annual awards for customer service or innovation, such as those offered by the University of Colombia (2015). You could use this as an opportunity to praise individuals for completing work on a specific project, or alternatively to recognize their skills or dedication to their job. Some organizations have annual awards ceremonies for all staff who work there (not limited to LKS staff), which may be organized around organizational values or objectives, e.g. Most Productive Team. Finally, you may be able to enter an individual or LKS team for awards presented by external associations or organizations.

In their Task Force which investigated staff recognition schemes with a view to implementing a local initiative, the University Library University of Illinois at Urbana-Champaign (2012) recommends that rewards offered should be:

- sincere
- meaningful
- adaptable
- relevant
- timely.

By nominating members of your team for awards, you are recognizing the good work that they do and demonstrating that you value their commitment and appreciate their contribution to the delivery of services, which can be great for motivation and productivity. If you nominate members of your team for awards within the organization, it will raise the profile of the individual or team and showcase the good work that they do. It can also serve to raise the profile of LKS generally, by sharing information about your work, which may not always be recognized throughout the wider organization.

LKS are filled with innovative individuals who are passionate about the services that they provide, but often our stakeholders do not have a full understanding of the scope and breadth of our activities. Celebrating and recognizing the achievements of your team members is a good way of building morale and creating a satisfied workforce who feel valued. Table 36.1 illustrates examples of awards.

🖒 Best for

- Employee awards enable you to recognize and reward the good work that your staff and teams are doing, either on a day-to-day basis or for innovative one-off projects.

Table 36.1 *Examples of awards*

Sally Hernando Award for Innovation in NHS Library and Knowledge Services (UK) www.libraryservices.nhs.uk/forlibrarystaff/lqaf/innovations.html
CILIP Libraries Change Lives Award (UK) www.cilip.org.uk/cilip/cilip-libraries-change-lives-award
Library Design Awards (UK) www.sla.org.uk/library-design-awards.php
School Librarian of the Year Award (UK) www.sla.org.uk/slya.php
I Love my Librarian Award (USA) www.ilovelibraries.org/lovemylibrarian
Lancashire Teaching Hospitals NHS Foundation Trust Quality Awards (UK) www.lancsteachinghospitals.nhs.uk/latest-news/news-220415-quality-awards-celebrating-staff-achievements-1804
The University of British Colombia Library Staff Recognition Awards (USA) http://about.library.ubc.ca/work-with-us/why-work-with-us/library-staff-recognition-awards

▶ More

- Decide what the awards will be in advance and publicize them. You will need to dedicate some funding to implement an internal scheme, as awards should be attached to some form of reward.
- If you don't have the resources to set up an internal awards scheme keep an eye out for external awards to nominate your teams for.

⚠ To think about

- If embarking on an awards programme, ensure that you have categories which can apply to people at all levels in the organization. They should be equitable, inclusive, tied to your organizational aims and include significant rewards to establish their value (University Library University of Illinois at Urbana-Champaign, 2012).

References

CIPD (2015) *Show Me the Money!: the behavioural science of reward*, www.cipd.co.uk/hr-resources/research/show-money-behavioural-science-reward.aspx. [Accessed 24 September 2016]

University Library University of Illinois at Urbana-Champaign (2012) *Library Awards and Recognition Task Force*, www.library.illinois.edu/committee/admin/supplement/2011-2012/Awards_and_Recognitions_Final_Report.pdf. [Accessed 28 December 2015]

37. Buddying

BUDDYING IS WHERE an experienced member of staff works with a new or inexperienced staff member to increase their confidence and expertise either generally or in a particular area. It is often used as part of the induction process as a means of giving a new member of staff a point of contact, other than their line manager, who can answer questions and provide one-to-one support. It tends to be a fairly informal relationship and lasts for as long as the person being buddied requires it.

Benefits of Buddying

Assigning a buddy to a new member of staff can really make a difference to the success of their induction. Having a buddy gives a new member of staff a friendly face they know they can seek support from in terms of explaining how things work and answering questions. This can help them to settle into their new role more quickly, and reduce the chance of them feeling isolated or unsupported.

Acting as a buddy also provides a good developmental opportunity for existing members of staff, giving them the chance to develop their communication skills and share their knowledge and experience.

University of Sheffield, 2014

Buddying offers development opportunities for both individuals in the relationship, not just the person who is being buddied. HR staff based at Manchester Metropolitan University (2015) have produced a guide on the skills, knowledge, expertise and behaviours that make a good buddy, from which the following list is taken.

Who Makes a Good Buddy?

A good buddy is someone who is prepared to be:

- A contact
- A friendly face
- An informal source of information on the team and department
- Someone who knows how things work across the organisation and is prepared to share that experience

Personal attributes of a good buddy include:

- The ability to listen
- Openness and commitment to being a buddy – it can be a learning experience for both parties

- Good time management and self management skills
- Relevant knowledge and experience to be able to provide the right level of support
- An honest and considerate approach to giving feedback and asking challenging questions including the ability to:
  - o give constructive feedback
  - o identify learning opportunities
  - o use questions to encourage new starters to think for themselves
- A willingness to learn

Manchester Metropolitan University, 2015

Figure 37.1 outlines a basic buddying process. The emphasis is on the person who is being buddied but should include opportunities for the buddy themselves to reflect on their own learning and development in the role.

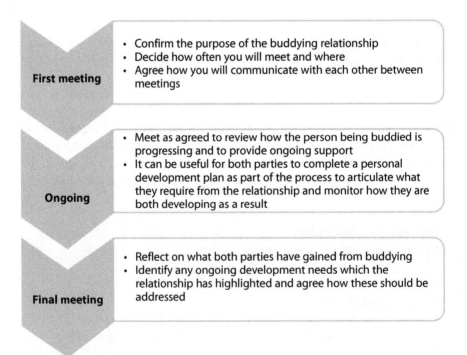

First meeting
- Confirm the purpose of the buddying relationship
- Decide how often you will meet and where
- Agree how you will communicate with each other between meetings

Ongoing
- Meet as agreed to review how the person being buddied is progressing and to provide ongoing support
- It can be useful for both parties to complete a personal development plan as part of the process to articulate what they require from the relationship and monitor how they are both developing as a result

Final meeting
- Reflect on what both parties have gained from buddying
- Identify any ongoing development needs which the relationship has highlighted and agree how these should be addressed

Figure 37.1 *The buddying process*

👍 Best for

■ Providing informal peer support to enable a new or inexperienced member of staff to increase their confidence and expertise.

■ Developing an existing team member by enabling them to share their skills, knowledge, expertise and behaviours with a new or inexperienced member of staff.

► More

■ There are some similarities to coaching and mentoring in that the skills required are similar. The main difference is that buddying is more informal. If you are thinking of using a buddy system then you might find it useful to read the Tips in this book (p. 100, p. 160 and p. 163) on coaching and mentoring.
■ Whilst most buddying relationships occur within the same team or department there are occasions when selecting a buddy for an individual from outside these parameters can be beneficial. Examples of this could include individuals from small LKS buddying up for extra CILIP qualification support or where individuals need to develop skills that are unique to their role. In these cases LKS staff working in other organizations or sectors could be approached. Understanding the development benefits to potential buddies is particularly important in such instances.

⚠ To think about

■ It is important to remember that this is a working relationship between equals. Buddying is not about being a counsellor for emotional issues or providing a confidant for an individual (Manchester Metropolitan University, 2015).

References

Manchester Metropolitan University (2015) *The Role of a Buddy/Mentor for New Starters*, https://www2.mmu.ac.uk/media/mmuacuk/content/documents/human-resources/a-z/guidance-procedures-and-handbooks/Buddy-Mentor_to_New_Starters.pdf. [Accessed 16 February 2016]
University of Sheffield (2014) *Buddying for New Starters*, www.sheffield.ac.uk/polopoly_fs/1.296199!/file/Buddying_for_induction.pdf . [Accessed 16 February 2016]

38. CILIP qualifications

CILIP (THE CHARTERED Institute of Library and Information Professionals) offers three levels of professional registration (see Table 38.1) which are available to all Members.

Table 38.1 *Three levels of CILIP professional registration*

Certification	**Who is it for?** 'Those who are at the beginning of their professional career or who want to gain some recognition for the knowledge and skills they have developed working in a library, information or knowledge role' (CILIP, 2014a).
	Members need to demonstrate they have: 1. Identified areas for improvement in their personal performance and undertaken activities to develop skills and enhance knowledge. 2. Considered the organizational context of their service and examined their role within the organization. 3. Enhanced their knowledge of information services in order to understand the wider professional context within which they work.
Chartership	**Who is it for?** 'Those working in the information professions who wish to be recognized for their skills, knowledge, and application of these in the form of reflective practice' (CILIP, 2014b).
	Members need to demonstrate that they have: 1. Identified areas for improvement in their personal performance, undertaken activities to develop skills, applied these in practice, and reflected on the process and outcomes. 2. Examined the organizational context of their service, evaluated service performance, shown the ability to implement or recommend improvement, and reflected on actual or desired outcomes. 3. Enhanced their knowledge of the wider professional context and reflected on areas of current interest.
Fellowship	**Who is it for?** 'The highest level of professional registration and if you're a Chartered member, hold a senior position in your organization, or have made a significant contribution to the information professions, it is appropriate for you' (CILIP, 2014c).
	Members need to demonstrate that they have: 1. Identified areas for improvement in their personal performance, undertaken activities to develop skills, applied these in practice, and reflected on the process and outcomes. 2. Examined the organizational context of their work and evidenced substantial achievement in professional practice. 3. Established their commitment to, and enhanced their knowledge of, the information profession in order to have made a significant contribution to all or part of the profession.

The process

The process of working towards professional registration will assist an individual in developing many skills which will have direct application in and benefit to the workplace. The process encourages critical reflection and evaluation. The selection and organization of the supporting evidence is a means for individuals to demonstrate their professional judgement. From an employer's point of view, supporting candidates working towards any of the levels of professional registration is valuable, as your organization will benefit from:

- the opportunity professional registration offers for career progression
- staff demonstrating their commitment to continuing professional

development and a structure to encourage improvement and development of skills
- the fact that your staff will help you to stay on top of industry developments through access to a network of committed individuals across the information professions
- the opportunity to benchmark against other organisations
- your commitment to staff improvement and a structure to encourage improvement and development of skills
- improved business performance through involvement in professional registration
- innovative thinking, practice, influence and improved reliance

Adapted from CILIP, 2015

As part of the process, candidates are required to complete two Professional Knowledge and Skills Base (PKSB) self-assessments (see Figure 38.1 below). Candidates undertake an initial assessment at the start of the process and a reassessment towards the end to see if their original learning aims have been met. If the candidate is happy to share their initial assessment with you this can be an effective way of incorporating the process into an individual's day job as it will identify development needs which you can work with them to fulfil. Additionally, it could flag up skills and knowledge which an individual possesses but which you were not aware of, as these are not directly connected to their current role.

Monitoring progress

Incorporating discussion on a candidate's progress into your regular one-to-ones is a useful way of monitoring progress and will assist the candidate in managing the process. It will demonstrate to the candidate that you are interested in them as an individual and that their continuing professional development is important to you, the team and the organization. It is important to be clear with the candidate that you are supporting them as their line manager. It is generally considered not appropriate for an individual's line manager to be their official mentor for professional registration. The application process is shown in Figure 38.1 overleaf.

Example from practice: Carol Brooks – LKS manager (public)

Over the years I have seen a number of para-professionals work towards Certification and have seen amazing results in both their levels of confidence about their work, their professionalism and their ability to move into higher level roles. Without a doubt, the process of focusing on their own development and reflecting on results has benefitted them as individuals and the service delivery they manage or provide.

Similarly qualified librarians have gained in confidence and determination to move forwards in their career through focusing on Chartership. It never ceases to impact on the service or the individual when reflective practice becomes a norm in considering what they are doing and how the results have benefitted the service users.

Stage 1 Getting started			
Join CILIP	Enrol on the VLE	Attend workshop	Find a mentor

Stage 2 Professional Knowledge and Skills Base (PKSB)
Complete your intital self assessment of your skills and knowledge using the PKSB. You will complete a reassessment as part of the final submission process

Stage 3 Developing yourself and collecting evidence
Develop your skills and knowledge, collect evidence of doing so and reflect on the process

Stage 4 Assembling your portfolio				
Evaluative statement	Evidence	CV and job description	Both PKSB assessments	Mentor form

Stage 5 Submit your application
Submit your portfolio for assessment using the CILIP VLE

Figure 38.1 *The application process for professional registration with CILIP*

👍 Best for

- Developing and applying an individual's skills and knowledge whilst demonstrating that they are committed to personal development and to their professional growth.

▶ **More**

- The support of the line manager is extremely helpful to an individual during the professional registration process, as well as that of the team and the organization. However, this is not the only course of support available to candidates. In addition to their mentor, candidates can also look for support within their regional member network, their Candidate Support Officer and the CILIP member services team.
- There is other support available through the CILIP VLE including sample portfolios, a list of useful publications and discussion forums. Additionally, there are a number of professional registration blogs which individuals can follow or contribute to. Twitter can be a useful source of support and help, via the hashtags #certification, #chartership or #fellowship.

⚠ **To think about**

- CILIP does not set any deadlines from when candidates register to when they submit. Deciding how long an individual needs to complete their submission is part of the process and will often depend upon the stage they are in their career. The downside of this is that it can be easy for the process to become drawn out and for the candidate to lose motivation. If this becomes an issue encourage the individual not to lose heart. Persuade them to talk to their mentor and their candidate support officer who can help get them back on track.

References

CILIP (2014a) *Certification: a guide for Members*, www.cilip.org.uk/sites/default/files/documents/Certification%20Handbook%200 70314.pdf. [Accessed 19 September 2015]

CILIP (2014b) *Chartership: a guide for Members*, www.cilip.org.uk/sites/default/files/documents/Chartership%2007 0314.pdf. [Accessed 25 October 2015]

CILIP (2014c) *Fellowship: a guide for Members*, www.CILIP.org.uk/sites/default/files/documents/Fellowship%20Handbook%2007 0314.pdf. [Accessed 30 October 2015]

CILIP (2015) *Information for Employers*, www.CILIP.org.uk/CILIP/jobs-careers/professional-registration/information-employers. [Accessed 19 September 2015]

Further reading

CILIP (2013) *Your Professional Knowledge and Skills Base: identify gaps and maximise opportunities along your career path*, CILIP, London.

CILIP (2015) *How to Access the VLE,*
www.CILIP.org.uk/CILIP/membership/benefits/virtual-learning-environment-vle/how-access-vle. [Accessed 19 September 2015]
Fisher, B., Ruddock, B., Young, G. and Brooks, C. (2013) *The CILIP Mentoring Award,* https://pteg.wordpress.com/category/cilip-mentoring-award. [Accessed 24 June 2016]

Acknowledgement

Many thanks to Matthew Wheeler, Development Officer (Member Support), CILIP – www.cilip.org.uk/cilip/about/cilip-people/staff/member-services/matthew-wheeler – for checking the information provided in this Tip.

39. CILIP qualifications – revalidation

REVALIDATION IS THE means by which holders of any of the three levels of CILIP professional registration can demonstrate that they have continued to learn and develop since obtaining their professional registration.

The process is simple (see Figure 39.1). Members need to log a minimum of 20 hours of CPD (continuous professional development) on the CILIP VLE and put together a 250-word reflective statement which demonstrates how they have developed their:

- personal performance
- organizational performance
- knowledge of the wider LIS profession.

How to Revalidate

To revalidate, access your space in the CILIP Portfolio section of the VLE and start logging any CPD activities that you've undertaken in the last year.

You should think broadly when considering what activities to include in your revalidation. Reading a professional publication, talking about professional issues with a colleague or engaging on social media are just as valid as attending a formal training course or a conference.

Once you've completed a minimum of 20 hours of CPD, submit this with a 250 word reflective statement focusing on how you've developed your knowledge over the year. All CILIP Members already complete more than 20 hours of CPD in a year. By revalidating, you will get professional recognition for doing so!

There is no charge for revalidation.

Figure 39.1 *How to revalidate (CILIP, 2014)*

Regularly revalidating professional qualifications enables individuals to develop a number of good habits, which line managers and organizations should encourage. Maintaining an ongoing record of CPD on a routine basis is good practice. It is useful in assisting individuals in preparing for annual appraisals or job applications and in identifying gaps in skills and knowledge.

Revalidation encourages a broad approach to CPD, as it is not just about attending training courses or conferences, which can be expensive and involve time away from the workplace. The Tips in this Activities and Tools section of this book provide a wide range of CPD suggestions that an individual can undertake which cost very little but offer benefits to them as an individual, their team and the wider organization.

Finally, revalidation is important from a professional perspective, as it demonstrates the importance of ongoing development. It brings the LKS profession into line with many other professions which require those practising in their field to demonstrate regular evidence of CPD throughout their career.

Example from practice:
Tracey Pratchett (2016) – LKS manager (NHS, FE and public)

I completed my first revalidation at a group session in September 2015. It was one of those things that was on my to-do list, but always slipped to the bottom of the pile. Making a commitment to attend a session meant that I was able to complete revalidation in a couple of hours, and it was great having support on hand. I've also encouraged members of my team to revalidate in this way.

I found that the process was very quick and easy, but also gave me the opportunity to reflect on what I had achieved over the past year, where I was now and what development needs I have for the future. Having changed roles 6 months earlier, this was invaluable. I have also used this information to support conference submissions, underpin appraisal discussions with my line manager and to update my CV. I now put an hour aside every month or two to keep my log updated with a view to making the next time even easier.

👍 Best for

■ Actively demonstrating an ongoing commitment to developing and applying skills and knowledge whilst maintaining a commitment to personal development and professional growth.

▶ More

■ CILIP recognize this achievement by maintaining a Register of Practitioners, which displays an individual's professional details alongside the date that they initially achieved their qualification, and also the last date they revalidated. This information is publicly available to employers, potential future employers and colleagues. Individuals are able to control the information displayed in the Register by editing their profile on the CILIP website.

■ There is a user called 'Example Portfolio Content' on the portfolio system which has a small number of examples of revalidation submissions. Additionally individuals can make their submissions available to their friends on the portfolio system for further examples.

References

CILIP (2014) *Revalidation*, www.cilip.org.uk/CILIP/jobs-careers/professional-registration/revalidation. [Accessed 8 November 2015]

Pratchett, T. (2016) *Revalidation in Action*, www.lihnn.nhs.uk/images/Documents/LIHNN/LIHNNK-Up/LIHNNK_UP_50_v8_lo-res.pdf. [Accessed 19 June 2016]

Further reading

CILIP (2013) *Your Professional Knowledge and Skills Base: identify gaps and maximise opportunities along your career path*, CILIP, London.

CILIP (2013) *Revalidating Using the CILIP Virtual Learning Environment*, www.cilip.org.uk/sites/default/files/documents/How%20to%20revalidate%20using%20the%20cilip%20VLE.pdf. [Accessed 8 November 2015]

CILIP (2015) *How to Access the VLE*, www.cilip.org.uk/cilip/membership/benefits/virtual-learning-environment-vle/how-access-vle. [Accessed 8 November 2015]

Acknowledgement

Many thanks to Matthew Wheeler, Development Officer (Member Support) CILIP – www.CILIP.org.uk/CILIP/about/CILIP-people/staff/member-services/matthew-wheeler – for checking the information provided in this Tip.

40. Coaching

COACHING AND MENTORING have similarities and the terms are often used interchangeably. They employ similar techniques, sometimes blurring the boundaries between the two approaches (Webster, 2014; Brewerton, 2002). Coaching derives from the sporting community and the coach is particularly concerned with improving performance and finding solutions. Coaches do not need to work in the same field as the person being coached, but rather bring a skill set which they use to help the individual to achieve their goals. A mentor is usually a more experienced professional working in the same field who will share their knowledge and skills with the individual being mentored.

Coaches use their skills in listening, questioning, challenging and being supportive, to focus on solving a specific problem or achieving a clear outcome, often within a short timeframe. This differs from a mentoring relationship, which is usually longer-term and more likely to be concerned with the learning elements of the relationship rather than performance. Hadikin (2004) states that there is no universal definition of coaching, that it is 'simply helping others to realise their potential' (Hadikin, 2004, 1).

Coaching is not necessarily career-focused and can be applied to all aspects of an individual's life. In the context of this book, we will emphasize the way that coaching provides a structured framework for an individual to work with a skilled professional to improve their performance and solve problems at work. Within this model of coaching, Whitmore (2009) indicates that the coach uses their expertise (without necessarily having knowledge of the coachee's specialism) to explore perceptions, unlock learning and draw new or unknown conclusions. CIPD (2009) states that coaching focuses on the individual and is not always work-related, so can be used to explore self-perception and personal responses to situations.

The GROW Model

Coaches often use frameworks to structure their sessions and Whitmore's (2009) GROW Model (Figure 40.1) is a simple yet common approach. This model is useful for keeping coaching sessions on track and ensuring that the individual being coached leaves with a tangible action plan that they can implement.

Employing an external coach for an individual or group may not be an option for your LKS, but some organizations have in-house coaching schemes to provide individuals with support. Rock and Donde (2008) highlight that whilst coaching is expensive for organizations, coaching can provide a tangible return on investment, resulting in staff who are motivated, good performers and able to lead and have reduced stress.

Coaching provides a space to explore challenging issues in a supportive environment with a skilled professional and can be an extremely valuable experience. It is not easy and will be challenging, and so will only work with someone who is committed to the process and prepared to explore uncomfortable self-perceptions and to act on their insights.

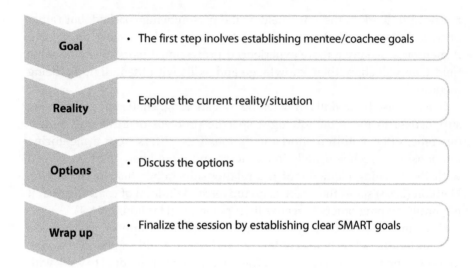

Figure 40.1 *The GROW Model (Whitmore, 2009)*

🖒 Best for

■ Working with a professional to explore problems in depth and to improve performance in the workplace.

► More

■ Coaching is similar to mentoring, so it is worth exploring both options to ensure that the most appropriate approach is selected (Tips 62, p. 160 and 63, p. 163).

⚠ To think about

■ Coaching will only work for individuals who are committed to the process and are prepared to implement change. This approach cannot be imposed on an individual who is not engaged.
■ Employing an external coach may not be a viable approach for your team, as it can be costly. Explore in-house organizational coaching opportunities and opportunities linked to professional bodies, which may be more affordable.

References

Brewerton, A. (2002) Mentoring, *Liber Quarterly*, **12** (4), 361–80.
CIPD (2009) *Mentoring – CIPD factsheet*,
    www.shef.ac.uk/polopoly_fs/1.110468!/file/cipd_mentoring_factsheet.pdf.
    [Accessed 6 April 2015]

Hadikin, R. (2004) *Effective Coaching in Healthcare*, Elsevier Science, London.

Rock, D. and Donde, R. (2008) Driving Organizational Change with Internal Coaching Programs: part one, *Industrial and Commercial Training*, **40** (1), 10–18.

Webster, M. (2014) *The Difference Between Coaching and Mentoring*, www.leadershipthoughts.com/difference-between-coaching-and-mentoring. [Accessed 6 April 2015]

Whitmore, J. (2009) *Coaching for Performance: growing people, performance and purpose*, 4th edn, Nicholas Brealey Publishing, London.

41. Collaborative working

REGARDLESS OF AN individual's level in an organization, at some point in their career they will have to work collaboratively. Within a LKS there will be opportunities for your team members to work with library staff from other teams, LKS staff from other organizations and your users. Nonthacumjane (2011) states that the expectation that LKS professionals will work in multidisciplinary contexts means that teamwork is one of the key skills for practitioners. The ability to work collaboratively as team leader and/or team member will ensure that working groups complete projects successfully and contribute to the achievements of the goals of the service and the organization (Nonthacumjane, 2011). This may be a challenge for those who enjoy working independently. However, it is a good opportunity for you and your staff to grow professionally by learning from other people's experiences and expanding existing networks.

Communication

Ensure that when individuals are involved in collaborative projects, communication is maintained, as without it things come to an abrupt standstill! When working with different groups it is vital that everything is communicated as clearly as possible. This is particularly important when working with a group for the first time where the members have no prior knowledge of each other's working practices. At the beginning of the process it is imperative to outline the objectives of the project, assign responsibilities based on skills and experience and agree the preferred method of communication. It is important that communication is proactive. If your staff advise that someone is not responding, encourage them to follow up the contact and not to worry about being impolite.

If things are not going so well, or if there is an unexpected change, remind your team members to keep focused and remember why the collaboration was started in the first place. Once this is done, they will find it easier to think of the bigger picture and begin allocating work. They will need to be flexible and use their organizational skills to ensure that they are able to adapt or change any existing plans.

If an individual takes on too much work or if something is not being completed or is not done within a certain timeframe you will need your team members to be assertive and allocate work to others. When things are not going so well, your role as a manager or supervisor will be to offer support and help them to work out in a calm manner what needs to happen. Ultimately, they need to be diplomatic and professional to prevent the collaborative effort from failing.

When staff enter into collaborations with people who they do not know well things can be difficult, particularly if the task or project is being organized virtually. Issues can arise if one of the team seems to take on more work than others in the group. As previously mentioned, this is where individuals will need to be diplomatic, assertive and willing to compromise. Here are some tips for successful collaboration:

- Communication is key.
- Staff should keep focused and be committed.
- Encourage individuals to be diplomatic when dealing with issues.
- Support staff to deal with unexpected changes.
- Help them to stay organized to prevent them from becoming overloaded.
- Remind them that the positives far outweigh any negatives.

Without the above, the barriers will overwhelm the individuals and ultimately impact negatively upon the success of the collaboration.

🖒 Best for

- ■ Projects where different skill sets are needed.
- ■ Improving communication and organizational skills for individuals and teams.

► More

- ■ Good for developing and increasing networks for the individual and your LKS.
- ■ Enables staff to identify the skill sets and strengths of others in the collaboration who they can turn to for future projects.
- ■ Learn from other collaborative projects by conducting wider reading, e.g. Goldsmith's (2014) summary of a presentation at the 2014 LILAC conference focusing on a collaborative project.
- ■ Collaborative working has been proven to be effective for saving money and making services more effective (Miles, 2011).

⚠ To think about

■ If the project has come to a standstill encourage the individuals to restore communication and use their new skills to drive the project forward.

■ If individuals feel that they are doing more than their share of the work support them to verbalize their concerns.

■ Ensure that they remain calm, objective and tackle any issues diplomatically.

References

Goldsmith, S. (2014) *10 Tips on Collaborative Working from Lilac 2014*, www.cilip.org.uk/cilip/blog/10-tips-collaborative-working-lilac-2014. [Accessed 24 January 2015].

Miles, E. (2011) *Collaborative Working: how publicly funded services can take a whole systems approach*, www.instituteforgovernment.org.uk/publications/collaborative-working. [Accessed 24 January 2015].

Nonthacumjane, P. (2011) Key Skills and Competencies of a New Generation of LIS Professionals, *IFLA Journal*, **37** (4), 280–8.

42. Communities of practice – internal

A Community of Practice can be described as a network of people emerging spontaneously, and held together by informal relationships and common purpose, that shares common knowledge or a specific domain, expertise and tools, and learn from one another.

van Wyk, 2005, 92

COMMUNITIES OF PRACTICE (CoPs) have been discussed in a number of sectors such as business, education and health and they are common in LKS. In fact we are all probably members of formal or informal communities of practice, even if we don't define them in this way. One problem with the literature is that definitions are varied and have evolved over time; however members of a CoP generally share common goals and motivations (Kimble and Hildreth, 2005). They can be created within a single organization, and often these CoPs are influenced by management goals and may be linked to the overall knowledge management (KM) strategy.

Example from practice: the Academic Library Service at the University of Pretoria (van Wyk, 2005)

The Academic Library Service at the University of Pretoria includes a collection of service units. Through interviews and focus groups, two types of CoP were identified: Cross-organizational CoPs and internal CoPs.

Cross-organizational CoPs are: Knowledge Management Practitioners Group of Pretoria; Gaelic Cataloguers and Technical Services Working Group; African Goats Group.

Internal CoPs are: Information Specialists Group; Digital Repositories Group; Information Network for E-Information Experts.

van Wyk (2005) found that these CoPs enabled members to work smarter, share knowledge and feel part of a wider network. They were also beneficial to the organization, as they helped to embed knowledge within the organization and avoid the loss of tacit information when individuals left. They also spread ideas across the organization and enabled innovation.

Whilst there are many benefits to organizational CoPs, van Wyk (2005) outlines a number of critical factors which can threaten the success of organizational CoPs. Management support, time to participate, workload, incentives, size of the CoP, trust and motivation can all provide challenges to a community of practice.

To summarize, CoPs within an organization can be very useful, especially when they have a clear and specific function and, crucially, if supported by management. They can be a great source of learning and networking for the individual and can also be an integral part of an organization's knowledge programme. Lesser and Storck (2001) believe that CoPs are valuable because they contribute to the development of social capital, which is necessary for knowledge creation, sharing and use (Cohen, 2006). CoPs can be varied in scope and design, as largely this will be influenced by the members, their interests and their preferences for ways of working. van Wyk (2005) found that the optimum number of members for a community of practice was 15–20 members.

As a supervisor or manager you can encourage your staff to become members of CoPs to increase their knowledge and ensure that learning across an organization is pooled and shared. In a large academic LKS, for example, you may encourage members from different teams to come together with a view to developing a digital strategy for your service or to plan marketing and promotional campaigns. In smaller LKS, you are unlikely to have internal CoPs. However, you can encourage staff from your team to become part of organizational CoPs, working with non-library staff to improve knowledge management activities, for example.

♖ Best for

- CoPs within organizations are great for sharing learning and building networks. They can be a useful tool for progressing an organization's internal knowledge management strategy and can be a useful means of transferring, capturing and harnessing knowledge and keeping it within the organization.

■ For the individual there are many benefits to working with like-minded people and CoPs provide an opportunity for your staff to broaden their learning and develop new skills and ways of working which could benefit your LKS.

▶ **More**

■ Due to the largely informal and spontaneous nature of organizational CoPs which are led by members, motivation levels can remain high if the right conditions are in place.

⚠ **To think about**

■ Without management support, leadership and direction to some extent, it can be difficult to maximize and capture learning within these often informal groups. If management do not embrace the CoP as an essential component of organizational learning, staff will be less likely to engage in the process, particularly if they are not given time and space to participate or the resources for success.

References

Cohen, A. (2006) Libraries, Knowledge Management, and Communities of Practice, *Information Outlook*, **10** (1), 34–7.

Kimble, C. and Hildreth, P. (2005) Dualities, Distributed Communities of Practice and Knowledge Management, *Journal of Knowledge Management*, **9** (4), 102–3.

Lesser, E.L. and Storck, J. (2001) Communities of Practice and Organizational Performance, *IBM Systems Journal*, **40** (4), 831-41.

van Wyk, J. (2005) *Communities of Practice in an Academic Library: a run on the wild side*, http://repository.up.ac.za/bitstream/handle/2263/6427/vanwyk.pdf?sequence=1. [Accessed 8 November 2015]

43. Communities of practice – external

LKS STAFF CAN become involved in communities of practice (CoPs) with staff from other sectors or other organizations. These are different to internal CoPs, which exist within the boundaries of a single organization, as they bring people together who have shared interests and a common purpose and tend not to be dictated by organizational priorities (van Wyk, 2005).

Connecting with people from outside the organization can be extremely beneficial for the personal development of the individual. By encouraging your staff to join external CoPs, you create opportunities for them to learn from others and to bring new ideas, perspectives, knowledge and innovations into your service. These groups are often informal and membership is likely to change as new people join and others leave when their interests change. External CoPs tend to be more flexible and all members usually have equal status. There is no hierarchical structure, even when people have defined roles within the group.

CoPs can provide opportunities for junior staff to work with senior staff from other organizations on an equal footing. Cohen (2006) states that the remit of external CoPs tends to evolve as new people join and according to group members' consensus. These differ from internal CoPs, which are likely to be driven by the need to fulfil organizational objectives; external CoPs are much more fluid and the relationships between members is of great value.

There are a large number of CoPs in the LKS sector, many of which exist in the virtual environment using mailing lists, forums and social media (Facebook, Twitter, blogs, etc.) to connect. In some cases these CoPs exist only in virtual spaces, but often will include some face-to-face contact to supplement this. The Michigan Library Association (2015) has developed a number of online 'Communities of Practice (CoPs) to create and archive knowledge, develop and document best practices, solve problems and build relationships among professionals'. These CoPs are not only about learning, but also about storing knowledge for reuse and are organized according to members' priorities.

Example from practice:
MAP Toolkit Project, a virtual community of practice

This project started in the North-west of England in 2008, when a group of eight health library staff – inspired by the LondonLinks Alignment Toolkit (LondonLinks, 2014) – came together to think about how they could share the good work happening in their region. They wanted to demonstrate the impact of their work and how it was implicitly linked to key drivers for their organizations, and to provide handy tools which could be used by others.

The group membership changed over time and expanded to include members across the country. The CoP has a small central group who drive change, but is also a wider membership of people who use the resources. As membership increased, meetings changed from face-to-face to virtual, using teleconferences and a blog to share learning and planning tools.

As time has moved on, social media has been exploited to share learning and developments more widely within the sector. The bulk of the learning and knowledge is captured in a single blog, the MAP Toolkit (2015).

👍 Best for

■ Providing opportunities for staff to learn from people outside your organization. This can be especially useful for smaller teams, or those working in specialist or isolated roles.

■ Bringing new ideas and approaches to problem solving as well as relationships which can help your service grow and meet its objectives.

■ Helping individuals to develop professionally and work with people who have shared ideologies and approaches to knowledge management. Can be really useful for formalized development, e.g. Chartership or revalidation.

▶ **More**

■ Virtual CoPs also provide access to a vast support network, without the need to travel far and wide. They can be a cost-effective and accessible solution for staff to gain development opportunities.

⚠ **To think about**

■ External CoPs are very much about the individual and their professional development, rather than the organization. As a manager or supervisor, you cannot dictate or control the agenda of these groups, as they exist outside your control.

■ It can be difficult to build virtual CoPs and to maintain integral relationships and some face-to-face contact can be useful as an opportunity to strengthen the group and refocus.

References

Cohen, A. (2006) Libraries, Knowledge Management, and Communities of Practice, *Information Outlook*, **10** (1), 34–7.

LondonLinks (2014) *LondonLinks Alignment Toolkit*, www.londonlinks.nhs.uk/resources/files/alignment-tool. [Accessed 20 April 2016]

MAP Toolkit (2015) *Making Alignment a Priority (MAP) Toolkit*, https://maptoolkit.wordpress.com. [Accessed 29 November 2015]

Michigan Library Association (2015) *Communities of Practice Listservs*, www.milibraries.org/prof-development-networking/communities-of-practice-listserves. [Accessed 15 November 2015].

van Wyk, J. (2005) *Communities of Practice in an Academic Library: a run on the wild side*, http://repository.up.ac.za/bitstream/handle/2263/6427/vanwyk.pdf?sequence=1. [Accessed 8 November 2015]

44. Conferences – attending

ATTENDING A CONFERENCE as a delegate is a rewarding experience. It provides numerous opportunities for learning, sharing ideas, meeting new people, building networks, visiting new places, generating new initiatives and providing time out from the day job for reflection (Baron, 2014). The benefits to both the LKS and individual development are varied and sometimes unexpected, whether attending or participating.

As a manager or supervisor you will need to balance your service needs with the personal development needs of individuals in your team, whilst trying to be fair and equitable to everyone. However, promoting conference attendance and attending conferences yourself proves your commitment to learning and professional development, which is vital in creating a successful team.

One way to make an informed decision about whether a member of the team should attend a particular conference is to ask them to provide you with a business case as to why they should attend. This means that they will really have to reflect on the conference and why their participation would be useful to them and to the LKS. You can also add the condition that, on their return, they will write up a report and give a short presentation on what they learned, in order to cascade knowledge to the rest of the team.

You could encourage staff members to give a presentation at the conference that they wish to attend. In fact some organizations make having a paper accepted at a conference a requirement for receiving funding to attend. If a member of staff does have a paper accepted, they get all the learning and networking benefits of attendance at a conference. They learn about presenting at conferences and they promote your project or service.

Obviously, attending a conference can be expensive in terms of the actual costs involved and the participant's time out of the office. There is preparation time if they are presenting, travel time, expenses and a possible overnight stay, all of which can mount up.

Local conferences can help to minimize costs and can be a great way of making connections with new people, creating local networks and building on existing knowledge and skills (Baron, 2014).

Attendance at a national conference may involve a member of staff travelling further, but will provide numerous opportunities including broadening their networking and raising the profile of your organization or initiative to a wider audience.

Finally, international conferences provide unique exposure to a wider global perspective and facilitate a cultural experience, as well as offering the chance to visit LKSs in different countries (Helregel, 2014). When the International Federation of Library Associations (IFLA) surveyed attendees, the key benefits for organizations were identified as: learning from other services, gathering ideas, identifying future trends and assessing your services against others. Personal benefits were identified as: networking with the international community, professional development, new ideas, inspiration, deeper learning and increased motivation.

Example from practice: Amy Finnegan – LKS professional (NICE)

I have been fortunate to work at an organization that encourages conference attendance and I try to attend at least one large conference a year. I select the sessions I want to go to as soon as the programme is released, first focusing on sessions that are relevant to my role so that I can feed information back to the team and then on topics that appeal to my personal interests.

Conferences are an excellent way to maintain a current awareness of trends within the library and information community and reflect on how such trends will impact your sector and role. Equally, conferences are a great opportunity to network with peers from outside your sector. Enthusiasm and creativity are palpable at conferences, so don't be surprised if you leave a conference with new ideas and potential collaborative projects with other attendees!

🖒 Best for

- Keeping staff learning and motivated in their profession whilst maintaining a sense of the bigger picture and wider implications. Attending conferences can really increase staff engagement and enthusiasm for their job and career.
- Attendees should come back inspired and full of innovative ideas which you could use to improve your service.

▶ More

- Networking with peers and librarians from other services and sectors is invaluable for providing staff with information on a wider professional context than their own organization.
- Promoting new initiatives, raising awareness of your service.

⚠ To think about

- Conferences can be costly both in time and money. Ensure that you can cover the service needs so as not to burden remaining staff and help staff to identify alternative funding streams and bursaries.
- Ensure that opportunities are distributed fairly amongst team members, to ensure that some staff are not seen to be getting favourable treatment.

References

Baron, C. (2014) *The Benefits of Attending Local Conferences*, http://hacklibraryschool.com/2014/11/19/the-benefits-of-attending-local-conferences. [Accessed 20 April 2016]

Helregel, N. (2014) *Top 8 Reasons to go to an International Library Conference*, http://hacklibraryschool.com/2014/02/10/international-library-conferences. [Accessed 20 April 2016]

Further reading

Bennett, M. (2015) *Top 10 Reasons Your Friends Members Should Attend the ALA Annual Conference*, www.ala.org/united/events_conferences/annual/attendingannual. [Accessed 20 April 2016]

Moira Fraser Consulting (2013) *The Benefits of Attending IFLA Conferences*, www.ifla.org/files/assets/services-for-parliaments/publications/ifla_conference_attendance_report.pdf. [Accessed 20 April 2016]

Potter, N. (2010) *The Echo Chamber, Live!* www.ned-potter.com/blog/1086. [Accessed 20 April 2016]

45. Conferences – organizing

GETTING INVOLVED IN organizing a conference is a great opportunity for all levels of staff. They will develop a range of skills, including networking, marketing, communication, presenting, negotiating, managing people, troubleshooting and budget management, to name but a few. In addition, they will find that creating something people enjoy and find useful is incredibly rewarding. If this is something you or your staff are interested in you can either look at joining the organizing committee for an established conference, such as the ones listed in the Further Reading section at the end of this Tip, or you could consider setting up a conference of your own if you can identify a gap in the LKS conference market.

Getting involved

If members of your staff are thinking of joining an established committee it is a good idea to think about the skills that they already have and identify any areas that they need to develop when allocating roles and tasks. Some areas that individuals can be involved in are:

- Chair
- Treasurer
- bookings
- call for papers

- sponsorship
- programme (what the delegates receive in their packs on arrival, brochure, badge, useful information, etc.)
- marketing and communications (website, social media, etc.).

Organizing your own conference

If you and your team decide to organize a conference yourselves there are a number of considerations to take into account. These include planning the programme, organizing the venue and attracting people to the conference, not just as attendees but also in terms of presenting papers and running workshops.

The theme of your conference should be relevant and informed by the target audience and their expectations. Once the theme is agreed the programme can be designed with a view to attracting attendees and interesting speakers or experts in the field can be invited to speak or present. It is usual to put out a general call for papers on the agreed theme which outlines the criteria for inclusion. It is not unusual for high-profile speakers to charge appearance fees or expenses and this should be factored into the planning process.

The event must be promoted using established methods to attract the desired audience in terms of interests and numbers. A website containing all the information that delegates might need, including details on the venue and location, as well as how to book a place, is essential. This is also a good focus for other promotional activities as it can link to your social media channels and mailing lists.

The venue for any conference will be dependent on the size and style of the event and you could encourage your staff to arrange small events at your workplace. Larger events will require venues that are designed specifically for holding conferences but they can be quite expensive, and so ensure that your team members ask for quotes before making a decision. Conference venues have the advantage of being purpose-built and have experienced staff who ensure that events run smoothly. Encourage anyone who is involved in organizing a conference to visit potential venues before making a decision as seeing them in person makes planning easier, providing the opportunity to experience the space and see what facilities are available.

For any conference which is longer than a day delegates will need accommodation, so ensure that staff planning a conference give this some consideration. If they are not arranging accommodation then delegates should be advised to make their own arrangements and information should be provided on the website about local hotels, etc. Alternatively, organizers can liaise with the local tourist board, who may offer preferential rates to delegates, but ensure that the conference team will not become liable for payment if hotel bookings are not taken up.

You need to be aware that during the conference members of the organizing committee will need to be on hand at all times, as the responsibility for a successful event rests with them. They will need to co-ordinate a range of tasks, including managing volunteers, introducing speakers, troubleshooting problems and working with the venue staff, presenters and attendees to ensure that things run smoothly. If you are supporting individuals within your team to be involved in organizing a conference, you need to ensure that they are released from their daily duties accordingly.

The work of the conference organizers is not finished once the conference has taken place. An after-conference meeting enables the team to review the success of the conference, including assessing any feedback, looking at what worked and what didn't and ensuring any further actions are agreed. Further actions might involve writing follow-up articles for relevant publications, ensuring that any profit is spent as agreed and providing feedback to speakers and the venue.

Example from practice: Lisa Jeskins – Co-chair of the LILAC Conference Committee and freelance trainer and consultant

LILAC is three days long and attracts approximately 300 delegates. We have a team of eight to organize the conference plus two local representatives from the host venue. As Co-chair I have learnt about every aspect of organizing events, from agreeing and planning the timetable to booking speakers and venues, managing the money, marketing the event and every other aspect imaginable. The skills I have developed are numerous and transfer into other areas of my professional life, particularly in my work as a freelance trainer and consultant. I have learnt how to negotiate fees with speakers, sponsors and venues, the value of quality promotional materials and how important things such as food and social events can be to the success of an event.

Organizing LILAC is challenging but working on creating something people enjoy and find useful is both incredibly rewarding and fun. Much of my learning has come through working with the other people on the organizing committee and it's provided me with many an opportunity to network with a wide range of other information professionals. The time commitment is considerable but the benefits to me as an individual more than make up for it. Organizing the annual LILAC conference is easily one of the most rewarding development experiences of my career.

🖒 Best for

- Developing a wide range of skills which can be transferred back to the workplace.
- Enhancing the professional network of the individuals.

■ A well organized event can boost the reputation of your LKS and individuals in your team.

▶ More

■ Is a formal conference the best approach or is an Exchange of Experience event, TeachMeet or Unconference (Tip 53, p. 132) more suitable?
■ Conferences usually charge delegates to attend, obtain sponsorship or charge exhibitors to cover costs. Advise the organizing team to agree this at the start, arrange a system for taking payment and agree how profit will be spent.

▲ To think about

■ This is a time-consuming process and you will need to allow individuals time away from their day job for meetings and to attend the conference.
■ Organizing an event of this type is hard work and can be stressful so consider how you will support individuals during this time.
■ A poorly run event can damage the reputation of your LKS and your staff, so ensure that the right people are given the right roles.

Further reading

BIALL (2016) *BIALL Conferences,* www.biall.org.uk/pages/conferences-biall.html. [Accessed 2 May 2016]

FIL (2016) *Forum for Interlending and Information Delivery,* www.forumforinterlending.org.uk. [Accessed 22 April 2016]

HLG (2016) *HLG Conference 2016,* www.cilip.org.uk/health-libraries-group/events-conferences-seminars/conferences/hlg-conference-2016. [Accessed 2 May 2016]

LILAC (2016) *LILAC,* www.lilacconference.com. [Accessed 22 April 2016]

UKSG (2016) *Annual Conference and Exhibition,* www.uksg.org/events/annualconference. [Accessed 22 April 2016]

46. Conferences – posters

PRESENTING A POSTER at a conference is a great way of delivering information on a new project or initiative and can be a good starting point for individuals who are not ready to deliver a formal presentation. Posters raise awareness of an individual's work or an LKS project and are often less intimidating than presenting a paper. This is an alternative opportunity for a member of staff who wants to gain presentation experience in a 'less scary' environment.

What is a poster?

A poster should be attractive and pleasing to the eye. Its primary function is to advertise and be decorative. People often use conference posters to present brief information about a project they are working on. During the scheduled poster session, the designer of the poster should be beside their poster to answer any questions that people might have. For this reason, a poster can also be considered as a means to generate discussion.

What should your staff consider when producing a poster?

- Any poster should be prepared in accordance with the conference guidelines, which will advise about acceptable size, orientation, structure and format.
- It should make an impact and use credible and professional images and fonts. Avoid Comic Sans and cartoon-like images.
- A poster full of text will not attract people. They will not be able to see quickly what it is about and a poster loses impact if people have to get really close to read it.
- Text must be clear and concise and broken up using headings and bullet points.
- Information must be illustrated visually using charts, graphs and photos to get the message across.
- Encourage staff to try using free graphic design tools such as Canva (2016), which can help to produce something professional-looking.
- Interactive posters can make an impact. Electronic posters can link to multimedia content and QR codes can enable your staff to link to videos or web-based content.
- Follow-up information can be provided via handouts or flyers that people can take away with them.
- Offer to proofread the poster before sending it to the printer.
- Consider giving your team member a small budget to get a professional to help design their poster. It could become a marketing tool and if accepted at more than one conference would provide a return on investment.
- Provide opportunities for team members to attend other conferences and attend poster sessions to collect ideas.
- Suggest that the member of staff asks for feedback using a paper survey, as this could provide useful learning for future posters.

👍 Best for

- Promoting and raising awareness of new research, initiatives or projects to a wide audience.

■ Providing staff with opportunities to develop their presentation skills at a conference in a less intimidating environment.

■ Helping team members to build a portfolio of experience which will enhance their CV and LinkedIn profiles.

▲ To think about

■ Make sure that there are no spelling mistakes or grammatical errors.

■ Ensure that guidelines are followed to the letter. An overlarge poster or one with a different orientation will stand out for the wrong reasons or be difficult to 'hang'.

References

Canva (2016) *Canva*, https://www.canva.com. [Accessed 20 April 2016]

Further reading

NYU Libraries have a good guide to producing posters:
   http://guides.nyu.edu/posters.
Examples of posters: http://archive.lilacconference.com/home/lilac-2014.
                     http://archive.lilacconference.com/home/lilac-2015.

47. Conferences – presenting

PROVIDING OPPORTUNITIES FOR your team members to present at conferences or events can be great for both your organization and the individual concerned. It raises the profile of your work and can help to develop the individual's skills and confidence.

Presenting at small events can provide good opportunities for staff to practise their first presentations. At larger conferences, short presentations or posters can also be less intimidating ways to present for the first time. Look out for TeachMeets (Tip 53, p. 132), PechaKucha (2003) or lightning talks to get a first taste of presenting.

Create and encourage an ethos of peer review within your team so that staff might practise on their colleagues and receive feedback. Provide other safe opportunities for staff to practise their presentation at team meetings or other local events.

If individuals are to have an impact when they present, they need to produce professional-looking presentations and posters. This means not overfilling slides or posters, not adding too much text and using quality images to illustrate the presentation. It is strongly recommended that you avoid using cartoons and cartoonish fonts. Presentation skills training can be invaluable in giving staff more confidence in their performance. There are courses staff can go on that will show them how to create great PowerPoints or how to use Prezi (2016).

Presenting at any conference helps the individual to develop skills in abstract writing, poster design, film production, negotiating, influencing, presenting and public relations (Blagden, Pratchett and Treadway, 2014), which can only be good for your service.

Example from practice:
Tracey Pratchett – LKS manager (NHS, FE and public)

I've presented at the Health Libraries Group Conference (CILIP, 2015) twice and have returned to the office with a new vigour, full of ideas and enthusiasm to try new things. On the other hand, I also felt guilty about the cost (I was lucky enough to obtain a bursary) and concerned about the impact that taking time away would have on my colleagues, as we were a small team.

When I presented at an NHS Procurement conference to senior finance and procurement managers, I was surprised at the positive reaction and interest in my role. Presenting at a conference outside the library and information sector took my work outside the 'Echo Chamber' (Potter, 2010) and generated debate and contacts to be followed up after the conference.

🖒 Best for

- Submitting a paper or a poster to present at a conference can be great for developing staff confidence and helping them to develop a range of skills which will benefit and improve your service.
- Promoting a new initiative or project.

▶ More

- If a member of your staff presents at a conference it raises the profile of your LKS to a wider audience.
- Team members become advocates for your local service and the wider profession.

⚠ To think about

- Staff may need additional support and time to prepare.
- There may be significant travel time and possible overnight stays.
- Although presenting at a conference can be rewarding, don't underestimate how stressful it can be, particularly for those who are less experienced.

References

Blagden, P., Pratchett, T. and Treadway, V. (2014) Supporting Advocacy Outside the Profession, *CILIP Update,* March, 42–3.

CILIP (2015) *Health Libraries Group,* www.cilip.org.uk/about/special-interest-groups/health-libraries-group. [Accessed 5 March 2015]

PechaKucha (2003) *PechaKucha 20x20: the art of concise presentations,* www.pechakucha.org. [Accessed 20 April 2016]

Potter, N. (2010) *The Echo Chamber, Live!,* www.ned-potter.com/blog/1086. [Accessed 20 April 2016]

Prezi (2016) *Prezi,* https://prezi.com. [Accessed 20 April 2016]

Further reading

For guidance on presenting and creating presentations read Tip 70, p. 179, and the following from Ned Potter:

- www.slideshare.net/thewikiman/stop-breaking-the-basic-rules-of-presenting.
- www.ned-potter.com/blog/the-4-most-important-powerpoint-rules-for-successful-presentations.

48. Conferences – sharing the learning

CONFERENCES ARE RICH learning events, where individuals participate in a range of activities, including attendance at workshops or presentations, participation in debates and networking with colleagues from different organizations who have similar professional interests. There is no doubt that the individual who attends a conference is likely to find the experience rewarding and will return to the workplace with a multitude of ideas that they can be put into practice. If you are sending a member of staff to a conference, they can do a number of things to share their learning to the benefit of the wider team.

Social media

Social media provides informal learning opportunities and conferences often tap into these platforms to disseminate information before, during and after the conference. These days, if there is a conference we want to go to, but can't afford it or if it clashes with something else, it doesn't matter; we can read the resulting articles, blog posts and tweets and watch videos and presentations, without leaving our desks.

Most conferences have Twitter (2016) accounts and use a designated hashtag (#) (see Tip 87, p. 231, for more information). Delegates are encouraged to post tweets about the conference using the hashtag, so that they can network and meet up with other delegates. They enable individuals to take notes, which can be referred back to, and to make comments about the things they are hearing. All tweets which have used the hashtag can later be saved or archived using a content tool like Storify (2016) or Paper.li (2016).

Tweeting from a conference is a good way of raising a team member's profile and will provide opportunities for others within your team or your LKS account to follow, comment and interact with the attendee. Social presentation tools such as Prezi (2016) or Slideshare (2016) provide the opportunity to share presentations via Twitter and other social media channels, enabling your staff to share their work.

It is a skill to take notes using a hashtag and it takes practice. You could encourage individuals to use a note-taking tool on their device and cut and paste what they want to tweet. Tweeting all of their notes can be tricky and, if they are not skilled at this, it may mean that they struggle to pay attention to the speaker, so Twitter may not be the best approach for them. You can encourage individuals to use these notes and tweets after the event to inform blog posts or articles reflecting on their conference experience. These can take the form of session write-ups, discussions on favourite speakers and presentations and reflections on learning and future application.

Sharing the learning

When your team member returns from a conference, it is vital that you provide opportunities for them to cascade their learning to colleagues within the team or organization. You could encourage them to write an article for a newsletter, a blog post or give a presentation to colleagues about what they learned and what could be the most useful information for your team. Support the individual to reflect on how they can practically apply what they have learned in their environment and whether any of this learning could solve problems within the team.

🖒 Best for

- Informal learning amongst team members without the cost of everyone having to attend the conference.
- Ensuring that any learning from the conference is beneficial for the LKS and your wider team.
- Raising the profile of individuals within your team and enhancing the reputation of your LKS.

⚠ To think about

- Warn individuals not to become so focused on searching for the 'tweetable' quote that they don't take away any real understanding of what speakers are saying.
- Not sharing learning within your team means that much of the value of an individual attending a conference is lost.

References

Paper.li (2016) *Paper.li*, http://paper.li. [Accessed 20 April 2016]
Prezi (2016) *Prezi*, https://prezi.com. [Accessed 20 April 2016]
Slideshare (2016) *Slideshare*, www.slideshare.net. [Accessed 20 April 2016]
Storify (2016) *Storify*, https://storify.com. [Accessed 20 April 2016]
Twitter (2016) *Twitter*, https://twitter.com. [Accessed 20 April 2016]

49. Conferences – volunteering

VOLUNTEERING FOR ANY project, working group or conference can be hugely beneficial to members of your staff and their careers. Volunteering at a conference may allow staff to attend the conference for free and, depending on what work they get involved in, can also improve their knowledge of a particular topic, their confidence, networking and other professional skills. It might even help staff develop skills that cannot be developed in the office. Perhaps you work for local government and staff are not allowed to create social media accounts, but they could run the Twitter feed for a conference. Maybe there are no opportunities for your staff to develop their staff management skills, but they could get involved in 'staff management' for a conference. This sort of volunteering can help progress a person's career and positively impact on their motivation, particularly if your organization lacks opportunities.

Levels of volunteering

There are different levels of volunteering for conferences. Sometimes conference organizers need more 'people on the ground', volunteers who can act as guides for delegates, showing them where the different rooms are, or 'runners' (running to get a tech problem solved), or sometimes just to help move equipment around. Sometimes library conferences approach local LKS courses and ask for student volunteers.

A member of staff could apply for a longer-term vacancy on a conference organizing committee or steering group. This would involve having a look at the conference website, seeing what the parent body is and then asking if there are any vacancies. If there are, is it a vacancy where the member of staff has a particular skill or knowledge that might help?

Staff should think about when the conference is being held and what they want to do. They can offer to help (one-off volunteering) in the run-up to the actually conference. If they want a longer-term position, they should watch mailing lists and social media (such as Lis-Link (JiscMail, 1998) or any subject-specific lists) for ads for conference committee vacancies. They should also talk to people who are already on a committee and ask questions such as:

- What is expected of you?
- How much work is involved?
- Is it all year round? Or are there peaks and lulls?
- What is your work load like? [An academic liaison librarian, for example, is unlikely to get support to volunteer if the conference clashes with the start of the September term.]

Table 49.1 sets out some questions to consider before volunteering.

Table 49.1 *Considerations for potential volunteers*
What should an individual considering volunteering think about?

• Is this conference on a topic that you are interested in?
• Is this a one-off or would you like to help with the future organization of the conference?
• Is this a topic you want to know more about or specialize in? How will this help you with your career?
• Where is this conference being held?
  – Depending on what type of volunteer you are, you might not get your accommodation or travel paid for. Is this an issue? If yes, choose local conferences so that this isn't a problem for you.
  – Ask your employer. You may well be volunteering because your employer doesn't have a budget for staff to attend conferences, but if they don't have to pay for the conference itself perhaps they might pay for your travel if it's not too far away.
• When is this conference being held?
  – Are there any work commitments that clash?
• Will your employer give you the time to go?
• If you are considering a long-term position, how much work is involved and will your employer support you?
  – How many meetings are you expected to attend and where are they?
  – How long is the conference? If you have to be there before and after, can work cope with you being out of the office for that long?
  – How many hours a week will you need for 'conference work'?
  – Can you do this during work time or will you have to do it in your own time?
  – What other responsibilities do you have?
• Is there a business case you could develop to show your employer why being the member of a conference committee would be beneficial to the team or organization?

You could encourage team members to look at roles within existing conferences, such as those outlined below and consider which role is most appealing and whether it links to prior experience or future career progression. They should also look at other conference committees and compare the range of opportunities to get involved to ensure that whatever they chose benefits their specific interests and career aims. The following is a list of roles on the LILAC Committee:

- Chair
- Treasurer, Marketing and Communications Officer (social media and website)
- Programme Officer (organizes all conference information into a booklet or programme)
- Deputy Chair
- Papers Team (organizes the call for papers, collates paper reviews and puts the timetable together)
- Sponsorship Officer and Awards Officer.

🖒 Best for

- Continuing professional development and providing opportunities not available in the immediate workplace.
- Great for developing new knowledge for projects and other work initiatives.

► More

- Developing new professional skills outside the current working context.
- Increasing knowledge of the wider professional context and networking with information professionals nationally and possibly internationally.

⚠ To think about

- It can involve a lot of work that is unpaid.
- Not all conferences need 'one-off' volunteers.

References

JiscMail (1998) *LIS-LINK*, www.jiscmail.ac.uk/cgi-bin/webadmin?A0=LIS-LINK. [Accessed 20 April 2016]

Further reading

Corey, K. (2014) *Why You Should Attend Professional Conferences*, http://studentlife.ryerson.ca/professional/why-you-should-volunteer-at-professional-conference. [Accessed 20 April 2016]

LILAC (2016) *LILAC,* www.lilacconference.com. [Accessed 20 April 2016]

50. Conferences – workshops

WORKSHOPS ARE USUALLY smaller and more informal than typical conference presentations. They are often used to teach new concepts or practical skills and involve delegates participating in individual and group activities. They are characteristically short (an hour to two hours in length), and so the facilitator should consider what they want to achieve and structure the workshop accordingly. It can also feel easier to 'team teach' or 'team present' a workshop, as working with a colleague can lighten the stress of a lone facilitator. When creating a workshop for a conference consider:

- Why is it being done?
- Who is the audience and what are their expectations?
- What is the purpose?

Planning

If the answers to these questions suggest that a workshop is the best way of getting the information across, the steps shown in Figure 50.1 should be

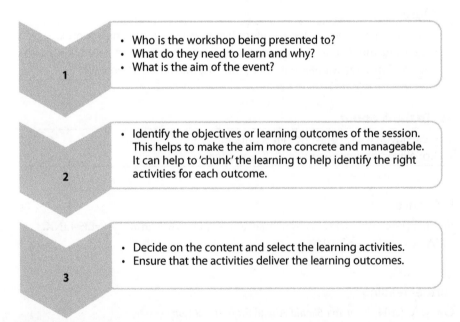

Figure 50.1 *Planning a workshop*

carried out in the planning process.

Once the programme is designed and the relevant activities are identified the visual aids, worksheets and handouts which summarize the workshop content can be prepared. The facilitator will need to consider what resources will be included, such as a PowerPoint or Prezi presentation, and whether the venue supports the technology. They may also need to check with the conference organizers whether they need to supply their own Post-its, flipcharts, pens and paper, to ensure that there are enough resources for all participants.

The workshop is likely to involve a mix of presentation and activities which are designed to deliver the learning objectives. It is important that the person presenting has a clear plan which sets time limits on any activities and enables them to monitor the progress of groups. They will also need to build in time to discuss the results of each exercise.

Practising

It is good practice to have a trial run of the workshop to ensure that timings and activities work. Provide opportunities for the individual to test the workshop with colleagues and encourage them to ask for feedback on the presentation style and the activities used. Individuals who are nervous about presenting may not want to try the session out in advance, but explain to them the benefits of this approach. The trial run will improve their confidence and highlight whether the activities are easy to understand and can be completed within the timescales outlined. They can then review their workshop and make amendments based on the feedback received.

Encourage the facilitator to rehearse the presentation aloud beforehand to ensure that the sentence structure and flow work. Practising in front of a mirror can help confidence, provide the opportunity to evaluate eye contact and show them how well they know the topic. If they are looking down and reading from their notes too much, they need more practice. It is acceptable to use notes as prompts as long as they do not interfere with making eye contact with delegates. Eye contact makes the facilitator appear more engaged and as a result their voice will be interesting and better modulated. It will seem that they are talking to the audience rather than just looking down and reading and they will have more confidence in what they are saying.

Delivering

On the day of the workshop the facilitator must make sure that they arrive in plenty of time. Suggest they check whether there is a session in the room before theirs and, if there is, suggest that they visit the room at the beginning of the day so that they can imagine themselves presenting there and can check:

- Is the room appropriate for a workshop?
- If there is anything that needs changing?
- Will there be enough time to prepare before participants arrive?
- What contingencies have been planned?
- What happens if the technology doesn't work?

These are all things that the facilitator needs to think about and prepare for before the workshop. The more preparation they do the more confident they will feel.

🖒 Best for

- ■ Creating a fun and memorable session which provides opportunities for delegates to participate.
- ■ Teaching participants a skill and enabling staff to develop workshop facilitation skills, which can be useful in their role.

⚠ To think about

- ■ Encourage the facilitator to consider the audience when planning the workshop, as some groups such as undergraduates and some international delegates may respond well to open questions. They could use group/pair work as an alternative approach or introduce participation in a safe, non-scary way, such as getting participants to write answers on Post-its, talk to their neighbour or a show of hands.
- ■ They should find out where the workshop is held, as lecture theatres or IT suites are not ideal for encouraging group work. Activities may need to be adjusted if the furniture cannot be moved around.
- ■ Ensure that the workshop does not involve too many activities, as credibility will be lost if it runs over. If delegates do not see the value of exercises it could become more stressful for the facilitator.

Further reading

Blake, J. (2016) *Webinar Recording: how to write and deliver a good workshop,* www.informationliteracy.org.uk/2016/02/webinar-recording-how-to-write-and-deliver-a-good-workshop. [Accessed 20 April 2016]

Community Tool Box (2014) *Section 4. Conducting a Workshop,* http://ctb.ku.edu/en/table-of-contents/structure/training-and-technical-assistance/workshops/main. [Accessed 20 April 2016]

51. Conferences – writing proposals for papers

PRESENTING AT A conference is a great experience for staff. It raises their profile, the profile of your organization and the work you are doing. However, to do this individuals first need to get their proposal accepted. If members of your staff are considering submitting a paper to a conference, they should think about the points below before beginning to write.

What and why?

- Ensure that they have chosen the right conference to present their paper, as relevance is a key criterion on which it will be judged.
- Investigate how original their presentation topic is; for example, submitting a paper to the LILAC conference on how to teach search skills in the LKS library might not be offering anything new to delegates, unless it is a revolutionary approach.
- The topic should be interesting, be up to date and reflect current trends in this area.
- If presenting research or any sort of new initiative include the methodology, ensuring that it is robust, tested and explained in the paper.
- The presentation should be about work which has been completed and should include the results. Delegates do not want to know what *will* happen, they are much more interested in what happened, the challenges, 'lessons learned' and future improvements.
- Reflect on how this research/project changed practice, successes, students' marks or behaviour.
- The presentation format should fit into the formats accepted by the conference, such as short papers, long papers and workshops. If a workshop is being facilitated, a lesson plan must be created.

Who?

The type of audience should be considered when planning the presentation:

- Why is the subject matter of interest to the delegates?
- Is this something that they will be able to take away and apply at their home institution?
- Why should they care and why should they listen?

Practicalities

- Read the conference guidelines carefully.

- Proofread the submission.
- Develop a catchy title to help your paper to stand out.
- Do not leave planning to the last minute.

👍 Best for

- Promoting and raising awareness of new research, initiatives or projects.

▶ More

- Getting a paper accepted on new research, initiatives or projects provides the opportunity to test public reaction or gain peer feedback on work.
- It can also validate work as of interest to a wider audience.

⚠ To think about

- Make sure that the submission is proofread, spell-checked and grammatically correct and remember to stick to the word limit. Errors and omissions will make a bad first impression.
- Ensure that planning takes place well in advance, to allow for unforeseen factors such as illness or technical problems.
- The majority of proposals are submitted 30 minutes before the deadline. This can test the robustness of any system being used and make submissions more liable to technological failure.
- Make sure that the paper is about a project which has been completed and can demonstrate tangible results.

Further reading

Aston, S. and DaCosta, J. (2015) *How to Create the Perfect LILAC Blossom*, www.slideshare.net/infolit_group/aston-da-costa. [Accessed 20 April 2016]

52. CVs

CVs **ARE RARELY** asked for within the LKS sector, although there are some exceptions which can include applying for committee positions, some job roles, applications for grants or bursaries and, of course, CILIP qualifications. It is therefore a good development activity to ensure that staff keep their CV up to date and reviewing a CV can form a useful part of the annual appraisal. A standard CV should be 2–3 pages, though an annotated CV running to four pages is ideal for personal use in keeping a record of development.

You should encourage your staff to think of their CV as a marketing tool to sell themselves. They are the only person who can communicate why they are suitable for the role, funding or qualification they are applying for. If they don't do it themselves no one else will be doing it for them. Worse, another applicant will be doing it and will be successful. Get them to really think about what they have done in the past and to what level. If they managed a project or wrote a guide then they need to say so. The example here outlines the value of maintaining an updated CV.

Example from practice:
Gil Young – LKS professional (academic, public and NHS)

In 2010 I was made redundant. At the time I was undertaking a qualification which required me to produce an updated CV and continuous record of development. Redundancy is never easy but having documents which had been produced when I was feeling good about things was really helpful. I used them as the basis for job applications, where they proved to be incredibly useful, as they reminded me of all the things I had done and achieved previously.

Having an up-to-date CV provided me with a template for application forms which could be copied and pasted from. This ensured that my applications were consistent and that important information was not left out when deadlines were tight. The CV and record of development helped me to think positively about myself at a difficult time. On reflection I do think that having current versions of these documents enabled me to get a suitable new job very quickly.

A CV needs to be clearly laid out and easy to read. Make sure the pages are numbered and use a modern-looking font, 11–12 point at a minimum, with clear headings for each section. There are plenty of online templates available for CVs if staff are finding it difficult to get started. The following is a suggested structure for putting together a CV.

Page 1 of the CV

The header should include name, address, e-mail and phone number(s) and can also include links to a LinkedIn profile, blog, Twitter, etc.

A short paragraph should follow, outlining an individual's unique selling points, tailored to each application, to explain the relevant skills and knowledge which match the position being applied for. For example:

I am a Chartered Librarian and Associated member of the CIPD with excellent interpersonal and communications skills. I develop and deliver innovative training programmes for library knowledge staff in the academic and health sectors. As the LILAC (Librarians' Information Literacy Annual Conference)

Co-Chair I have extensive experience of organizing a successful annual conference. My professional interests include cataloguing, UX, facilitating access to e-resources, statistics and development opportunities for new professionals.

Then list key skills and knowledge, using roughly 6–8 bullet points. As with the paragraph itemizing the applicant's unique selling points, this should be amended each time the CV is used. For example:

Key skills and knowledge

- Excellent interpersonal and communications skills; works well with others, motivates and encourages
- High level knowledge of training and development, particularly for library knowledge workers
- Experienced committee member, including chairing and servicing of a variety of groups
- Mentoring skills
- Good strategic appreciation and vision; able to build and implement sophisticated plans
- Seeks new responsibilities and uses initiative; self-sufficient
- Strong planning, organizing and monitoring abilities; an efficient time-manager
- Good IT skills, including full knowledge of Microsoft Office applications
- Knowledge of a variety of sectors, including academic and health
- Good networking and influencing skills.

Encourage staff to spend time thinking about the language they use in their introduction and the bulleted list. If they have excellent knowledge of something then make sure they state this rather than just saying 'I have an understanding of'. This is not about exaggerating what they do and know but about being honest about their knowledge, skills and experience.

After detailing their key skills and expertise suggest that they include two or three career highlights. These could take the form of short case studies. The model in Figure 52.1 can be a useful way of thinking about structuring these.

Figure 52.1 *Model for structuring career highlights, adapted from Open University (2016)*

Pages 1–2 of the CV

Next the individual should list their roles, starting with the most recent. Generally speaking their current or most recent role should take up the most space and cover at least half a page. They should list the job title, organization and dates covered, followed by an outline of key tasks. Stress the importance of being reflective whilst focusing on their achievements and remind the team member to be specific about what they did and the outcomes.

Pages 2–3 of the CV

On these pages the individual should list the rest of their roles. For roles that were a long time ago or not particularly relevant just get them to put the bare details and a line outlining their key development from the role.

Pages 3–4 of the CV

- Education – include the most recent first.
- Training and development – only include that which is relevant to the application.
- Papers and publications – if any of these are online then a link should be included.
- Referees – at least three, one of which should be their current employer, as people will wonder why they are not included if they are not listed.
- At the end of the CV suggest the member of staff includes two or three personal recommendations written by people they have worked with/for. As their line manager you could write one of these.

👍 Best for

- Personal marketing and applying for jobs, committee roles, grants, bursaries or CILIP qualifications.
- Monitoring the career progression of the staff you manage.

⚠ To think about

- Make sure staff are clear about the type of CV required and encourage them to make it interesting and varied. If asked for an annotated one then they must provide one. If it is just a standard CV then it should be no more than two or three pages.

References

Open University (2016) *STAR Technique*,
    www2.open.ac.uk/students/careers/applying-for-jobs/pdp-star-technique.
    [Accessed 1 August 2016]

Acknowledgement

Some of the suggestions in this Tip were based upon these provided by The CV and Interview Advisors – www.cvandinterviewadvisors.co.uk – in a series of webinars they ran for CILIP in 2015–16.

53. Exchange of Experience events, TeachMeets and Unconferences

TEACHMEETS, UNCONFERENCES and Exchange of Experience events provide opportunities to share good practice and to discuss issues, problems and potential solutions. They are largely informal events which encourage active participation from attendees. They facilitate networking, as attendees are sharing these experiences with those from outside their workplace. Attendees are able to gain an insight into different sectors and roles, due to the variety of topics covered. Such events offer a number of development opportunities, ranging from attendance through to organizing an event.

These types of events have gained momentum amongst the LKS community in recent years as an inexpensive means of bringing together like-minded people to discuss new approaches, share ideas and solve problems. The format of these events can overlap and it can be difficult to clearly identify differences between them. They often consist of a mixture of informal and formal sessions. Table 53.1 gives a brief overview of each of the formats but none of them are set in stone and they are interchangeable. The guiding principle for all of them is that attendees are given as many opportunities as possible to contribute and to engage with each other.

Exchanges of Experience, TeachMeets and Unconferences are an effective and inexpensive way, given the emphasis on informality, to enable sharing of experience and networking of colleagues locally across the various sectors. They offer a convenient opportunity to meet up with colleagues outside (expensive) conferences or other large-scale training events (Tumelty, Kuhn and Birkwood, 2012). With no big-name speakers there is a greater sense of collaboration and a level playing field, removing hierarchies and the idea of learning from experts (Lawson, 2014).

The knowledge/skills gained from the sessions can immediately be put into practice by attendees or followed up with speakers to find out more if needed. They support continuing professional development for the organizers as well

Table 53.1 *Description of Exchange of Experience, TeachMeets and Unconference events*

Exchange of Experience	The theme and agenda for the events are agreed in advance. Presenters may volunteer themselves to speak or the organizer might approach people to present if they know they have valuable experience of the topic under discussion.
	Participants deliver a short talk on their experience of the theme under discussion to the rest of the group. Generally speaking, these presentations are delivered to the group as a whole. The use of visual aids is left up to the individual presenter.
	Opportunities for questions are provided after each presentation. There is usually a facilitator who will manage this process and who will provide a summing up of the main points raised at the end of the event.
TeachMeet	Presentation topics are usually registered in advance using a wiki, but the order of speakers is selected at random on the day (Tumelty et al., 2012).
	Presenters deliver a short talk on an aspect of their role. This generally means that a number of talks are occurring simultaneously with presenters sitting at different tables.
	The events themselves consist of 7-minute micro presentations and 2-minute nano presentations; however, this can vary depending on what you think would work best, e.g. 5-minute micro presentations. Presenters are encouraged to talk about a tool or technique they have tried themselves.
Unconference	People are invited to submit and 'pitch' topics in advance to provide opportunities for networking and collaboration on sessions.
	The agenda is set on the day by the participants and presenters are not expected to bring formal PowerPoint presentations, there is no keynote speaker and the attendees are seen as the experts. Sue Lawson says that this spontaneous approach allows the event to be 'more current or responsive to events than a traditional conference, as the agenda is set on the morning of the event, rather than a year before' (Lawson, 2014).
	Sessions are usually informal and range from short presentations, group discussions, posing a question or demo-ing something; often participants discuss an issue with a view to helping the session lead solve a problem or answer a question.

as the attendees, and the welcoming and accessible format of these events can be a supportive environment to encourage first time presenters (Tumelty, Kuhn and Birkwood, 2012). The quotes below are from one of the organizers and two attendees at LibraryCamp and demonstrate the development value of such events. LibraryCamp is a UK-based unconference which has been running since 2011. It is described as a 'user generated conference for people interested in libraries' (LibraryCamp, 2014) which is free to attend and funded through sponsorship.

Example from practice: Sue Lawson – LKS professional (public)

From a personal perspective organizing LibraryCamp has given me much more confidence in a number of areas, including attending other conferences, in work (more confident in suggesting ideas and projects to managers) plus delivering presentations at meetings and online. At the first LibraryCamp in 2011 I was so shy I couldn't introduce myself to the room during the icebreaker. At the second LibraryCamp I jointly proposed a session after much encouragement from a more experienced unconference goer. By the last two camps I was introducing the event and running sessions and I recently delivered a presentation at the launch of the Carnegie LibraryLabs project.

Unconferences involve active learning. You can present an idea, get involved in a discussion, teach others, and share your knowledge. This can continue after the event when you can take back what you've learned to your workplace. The fact that we try to keep them a PowerPoint-free zone means you can experiment with different formats and workshop styles.

Example from practice: Kieran Lamb – LKS manager (NHS)

Gets you out of the sector echo chamber and has cake! Love LibraryCamp.

Example from practice: Emily Hopkins – LKS manager (NHS)

I think my tip about Unconferences would be not to be afraid to contribute – it's not necessarily about just listening to a talk from an 'expert', but about sharing ideas and discussing things, it's about the exchange and the 'meeting of minds' as much as it is about listening to one person give a structured presentation. It's an opportunity to ask questions and have a discussion. It could also be a good way to practise speaking in a less pressured environment than a formal conference. I think the most interesting and exciting sessions I've been to at Unconferences are those where it's been a discussion session that's drawn out expertise and answers from attendees within the room, as everyone knows something about something – it's the knowledge management adage of 'all of us are smarter than any of us' in action! Go to sessions that interest you and be prepared to share your knowledge – and go to sessions you know nothing about just to listen, learn and ask questions – either way, enjoy it!

👍 Best for

- Networking, sharing ideas and identifying innovative practice. The nature of the events means that sessions enable participants to be involved in discussions and problem solving.
- Good opportunities for participants to deliver sessions either alone or collaboratively and try new training techniques. Can also help people to develop new skills and confidence.

▶ **More**

■ Anyone can plan and arrange an unconferencing event, with some sponsorship, a venue and eager participants to drive the agenda.

■ The Library TeachMeets wiki (Library TeachMeets, 2016) provides a list of upcoming events, a place to gather together resources from those events and share tips on running TeachMeets. If there isn't a TeachMeet being organized in your area why not use the tips provided to organize your own. However, it is important to remember that collaboration is an important aspect of TeachMeets; therefore you should ensure that the sessions provide opportunity for audience participation/questions as people may feel that they have just been 'talked at'.

■ Cake, there's always cake.

⚠ **To think about**

■ Many, although not all, of these events take place in the evenings or at weekends, so staff should be prepared to give up some of their own time to attend these rewarding events.

References

Lawson, S. (2014) 'Unconferences: 101 Tips to developing staff', e-mail to T. Pratchett, 18 November 2014.

LibraryCamp (2014) *LibraryCamp*, www.librarycamp.co.uk. [Accessed 2 March 2016]

Library TeachMeets (2016) *LibTeachMeet – Librarians Sharing Teaching Ideas*, http://libTeachMeet.pbworks.com/w/page/64677116/FrontPage. [Accessed on 23 February 2016]

Tumelty, N., Kuhn, I. and Birkwood, K. (2012) *TeachMeet: librarians learning from each other*, https://www.repository.cam.ac.uk/handle/1810/244069. [Accessed 23 February 2016]

Further reading

Hamlin, K. (2010) *unConferencing – How to Prepare to Attend an Unconference*, www.unconference.net/unconferencing-how-to-prepare-to-attend-an-unconference. [Accessed 2 March 2016]

54. Formal qualifications

FORMAL TRAINING FOR librarians in the UK dates back to the late nineteenth century (Broughton, 2010). Professional (rather than academic) qualifications are managed by CILIP; presently the normal route is postgraduate study, e.g. a Masters in Library and Information Studies or equivalent (Broughton, 2010). By focusing on assignments that mirror professional activities students develop a more professional mindset and capabilities; this can include briefing papers, competitive intelligence reports, new designs for libraries, delivering information literacy teaching and evaluating it, presentations, and web pages which are much closer to the reality of professional writing and activity (UKLIBCHAT, 2015a).

In order to facilitate your staff in achieving their qualifications support can be provided in a number of ways, including releasing staff from work for studying and helping with flexible hours. Working whilst studying has been reported (UKLIBCHAT, 2015b) as being beneficial, as it helps people finance their qualification and provides access to useful resources and advice from their colleagues. For staff considering undertaking a formal qualification where financial support is unavailable from the workplace other support/ funding is available; this includes the John Campbell Trust Award, disabled students allowance and/or career development loan.

Modes of study

There are different modes of study available for staff wanting to undertake a formal professional qualification whilst working; these include distance learning and part-time study. Both distance learning and part-time study were considered amongst contributors to a UKLIBCHAT (2015b) Twitter chat to have the advantage of being more affordable, as students could continue working to finance the course and did not have to take a career break to gain the qualification. In addition, students who are already working in LKSs were able to immediately put into practice the skills they were gaining as they were learning them (UKLIBCHAT, 2015b).

Out of these two modes of study, distance learning is considered advantageous because of its flexible nature and the need for self-motivation, e.g. self-set deadlines. Conversely, it is purported that there is a lack of regular contact with fellow students and tutors; in addition, flexibility can lead to time management and motivation issues (UKLIBCHAT, 2015b). However, this lack of regular contact can be combatted by support from work colleagues. Time management is cited (UKLIBCHAT, 2015b) as an issue for those undertaking part-time study as well as working and can lead to the individual becoming tired and extremely busy, with limited down-time and struggling to fit their studies around work.

The professional qualification (MA LIS or equivalent) is topped up by a professional portfolio leading to Chartership, and the award of MCLIP. Certification or ACLIP (affiliated status) is available for paraprofessionals; possession of ACLIP allows paraprofessionals to embark on the Chartership process (Broughton, 2010).

Example from practice:
Katie Nicholas – Knowledge Officer (Health Education England)

Over the past two years I have been undertaking an MA in Library and Information Management. Undertaking the course part-time has inevitably enhanced my time- and project-management skills, as well as developing my report-writing and editorial skills. Attending lectures, reading for, preparing and submitting quality assignments for a deadline whilst working full time and maintaining a personal life has been difficult but through organization and prioritization I have successfully completed the taught part of the programme – having honed these skills throughout the course I now feel armed to meet the demands of a longer research project and prepared to tackle more complicated projects in a work environment.

The most rewarding aspect of the course has been learning from, and working with, my course peers. Their varied backgrounds and experiences of working in organizations other than my own has widened my understanding of the information landscape and given me new ideas to bring to my own organization. As we progress and change roles peers become a reliable network of professionals who can offer support, advice and suggestions. The collaborative skills developed are priceless in a working world which increasingly demands partnership working and the sharing of resources. This environment has given me the confidence needed to share my own experiences and perspective. I have refined my advocacy skills and feel more comfortable speaking with other professionals, which has encouraged me to 'say yes' to opportunities including delivering workshops, giving presentations and attending conferences both as a delegate and presenter.

🖒 Best for

- Developing a more professional mindset and capabilities through varied course activities.
- A formal way of validating ongoing professional development.

▶ More

- In addition to releasing staff from work for studying/helping with flexible hours, staff can be supported by advice from their colleagues.
- Knowledge/skills gained whilst studying can immediately be put into practice.

▲ To think about

- For staff who are struggling to manage their time or feeling despondent, extra support may be needed.

References

Broughton, V. (2010) *LIS Education: United Kingdom provision*,
    www.ucl.ac.uk/infostudies/unc-summerschool/LIS%20Education.ppt. [Accessed
    20 April 2016]
UKLIBCHAT (2015a) *Feature 22a: Career Support for LIS students – March
    2015 | #uklibchat*, https://uklibchat.wordpress.com/2015/02/26/feature-22-career-
    support-for-lis-students. [Accessed 20 April 2016]
UKLIBCHAT (2015b) *#uklibchat summary – Library Student SOS – March
    2015 | #uklibchat*, https://uklibchat.wordpress.com/2015/07/24/uklibchat-summary-
    library-student-sos-march-2015. [Accessed 20 April 2016]

Further reading

CILIP (2014) *Certification: a guide for Members*,
    www.CILIP.org.uk/sites/default/files/documents/Certification%20Handbook%20
    070314.pdf. [Accessed 19 September 2015]
CILIP (2014) *Chartership: a guide for Members*,
    www.CILIP.org.uk/sites/default/files/documents/Chartership%20Handbook%200
    70314.pdf. [Accessed 25 October 2015]
CILIP (2014) *Fellowship: a guide for Members*,
    www.CILIP.org.uk/sites/default/files/documents/Fellowship%20Handbook%2007
    0314.pdf. [Accessed 30 October 2015]

55. Funding for CPD

ATTENDING CONFERENCES, TRAINING EVENTS, formal courses and being involved in research can bring huge benefits for both your service and individuals in your teams (CIPD, 2015). These activities provide the opportunity for staff to build networks, bring new ideas and innovate. As a result of participating, individual team members are likely to be more motivated, engaged and generally happier in their careers, which can only be good for your service. Ongoing personal development for team members is vital for the success of your service; however, as LKS budgets are cut and we see more UK libraries under threat of closure, it is no surprise that funding for staff development is one of the first areas to be hit.

Costs

If you need members of your team to undertake training or attend conferences as part of their personal development objectives and your service strategy, then you will be expected to cover some or all of the costs from your staff development budget. Sending staff members to national and international conferences or on accredited training can be a rewarding experience, but the cost for one individual could wipe out your annual staff development budget. Travel, accommodation and providing cover for your service adds to the overall cost of activities.

Bursaries and grants

Whilst conferences and research projects can give you great insights into your service and can be of huge benefit to individuals in your teams, they can also be costly in terms of time, resources and training requirements for individual researchers. Bursaries and grants can be a great way to cover some of these costs and in this Tip we will consider what is available to support your teams. Competition for funding is fierce, with many applicants fulfilling all the criteria. This means your member of staff will need to make their application form stand out, ensuring that it does more than just meet the criteria outlined in the application form.

Most bursary applications give candidates at least a month to apply, so it is important that applications are not rushed. You must make sure that the staff member has fully addressed all of the criteria and included relevant examples or 'evidence' of how they meet the particular points. Most conferences will have issued their programme by the time the bursaries have been released so it is essential that staff applying spend time identifying subject matter relevant to them and/or areas where they require development.

Conferences

For conferences, panel members will look for evidence that the candidate has read the programme and outlined which sessions they will attend. They want to know why these have been chosen and how they are relevant to projects and issues at their workplace or beyond. Successful applicants are those whose applications discuss how they will reflect on and practically apply the knowledge gained from the conference and how they will use the new information to address specific challenges in their studies or at work.

Research projects

Panel members for research project funding applications will be looking to see whether the research is innovative and what it will add to the evidence base for the LKS profession. Any submission should be clearly underpinned by existing evidence and outline how the money will be spent on staff time, resources and conference attendance. At the application stage it is worth spending some time with the individual to work out a basic project plan with timings to ensure that everything is covered at this early stage.

Applying

Whatever the individual is applying for, encourage them to contact previously successful applicants and ask to view their applications, as these will provide insights into what the panel members are looking for. It can also help to see what makes an application have impact. Once the application is drafted, ensure that it is proofread for spelling mistakes and grammatical inaccuracies.

Example from practice:
Rachel Bickley sponsorship for Umbrella 2011 (2012)

In 2011 Rachel Bickley was awarded sponsorship to attend the Umbrella conference and has more recently judged applications for a conference. Some of her top tips for funding applications are summarized below:

■ Find details of bursaries or sponsorship via mailing lists, social media platforms, professional bodies, associations and special interest groups.
■ Check the applications criteria to ensure that the individual is eligible.
■ Emphasize how the learning will improve practice for the individual and their service.
■ Link your application to the theme of the conference.
■ Be prepared to share learning after the event by writing an article or presenting after the event.
■ Support individuals to 'go for it' – they have nothing to lose.

National and international bursaries and grants

Below is a list of some national and international bursaries and grants which are available to support training, research projects and conference attendance. This is by no means an exhaustive list and is likely to be subject to change, but tries to cover funding opportunities available in a variety of sectors. It is also worth exploring local networks and within your organization for additional staff development funds which may support CPD activities. For example, in the north-west of England, library staff working in the health sector can apply for bursaries from the Library and Information Health Network NW (LIHNN) or Healthcare Libraries Unit (HCLU) (HCLU, 2015).

UK
• CILIP offers a range of grants and bursaries to its Members:
www.cilip.org.uk/membership/membership/benefits-membership/
grants-and-bursaries.

- BIALL offers bursaries to attend an overseas law library conference: www.biall.org.uk/pages/overseas-conference-bursaries.html.
- SLA Europe provides awards for those early in their career: www.sla-europe.org/early-career-conference-award.
- Funding Opportunities for Research in Information Literacy: www.informationliteracy.org.uk/research/funding-opportunities.
- CILIP Health Libraries Group Awards: www.CILIP.org.uk/health-libraries-group/awards.
- CILIP Information Literacy Group Funding: www.CILIP.org.uk/information-literacy-group/sponsorship-and-bursaries.

International

- American Library Association offers a large number of grants and bursaries to its members: www.ala.org/awardsgrants/awards/browse/grnt?showfilter=no.
- Library Land Index lists a range of organizations that provide scholarships and grants for library staff: www.librarylandindex.org/scholarships-grants.html.

🖒 Best for

■ Making the most out of your staff development budget. By encouraging individuals to apply for external bursaries and supporting them through the process, you will be able to contribute to more developmental activities.

▶ More

■ Make sure the application form isn't rushed, to avoid any unnecessary mistakes, and get someone to proofread it.
■ Encourage staff to pair up to write applications. Buddying in this way can be useful to ensure that strengths are highlighted.

⚠ To think about

■ You will probably still need to contribute to the costs of attendance, even if the individual is successful in their application.
■ Decide whether you can support the individual with the full costs from the beginning and be clear about what you can afford to contribute.
■ Make sure staff have read the criteria carefully and have addressed all points and that they have enough time to write and rewrite their applications, making notes of deadlines in advance.

References

Bickley, R. (2012) *Tips for Applying for Conference Bursaries/Sponsored Places*, http://rachel-s-b.blogspot.co.uk/2012/06/tips-for-applying-for-conference.html. [Accessed 5 March 2015]

CIPD (2015) *Benefits of CPD*, www.cipd.co.uk/cpd/benefits.aspx. [Accessed 30 March 2015]

HCLU (2015) *Course/Conference Sponsorship*, www.lihnn.nhs.uk/index.php/hclu/training-and-development/course-conference-bursaries. [Accessed 30 March 2015]

56. Group conversations

LEARNING FROM COLLEAGUES and peers through conversation has become a popular development activity in recent years based on the principle that:

> Conversation, more than any other form of human interaction, is the place where we learn, exchange ideas, offer resources and create innovation.
>
> Art of Hosting, 2016

Gurteen (2015), through his work in running Knowledge Cafés, has identified the following advantages of hosting group conversations:

- turn a traditional chalk and talk, death by PowerPoint presentation or meeting into an engaging learning event
- transform an internal conference from a series of boring lectures into an exciting day
- transform traditional management training courses where younger managers learn from more experienced ones
- as a powerful sales tool to engage customers in conversation and thus better understand their needs and for them to better understand your product or service
- surface hidden problems and opportunities that exist in the organisation or in a department or project – especially ones caused by lack of communication
- break down organisational silos
- encourage knowledge sharing and the creation of a knowledge sharing culture
- give people a voice so that they feel heard and are thus less cynical and more engaged in their work
- bring managers and technologists together after a merger to build relationships, surface new opportunities and address cultural issues
- build and improve relationships
- improve business networking and make new connections

- solicit input and obtain buy-in for a new project or initiative
- as part or replacement for a paper survey or interview (the problem is that until people talk – their knowledge fails to surface)
- as a stimulus to innovation: Knowledge Cafés connect people to people; people to ideas and ideas to ideas; they challenge people to reflect on their thinking; surface new ideas and make new connections.

Gurteen, 2015

Creating a space for individuals to have meaningful conversations is meant to provide a more relaxed environment which encourages every-one to share and contribute. Most activities of this type are based on a version of the three principles in Figure 56.1.

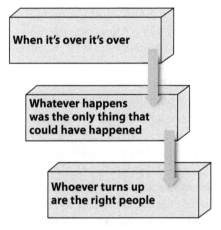

The absence of both hierarchy and an overtly formal agenda aims to encourage participation from all attendees. Although such events are informal in style they do require planning and organization to ensure that the conversations are constructive, that everyone has the opportunity to contribute and to facilitate learning.

Figure 56.1
Creating spaces for conversations, adapted from NHS Research & Development North West (2012)

Factors to take into account when planning a group conversation event include:

- What is the topic under discussion? Specifics can be agreed on the day of the event with attendees but it helps if people have at least a broad idea of why they are being asked to attend.
- Are participants to be invited or is the event open to anyone who might have an interest in the topic under discussion?
- What size should each discussion group be?
- Who will facilitate each group?
- How long will each conversation last?
- How will the conversations be recorded?
- How will the outcomes of the conversations be shared and further actions agreed?

The process suggested in Figure 56.2 is taken from the World Café (2016a) method.

Example from practice:
Dan Livesey – LKS manager (Mental Health and Social Care Trust)

In May 2016 I facilitated a knowledge sharing event for mental health librarians across the North of England. The purpose of the event was to provide library and knowledge service staff with the opportunity to discuss challenges, best practice and ideas for future collaborations. The event attracted representatives from 15 different mental health trusts and focused on the patient/public information agenda, which is a key part of the work for Knowledge for Healthcare (Health Education England, 2014).

Taking the lead on the session was a new experience but I discovered that there is a real desire amongst library and knowledge service staff within mental health to share resources and ideas. The session presented some interesting conversations and highlighted some practical challenges which I had not considered before. Taking the lead during the session also allowed me to articulate the vision for the national patient/public information agenda to my colleagues and I found their feedback extremely valuable.

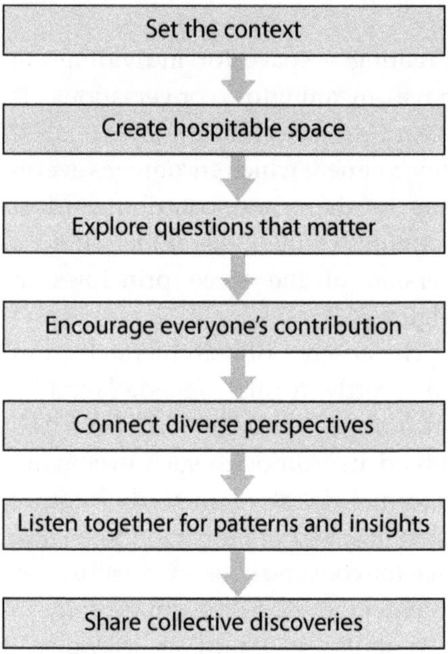

Set the context

Create hospitable space

Explore questions that matter

Encourage everyone's contribution

Connect diverse perspectives

Listen together for patterns and insights

Share collective discoveries

Figure 56.2
The World Cafe method (World Café 2016a)

👍 Best for

- Getting people working together in creative and inclusive ways through meaningful group conversation.

► More

- Three of the best known methods for hosting group conversations are The World Café (2016b), Knowledge Café (Gurteen, 2015) and Open Space Technology (Open Space World, 2016). A quick search on the internet for case studies using these methods will provide you with numerous examples of how the models have worked in practice.

References

Art of Hosting (2016) *What is the Art of Hosting Conversations that Matter?*, www.artofhosting.org/what-is-aoh. [Accessed 20 March 2016]

Gurteen, D. (2015) *Knowledge Café*, www.gurteen.com/gurteen/gurteen.nsf/id/kcafe. [Accessed 2 April 2016]

Health Education England (2014) *Knowledge for Healthcare: a development framework*, https://hee.nhs.uk/sites/default/files/documents/Knowledge%20for%20healthcare %20-%20a%20development%20framework.pdf. [Accessed 14 June 2016]

NHS Research & Development North West (2012) *Open Space Explained*, www.youtube.com/watch?v=4vEBcr_YkHU#t=218. [Accessed 20 March 2016]

Open Space World (2016) *Welcome to Open Space!*, http://openspaceworld.org/wp2. [Accessed 17 March 2016]

World Café (2016a) *Design Principles*, www.theworldcafe.com/key-concepts-resources/design-principles. [Accessed 2 April 2016]

World Café (2016b) *The World Café*, www.theworldcafe.com. [Accessed 17 March 2016]

57. Job rotation

JOB ROTATION CAN help you to provide additional opportunities for members of your LKS team. By carrying out different job roles within your service, team members are able to build upon their existing experience and develop new skills. In addition, job rotation can encourage greater understanding across your different teams and share learning and knowledge more widely. Bennett (2003) defines job rotation as the systematic and planned movement of staff and indicates that there are two forms of this approach: within-function rotation and cross-function rotation.

Within-function rotation

Within-function rotation is the movement of staff between jobs with comparable responsibilities or within the same area of your service; an example of this could be rotating a newly appointed subject librarian between different subject areas, thus enabling them to carry out the same activities, e.g. training, but within an alternative subject area and with different user groups.

Cross-function rotation

The above differs from cross-function rotation, which describes the movement of staff members between different areas of the service. For example, you could provide opportunities for members of your web development team to work in reader services. In this scenario, experience gained in a cross-function rotation could provide excellent learning which could influence the design of the website as a direct result of the experience of working more closely with front-line staff and user groups.

Opportunities

Whilst opportunities for rotation may be fewer for smaller services, job rotation can enhance the knowledge base of individuals, develop greater understanding between team members and create opportunities for innovation. Smaller services could provide job rotation opportunities for staff to work in all areas, which would mean that staff would be able to cover roles when needed. Bennett (2003) also indicates that providing opportunities for staff to work in a range of areas can relieve boredom, increase motivation levels, improve productivity and keep staff engaged. By systematically moving employees around, individuals develop a wider skill set which can only enhance your service.

Succession planning

Succession planning is the planned approach of identifying, training and developing talent within your organization or the sector as a whole, with a view to filling 'business-critical' positions in the future (CIPD, 2015). This is particularly important when your employees are approaching retirement age. Job rotation can be used in the succession planning process to ensure that crucial knowledge is maintained. Pennell (2010) indicates that job rotation is an integral part of the succession management process, enabling talented employees to gain a wider understanding of the organization whilst also enabling them to achieve their personal career goals.

Example from practice: a job rotation programme at the Niger Delta University Library (Baro, 2012)

This LKS introduced a programme of job rotation to improve the skills of newly appointed staff by rotating them around different departments in an academic LKS. The project evaluation outlines the following benefits and challenges for the individual librarians who participated in the project and the challenges of implementing the programme for the LKS:

Benefits for individuals
- improved ability to use computer systems
- made the job more interesting

- made friends and developed networks
- developed skills and learning
- improved effectiveness
- increased understanding of organisation
- opportunities to be involved in other activities.

Challenges for individuals
- not enough time to learn a specific department
- some department leads not prepared to train new staff.

Challenges for LKS
- individuals were not always motivated to learn the work of other areas if perceived too difficult
- supervisors were not always prepared to share practical knowledge/skills with new staff
- time constraints – varied length of time in different departments.

👍 Best for
- Providing opportunities for employees to develop a range of skills and undertake different duties.
- Can help to keep employees interested in their work, can improve motivation and productivity and can reduce boredom.
- Giving employees a broader understanding of the organization and different elements of the LKS. Trained staff can be used to alleviate manpower pressures if a specific area is short-staffed and could also provide opportunities for innovation and service redesign.

► More
- Can contribute to succession planning by providing opportunities to plan for replacing retiring employees and to keep tacit knowledge within the LKS.

⚠ To think about
- If you don't ensure that the employee is trained effectively to complete the tasks required in the job rotation, this could present a risk to successful delivery of LKSs.
- Job rotation can cause resentment amongst employees who are not selected for job rotation opportunities, as they could perceive those that are as receiving special treatment (Bennett, 2003).

References

Baro, E. E. (2012) Job Rotation Program Evaluation: the Niger Delta University Library, *Aslib Proceedings: new information perspectives*, **64** (4), 388–404.

Bennett, B. (2003) Job Rotation, *Development and Learning in Organizations*, **17** (4), 7–9.

CIPD (2015) *Succession Planning*, www.cipd.co.uk/hr-resources/factsheets/succession-planning.aspx. [Accessed 8 March 2016]

Pennell, K. (2010) The Role of Flexible Job Descriptions in Succession Management, *Library Management*, **31** (4/5), 279–90.

58. Learning logs and journals

LEARNING LOGS AND learning journals are often used as part of educational programmes or courses to monitor learning and identify areas for improvement. They can be an equally useful tool to promote a learning environment in the workplace and to capture and monitor both individual and team learning as it occurs. Whilst a learning log will probably have a more defined structure than a journal, the principles of maintaining them are the same. They are both used to keep a record of all learning experiences, not just those acquired through formal routes, and should also provide a space to encourage deeper critical reflection of experiences which can be used by both managers and individuals to identify areas for improvement on an ongoing basis. These insights can feed into both personal development and team planning processes.

As a supervisor or manager, you could build learning logs or journals into your programme of staff development by encouraging your team to keep records of all learning activities. They can be particularly great for analysing learning experiences which are not formal, but may result in a personal change in practice or improvement to how services are delivered. Logs and journals are not just about keeping a record of activities and incidents; individuals need to be prepared to be open and honest about their experiences and their role in what happened. By supplementing the record with focused critical reflection, individuals can identify where the real learning occurred and plan to make future changes. It is useful for each learning event to draw conclusions and include an action plan to ensure the application of this knowledge in the future.

Learning from experiences

Learning from experience is central to Kolb's cycle (McLeod, 2013) which is discussed in Tip 2 (p. 4) in more detail, but essentially includes a four-stage process of experience, reflection, learning and action. This is demonstrated as a continual cycle of learning, rather than a linear process. Barclay (1996) suggests that activities be recorded in a structured way, one based upon Kolb's learning cycle. If individuals prefer to work in a less structured way, the journal approach may work better for them, but guidance should be provided to facilitate deeper learning. Having a structured guide can be really useful, providing prompts for those to whom reflective practice does not come easily; for more information about how to facilitate reflection, read Tip 74 (p. 192).

Templates

To support individuals, create a structured template to inform the process, including:

- a description of the event/incident
- what happened – what went well, what could be improved upon
- how did they feel and how do they think others felt
- analysis of what they learned
- recommended actions for future.

Learning styles

Barclay's (1996) research analysed whether learning logs suited all of Honey and Mumford's learning styles (Tip 3, p.8) and they found that whilst reflectors and theorists enjoyed the process of keeping learning logs, activists were more resistant to this approach. It is important that you provide as much support and guidance for your team as possible and give them clear instructions as to how much they are expected to write, how regularly they should submit activities to their log or journal and how this will feed into their ongoing performance reviews and appraisal processes. Whilst for some individuals keeping learning logs and journals can be challenging, the benefits shown in Table 58.1 have been reported (Barclay, 1996).

Table 58.1 *Benefits of learning logs and journals (Barclay, 1996)*	
For the individual	**For the manager**
• helps to monitor progress against individual personal development plans • identifies future learning needs • improves individual self-awareness • increases ability to identify learning opportunities • individual becomes more positive about professional development.	• useful tool for monitoring progress • can feed into the appraisal process • can link the learning to LKS business plans.

Tools

One final point – logs can be produced in a number of ways, so encourage your teams to explore the range of tools available. Some may provide the traditional method of handwriting a journal, but others may want to tap into the range of tools and applications which may suit their need, such as the following:

- CILIP (2013) provides an online VLE for its Members, which has an area for recording learning for Chartership and revalidation. Candidates who use this as their learning log will be able to use the content for a dual purpose.
- Google docs are available from anywhere and spreadsheets or Word documents can be accessed on a number of devices.
- Online applications can be synched to various devices such as mobiles, PCs and tablets. Examples include:
  — I done this, https://home.idonethis.com
  — Evernote, https://evernote.com.
- Wordpress or other blogging software can be useful for reflection and sharing learning more widely with peers. Check out Jo Alcock's (2014) post on recording CPD to get some ideas and read the example from practice below.

Example from practice: Jo Alcock – LKS professional and researcher

For almost 10 years, I've kept a personal blog that I use to reflect on my professional development. The focus has changed as I have developed, but it's remained a useful tool to write about what I've learned, reflect on my development and share ideas for future. I find it an incredibly useful way to consolidate my thoughts and structure them in a coherent manner, and I enjoy sharing them with others in a format that suits my style of reflection. The fact it is public also enables me to encourage discussion and conversation and I've learnt a lot from this engagement. Having it there as a record is also useful for me to reflect back on previous learning and act as a reminder. Writing a blog has helped me develop my reflective practice and my communication skills, as well as strengthen my network and further develop my learning.

I also keep a learning log in the CILIP VLE, and use this to record my professional development activities to support my revalidation. This also allows for reflection but for me is more so an opportunity to keep a record of my development. I used to store this on iDoneThis (a free online tool) but now use the 'CPD Log' feature in the CILIP VLE. At the end of each month I add details of any professional development activities and brief notes about what I learnt. I find this a very useful process to gain an overview of my development and to help me prioritize future development.

🖒 Best for

- Useful to encourage team members to identify learning opportunities within their day-to-day work, especially when more formal training opportunities are not available due to funding restrictions.
- Keeping a learning log is integral to an individual's professional development, and by doing this as part of their work, they can make it easier to maintain their professional status, for example the ongoing revalidation of Chartered Members of CILIP.
- Monitoring continual professional development through regular one-to-ones and appraisal meetings.

▶ More

- Recommend to your team members that they make a weekly or monthly note in their calendars to remind them to record their CPD, ensuring that they update it as they go along.
- Provide individuals with flexibility as to how they go about recording this activity. If they are happy with the method of recording, they are more likely to embrace it as part of their professional development.

⚠ To think about

- Need to take into account that everyone has different learning styles and preferences and there is no one single method of logging learning experiences that will work for everyone. Ensure that there is flexibility in the approach and individuals are more likely to engage.

References

Alcock, J. (2014) *CILIP Revalidation Hints and Tips – Recording your CPD*, www.joeyanne.co.uk/2014/08/19/CILIP-revalidation-hints-tips-recording-your-cpd. [Accessed 12 March 2016]

Barclay, J. (1996) Assessing the Benefits of Learning Logs, *Education and Training*, **38** (2), 30–8.

CILIP (2013) *CILIP VLE*, www.cilip.org.uk/news/cilip-vle-launched. [Accessed 12 March 2016]

McLeod, S. (2013) *Kolb – Learning Styles*, www.simplypsychology.org/learning-kolb.html. [Accessed 12 March 2016]

59. Meetings – attending

MANY OF US spend a significant proportion of our working week in meetings. Good meetings get things done, they move projects on, assist in achieving individual, team and organizational objectives and can be an excellent way of facilitating communication. Bad meetings are a waste of time and resources that can leave participants feeling demotivated and frustrated. Getting the most out of attending meetings is a key skill for everyone in the workplace. As a line manager you need to work with your team members to enable them to benefit from attending meetings and to demonstrate the value their attendance brings to others at the meeting.

The best meetings have a specific aim or purpose with clearly set objectives. They start and finish on time. They allow for debate, facilitate discussion and encourage creativity. At the end of a meeting decisions should be made and actions agreed.

Attending meetings gives participants numerous opportunities to develop a wide range of skills. Having good communication skills is essential if your staff are to get the most out of meetings. If they have been asked to attend a meeting it is usually because it is believed they can contribute something to achieving the purpose of the meeting. When speaking in a meeting ensure your team members aim to be clear and concise. They should not be speaking just for the sake of it or deviate from the point in hand. Make it clear to them that meetings are not the place to rehash old arguments or to try and point score off other colleagues or teams.

Presenting

If your staff member is at the meeting to present a proposal or introduce a new project then you should encourage them to prepare in the same way they would for any other presentation. Ask them to agree with the Chair in advance how long they will have for their presentation and how long is to be allocated for discussion. They should find out who will be attending the meeting and aim to discover as much as they can about them in advance. This may be their one opportunity to influence those people who will ensure the success of their project.

Active listening

Actively listening in meetings can be challenging but it is an essential skill to master. Active listening means concentrating fully on what the speaker is saying as opposed to thinking about what the listener wants to say in reply or letting their mind wander on to another subject completely. Talk to your staff members about how to develop this skill and offer them the following pointers:

- Don't interrupt when someone else is speaking.
- Make a note of questions and ask them at the end.
- Aim to be positive when commenting on what someone else has just contributed.

Networking

Meetings can provide excellent opportunities for networking. Even if individuals are not presenting at a meeting it is still worth their researching the roles and professional interests of the other attendees. Prior to a meeting remind individuals to make a point of introducing themselves to people they haven't met before.

⚐ Best for

■ Meetings can have numerous purposes a number of which are listed below (Chapman, 2015):

- giving information
- training
- discussion (leading to an objective)
- generating ideas
- planning
- workshops
- consulting and getting feedback
- finding solutions/solving problems
- crisis management
- performance reporting/assessment

- setting targets and objectives
- setting tasks and delegating
- making decisions
- conveying /clarifying policy issues
- team building
- motivating
- special subjects – guest speakers
- inter-departmental – process improvement.

▶ More

■ It is important that the right people attend a meeting. This is about ensuring that people who can contribute to moving the work forward are invited. If people are invited who have nothing to contribute they will get frustrated and ultimately the purpose of the meeting will not be achieved.

⚠ To think about

■ Make sure that your team members only commit to actions that they are prepared to do.
■ It is important to review the purpose of regularly held meetings. If the

meeting has become a habit and is no longer a productive use of attendees' time then it might be time to stop holding the meeting.

References

Chapman, A. (2015) *Running Meetings*, www.businessballs.com/meetings.htm. [Accessed 1 May 2015]

Acknowledgement

Many thanks to Deborah Dalley from Deborah Dalley and Associates – www.deborahdalley.com – for permission to base this Tip on materials used within her training sessions.

60. Meetings – chairing

CHAIRING A MEETING is a good opportunity for individuals to develop a number of important and transferable skills. These include, but are not limited to, time management, negotiation, active listening, questioning and summarizing. The example from practice here outlines the skills developed by one individual as a result of undertaking a chairing role.

Example from practice: Jane Roberts – LKS professional (NHS)

When I was first asked to become co-chair of the LIHNN Trainer's Group it felt quite a daunting task, as I had never chaired a meeting before. It was reassuring that I shared the job with a colleague from another North West library who was also new to chairing, so we could learn together. The role gave me the opportunity to develop my organizational skills, I had to book meeting venues, arrange catering and sort out the agenda for each meeting – which included booking guest speakers. Chairing meetings increased my confidence in addressing a large group of people and leading discussions whilst ensuring all group members had their say on a particular item. I also used the experience for evidence for my Chartership portfolio.

If a member of your team is required to chair a meeting then you will need to think about what is required in advance and plan, with them, how to get the most out of the experience.

Role of the Chair

As Chair they should agree the agenda in advance of the meeting with the note taker and check that it, along with any other relevant papers, is circulated to all of those invited to attend the meeting. It is the responsibility of the Chair to ensure that the right people are invited to the meeting and that they are clear about why they have been asked to participate.

At the first meeting of a group the Chair needs to agree ground rules and any matters of confidentiality with attendees. Written terms of reference can be a useful tool, as they give group members something to refer back to, which clarifies the purpose of the meeting and what the group is aiming to achieve.

It is important that meetings start promptly. At the start of each meeting the Chair should welcome everybody and ensure that they all know the names, roles and areas of interest/expertise of the other attendees. It is a good idea to outline the purpose and objectives for the meeting, to remind everyone of why they are there and what they are working towards. Remind your team member that they will need to state who is taking the notes, the form these will take and how attendees will be able to access them.

The main role of the Chair, for the major part of any meeting, is to move through the agenda. It is important that each item is given enough time to be discussed properly whilst also ensuring that the meeting keeps to time. The Chair needs to control the discussion by clarifying points as required, summarizing the discussion at the end of each item and ensuring that everyone is clear about the agreed decisions and actions. It is the Chair's responsibility to keep the discussion on topic and not allow attendees to digress.

At the end of the meeting the Chair needs to thank everyone for their contribution, remind them of agreed actions and deadlines, and agree a time, date and location for the next meeting. Once the meeting is over it is up to the Chair to ensure the actions progress and to agree the draft minutes with the note taker. They will need to agree how actions will be monitored and what to do if deadlines are not met as part of the terms of reference for the group. At all times the Chair needs to keep in mind that the purpose of a meeting is to get things done and, if this is not happening, to implement measures to rectify this.

Managing personalities

One of the most important, and often the hardest, parts of chairing a meeting can be managing the personalities around the table. The Chair needs to ensure that everybody gets the opportunity to contribute and that no one person is allowed to dominate the discussion. It is a good idea to discuss these issues with your team member before they chair their first meeting and to consider how they will deal with this situation if it occurs.

If they notice that someone is not contributing, they should speak to that individual, preferably in a break, at the end of the meeting or very soon afterwards. They should check whether the individual is okay and establish why they are not contributing. Is it because they feel shy or inexperienced or is it because they are the wrong person to be there? If it is the former then the Chair should discuss with them how to proceed. Would they like to be asked their opinions directly on certain matters, which can be agreed upon in advance, or could they be allocated a particular agenda item to lead on?

The Chair should not draw their lack of contribution to everyone else's attention in the meeting by putting them on the spot and asking if they have anything to add. In addition to developing their personal skills, a large part of the Chair's role is to facilitate an environment where other attendees can develop their skills, too. Alternatively, if someone insists that they are the wrong person to be at the meeting, the Chair should explore with them why they were asked to attend and come to a decision about further participation together. If they are just there to listen and to report back then that is fine.

The other main issue with personalities is when one person dominates the conversation. This often happens when someone is very enthusiastic or excited about the topic under discussion. In your role as a supervisor or line manager, you can help your team member develop a strategy to deal with the overenthusiastic individual in a sensitive way. This is a good skill to develop to ensure that the individual does not continue to dominate, but maintains their enthusiasm, which may be essential for the successful outcome of the meeting. No one should be allowed to interrupt someone else in a meeting but a Chair can step in to summarize what has been said and say that the meeting needs to move away from this point. If the problem continues then the Chair should speak with the dominating individual away from the rest of the group. It is important to let them know their contributions are valued but that other people must be allowed to contribute.

👍 Best for

- Ensuring the meeting achieves its aims and objectives.
- Developing individual skills around communication, time management, negotiating and group management.

▶ More

- Not all meetings will be face to face. Chairing phone, video and other virtual meetings can be more challenging. Ensure that your team members understand the technology and that they are carefully monitoring who is contributing and who isn't.

- It can be useful to regularly review how well a meeting has gone. This applies to new and established meetings. Taking five minutes at the end of a meeting to ask what attendees thought went well and what they want to work better next time can be extremely beneficial to the future success of meetings.
- Changing the location or format of a meeting can help to re-energize a tired group. If a project has got stuck then suggest to your team that they consider holding the next meeting off premises, running a brainstorming session or inviting an external speaker. Alternatively they might need to consider some of the work being undertaken by smaller working parties or task and finish groups. Ensure your staff member has considered how these will report into the main group so that work doesn't get duplicated and people don't lose interest in the overall aim of the work.
- Some groups will have rolling Chairs to ensure that all group members get the opportunity to develop their chairing skills.

⚠ To think about

- There will be times when people will not agree on a decision or action. It is the role of the Chair to manage this. Talk with your team member about how to stay neutral and listen to what is being said. If the argument is relevant and useful to the work being undertaken then such discussions can help move things on. As long as things do not get personal or overheated it is fine to let people disagree. The Chair can slow the argument down by bringing in the views of other group members and summarizing the opposing points of view. Referring back to the terms of reference can be useful in these circumstances.
- Chairing as well as leading on an item can be difficult. If your team member is there to lead on something it is often best to hand the Chair to someone else for that item. This should be agreed with them in advance and attendees should be told that it is going to happen and the reason for it.
- The basics are important. People do not do their best work when they are too hot or cold, thirsty and hungry or needing the loo. If it is a long meeting then encourage the Chair to schedule in breaks and provide refreshments. If refreshments are not available then it is a good idea to make this known in advance so participants can make their own arrangements.

Acknowledgement

Many thanks to Deborah Dalley from Deborah Dalley and Associates – www.deborahdalley.com – for permission to base this Tip on materials used within her training sessions.

61. Meetings – note taking

MOST OF US have been in a meeting where the first question the Chair asks is, 'Will someone volunteer to take the minutes?' At this point everyone looks down at the table until someone gives in and volunteers. Whilst this is a better situation than the one in which someone asks, either halfway through the meeting or at the end, 'Who is taking the minutes?' and it turns out no one is, it is not ideal. Taking the notes at a meeting can be a valuable development activity but it requires some thought and preparation in advance if the note taker is to get the most out of the experience and if the notes are to provide a useful record of the meeting.

Note taking develops a number of skills including time management, written communication and active listening. Note taking can be a particularly good development activity for junior staff as a means of enabling them to understand how meetings work and how things get done within their organization.

Good practice

It is good practice to agree a note taker in advance of the meeting. The Chair and the note taker should then get together, either face-to-face or virtually, to agree the agenda and the type of notes required. The agenda needs to be clearly laid out and it is a good idea to include timings and who is leading on each item. The most important items should appear first on the agenda. The agenda, along with any other papers and the notes from any previous meeting, should be circulated well in advance of the meeting. The note taker should bring along spare copies of all papers to the meeting.

The note taker needs to be clear about how much detail is needed and how the notes are to be used by both group members and other stakeholders. Do they need to be a verbatim account of what is said or just a summary? Can only decisions and actions be recorded? Would a separate action plan be a useful document? The more detailed the minutes, the harder it is for the note taker to contribute anything else to the meeting. This is one of the reasons for deciding in advance of the meeting who the note taker will be and the format the notes will take.

Names of participants should be clarified at the start of the meeting and encourage your team member to be aware of the correct spellings. Once they have everyone's name noted at the start of the minutes it is fine to use initials throughout the notes. Do make sure that they clearly differentiate between people with the same initials.

When writing notes there are numerous formats and systems your team member can use. A quick search on the internet will give the note taker lots of ideas. As long as they are clear about the type of notes they are required to take they should use a method which works for them. The important thing is that they are clear and easy to follow and all actions need to include timescales and leads. The note taker must be reassured that they should not be afraid of clarifying points throughout the meeting.

After the meeting has taken place it is a good idea for the note taker to agree the notes with the Chair. They can then be circulated to other attendees, along with the action plan if there is one. If the group has a place for storing notes, such as a wiki or a web page, then encourage your staff members to make them available as soon as possible and to let group members know that they are there.

🖒 Best for

- Keeping a record of meetings held including decisions reached and actions agreed.

▶ More

- If it is not feasible for someone to attend just to take notes ask everyone to make a note of their actions and add them to an agreed plan at the end of the meeting. This can save time if a group is simply required to complete a project and does not have to demonstrate how decisions have been reached.
- Notes do not have to follow a formal written structure. If using something such as a mind map works better for the attendees then this method is fine.
- When notes are available electronically include hyperlinks to link to other relevant resources.

⚠ To think about

- If the note taker changes for every meeting then agreeing a structure for how notes should be presented is particularly important. It needs to be as simple and clear as possible so that each note taker can concentrate on taking the notes as opposed to making them 'fit' into the agreed format.
- Really think about the purpose of the notes. If very detailed notes are required then the group might require someone who is experienced in taking minutes. Be clear about what is important. Is it what the group does or how it gets there? Keeping it simple is generally the best option.

Acknowledgement

Many thanks to Deborah Dalley from Deborah Dalley and Associates – www.deborahdalley.com – for permission to base this Tip on materials used within her training sessions.

62. Mentoring – external

FINDING A MENTOR from outside your organization or team can provide a beneficial professional learning experience for your staff or colleagues. It is also a good opportunity for more experienced staff to share their learning and experiences with new members of the profession. A mentor is usually:

> a more experienced individual willing to share their knowledge with someone less experienced in a relationship of mutual trust. A mixture of parent and peer, the mentor's primary function is to be a transitional figure in an individual's development.
>
> Clutterbuck, 1991, cited in Brewerton, 2002

Generally speaking, the mentoring relationship involves a more senior colleague who will pass on their knowledge to more junior staff members (CIPD, 2009). This relationship should be built on trust, with the mentor using their skills and experience to encourage the mentee in order to help them attain their career goals and unlock their potential.

Role of the mentor

A good mentor will encourage, challenge and provide advice and may be able to help the mentee to make contacts within the profession. The logistics of the relationship will be discussed at the beginning and the pair may draw up a formal agreement to ensure that both parties have shared expectations, including:

- length of relationship
- method of meetings (face to face, webcam, online, telephone)
- regularity of meetings
- location
- objectives.

As a manager or supervisor, it would be difficult for you to mentor staff in your teams as conflicts of interest may arise. An external mentor can support the mentee objectively, and is positioned to avoid competing interests, perceived bias and internal politics. Should you try and mentor one of your team members, this could be interpreted as favouritism by others, or could make it difficult for you to discipline them in your management or supervisory role, as boundaries become blurred. It is worth noting that individuals looking for a mentor may meet a number of potential candidates before a suitable match is identified, as the mentee may be looking for certain characteristics or background experience. If the mentee wants to learn about web design, the mentor may not necessarily be from a library background, but should have recent experience in that area. Personal characteristics and approaches to learning may also be important for a successful mentoring relationship.

Benefits

Clutterbuck (2004) explains that there are a number of benefits for both the organization and the individual when mentoring is established. Mentoring arrangements benefit businesses by improving staff retention, adapting to change, effective succession planning and increased productivity. Individual mentees improve their knowledge, technical and behavioural expertise, manage their career goals, influence others, have increased confidence and self-awareness and demonstrate greater focus and engagement.

Mentor schemes

Some organizations provide internal mentoring programmes, so you may be able to link your staff with a mentor from another department in the organization. It is however, worth considering other regional or national programmes which may be of interest to your teams. The NHS Northwest Mentoring Scheme provides opportunities for staff from health and social care roles with an interest in mentoring to be matched with a mentor or mentee with a view to 'develop staff leadership abilities to lead to innovation and integration of services' (NHS Northwest Leadership Academy, 2015). In the UK, candidates preparing for Chartership certification must enter into a mentoring relationship to guide them through the process and a list of available mentors is provided on the CILIP website (CILIP, 2014).

Example from practice:
LLAMA Mentoring Program (2016) (American Library Association)

In the United States, the LLAMA Mentoring Program (Okuhara, 2012) was developed by the American Library Association to pair leaders with aspiring leaders. This provides a chance for existing leaders to pass on their knowledge and expertise to enthusiastic colleagues. Mentees are given the opportunity to explore their potential, demonstrate current leadership capability and develop skills. The program runs from June to April with applications typically closing in March.

Example from practice:
SLA Mentoring Scheme (School Library Association)

Working in a school library can often be an isolating experience, as librarians in this field often work alone. The School Library Association provides a mentoring scheme for new solo librarians who may not have worked in a school before and could benefit from support from experienced professionals working in similar roles who understand the challenges associated with this unique role.

⍟ Best for

- Expanding the knowledge and expertise of your staff in a cost-effective way.
- Introducing new ideas and innovation into your organization and keeping your best staff.
- Developing individuals in their career, providing contacts outside the organization and offering support during difficult periods.

▶ More

- Explore the range of mentoring opportunities which are available to your staff and provide advice and guidance to ensure that a suitable match is found.

⚠ To think about

- Not all mentoring relationships work out, so ensure that ongoing evaluation occurs and unsatisfactory mentoring relationships end as needed.

References

Brewerton, A. (2002) Mentoring, *Liber Quarterly*, **12**, 361–80, http://liber.library.uu.nl/index.php/lq/article/viewFile/7703/7739. [Accessed 2 January 2015]

CILIP (2014) *Becoming a Mentor*, www.cilip.org.uk/cilip/jobs-and-careers/qualifications-and-professional-development/mentoring/becoming-mentor. [Accessed 19 June 2016]

CIPD (2009) *Mentoring – CIPD Factsheet*, www.shef.ac.uk/polopoly_fs/1.110468!/file/cipd_mentoring_factsheet.pdf. [Accessed 31 December 2014]

Clutterbuck, D. (2004) *Everyone Needs a Mentor*, 4th edn, CIPD, London.

LLAMA (2016) *LLAMA Mentoring Program*, www.ala.org/llama/llama-mentoring-program. [Accessed 19 June 2016]

NHS Northwest Leadership Academy (2015) Mentoring Scheme, www.nwacademy.nhs.uk/mentoring. [Accessed 28 September 2016}

Okuhara, H. (2012) LLAMA Mentoring Program: an evolving model, *Library Leadership and Management*, **26** (2), 1–3.

School Library Association (2007) *SLA Mentoring Scheme*, www.sla.org.uk/blg-sla-mentoring-scheme.php. [Accessed 1 March 2015]

63. Mentoring – peer

PEER MENTORING OR co-mentoring is used in the academic world. It brings students together, sometimes from different year groups or specialisms, and they enter into a one-to-one learning relationship. This partnership 'provides for a collaborative learning environment where students can be both experts and learners' (Peter, 2013, 454). In one case study, Peter (2013) outlines how students in the information profession act as first-line support to help other students to navigate the library and information world.

Whilst the traditional mentoring relationship usually involves an older, more experienced individual sharing their wisdom and knowledge with someone less experienced (Clutterbuck, 1991, cited in Brewerton, 2002) a peer mentoring relationship provides the opportunity for an individual to learn from a colleague with similar experiences. This relationship rejects the hierarchical structure, indicating that all participants are able to learn from each other (Goosney, Smith and Gordon, 2014). As an added bonus, peers who are partnered with a colleague also have the opportunity to develop their own coaching and mentoring skills outlined in Tips 40 (p. 100) and 62 (p. 160).

Building this type of supportive relationship is useful for your staff, and could help them to work through problems and develop new ideas outside their day-to-day work. It can also be useful for staff to develop a learning relationship with colleagues from other departments or from other organizations. These relationships promote an overall learning culture, with peers providing opportunities for learning whilst also being encouraged to learn new skills (Wilson, Gaunt and Tehrani, 2009).

Collaborative approach

At the heart of the peer mentoring relationship is a collaborative approach to learning and sharing of expertise and knowledge.

> Co-mentoring is not based on a traditional teacher/student model but rather on the principle of equal, mutually beneficial relationships in which each member of an LC [Learning Contract] functions as both mentor and mentee: bringing knowledge, questions, and ideas to the group and benefiting equally from discussion, reflection, and exploration.
>
> Mullen, 2000, cited in Peter, 2013

The International Librarians Network (ILN) is a volunteer-led peer mentoring programme which aims to help librarians to develop international networks. Applicants are partnered with colleagues from different countries, at different stages of their careers and with similar interests. The partnership operates on an equal basis, with both parties approaching the relationship as both protégé and mentor. This peer mentoring relationship occurs online and a range of communication methods are recommended, details of how to apply are available via the ILN website (International Librarians Network, 2015).

Reflective mentoring

In their case study, Goosney, Smith and Gordon (2014) developed a reflective peer mentoring programme to bring together groups of librarians involved in teaching information literacy. These groups came together as small learning communities to share ideas, troubleshoot problems and participate in structured reflective conversations with a small number of colleagues. This differs from the earlier example, in that the learning community involves 3–4 members, rather than a one-to-one ongoing relationship. The programme is based on the three-step model shown in Figure 63.1.

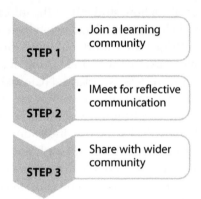

STEP 1 • Join a learning community

STEP 2 • IMeet for reflective communication

STEP 3 • Share with wider community

Figure 63.1
Learning community: three-step model (Goosney, Smith and Gordon, 2014)

Collaborative networks

Individuals may often benefit from informal peer mentoring relationships by being part of collaborative networks. It is a useful approach which can be adopted in many ways to support team members. You could support the individual to find a peer mentor from within your organization or a different organization and help them to set up regular meetings. Alternatively, you could encourage your staff to participate in formal or informal peer mentoring programmes such as the ILN program outlined above.

🖒 Best for

- Developing mentoring, coaching and leadership skills within the workforce.
- Useful for staff who are part of a small team and do not work alongside others with similar skill sets. It can be really good to help them to develop new skills or just have someone to bounce ideas around with.

▶ **More**

■ Providing opportunities to learn from and network with colleagues in a non-hierarchical relationship.

⚠ **To think about**

■ Staff entering into a one-to-one mentoring relationship should use the information outlined in Tip 62 (p. 160) to establish a contract underpinning mentoring arrangements. Not all mentoring partnerships will work, so agreeing expectations at the outset can future-proof the partnership.

References

Brewerton, A. (2002) Mentoring, *Liber Quarterly*, **12**, 361–80, http://liber.library.uu.nl/index.php/lq/article/viewFile/7703/7739. [Accessed 2 January 2015]

Goosney, J. L., Smith, B. and Gordon, S. (2014) Reflective Peer Mentoring: evolution of a professional development program for academic librarians, *Canadian Journal of Library and Information Practice and Research*, **9** (1), 1–24.

International Librarians Network (2015) *About ILN Networks*, http://interlibnet.org/how-the-program-works/matching-program-participants. [Accessed 6 April 2015]

Peter, K. (2013) *'Once a Library Ambassador, Always a Library Ambassador!': using peer mentoring to integrate the library into the first-year academic experience and beyond*, www.ala.org/acrl/sites/ala.org.acrl/files/content/conferences/confsandpreconfs/2013/papers/Peter_Ambassador.pdf. [Accessed 6 April 2015]

Wilson, M. C., Gaunt, M. I. and Tehrani, F. (2009) Mentoring Programs in US Academic Libraries – a Literature Review. In *Strategies for Regenerating the Library and Information Profession, 8th World Conference on Continuing Professional Development, Bologna, Italy* (18–20 August 2009), 84–95.

64. Minutes of madness

MINUTES OF MADNESS can be an effective means of encouraging staff to present. The principle is that the presenter speaks for one minute on their topic. In many cases a timer is used and the speaker is cut off when the minute comes to an end.

Minutes of madness can be used for numerous purposes. These include but are not limited to:

• poster presentations at conferences
• feedback at team meetings

- sharing achievements
- introductions
- session pitches
- awards.

Although only a minute long these presentations can be a very effective development activity, not only for developing presentation skills but also for encouraging networking, team building and marketing services. It can be a useful means for getting staff to understand what is important in the message they want to deliver by identifying what is core to their message.

To work well a minute of madness does require preparation (see Tip 70, p. 179). Practice is particularly important if a timer is going to be used and the speaker will be cut off when the minute comes to an end. The speaker needs to be sure they have delivered their message before this happens.

Example from practice: Library and Information Science Research Coalition (2012) Conference

Stella Wisdom chaired our whirlwind tour through the 13 quick-fire presentations, in which participants had just one minute to share their experiences of stepping out of their own research comfort zone.

Session Format: Those that signed up for a slot related to the audience how they have explored the use of research methods from other disciplines, worked on research projects with others with completely different research backgrounds, applied LIS research techniques to new research areas, discovered new ways to disseminate their work, or found a new network of relevance to their research efforts. Some took the opportunity of a slot in this session to put out a call to invite others to join them as they take their first steps out of the comfort zone. Each had just one minute to make their points, which was strictly enforced by Stella Wisdom and her horn. They were accompanied by a single slide providing their name, the title of their talk and their contact details so that members of the audience could get in touch to follow up on any points of interest or overlap.

🖒 Best for

■ Getting a simple message across in a quick and effective way. Especially useful in situations where a large number of people are required to share information or wish to speak.

▶ More

■ Visual aids can still be used.

- The minute doesn't have to be a standard presentation. Presenters could do a song, poem, limerick or short film. Encourage staff to use their imagination.
- You don't have to limit speakers to a minute. The important point is that speakers are clear as to how long they have and what will happen if they go over the allocated time.
- There are lots of free online timers available. If you do a search for 'online stopwatch timer' you will be provided with a number of options.

⚠ To think about

- Preparation is very important. The aim is to get the message across clearly, not to cram five minutes of information into one. Presenters need to work with the format, not against it.

References

Library and Information Science Research Coalition (2012) *One Minute Madness*, https://lisresearch.org/dream-project/event-1-presentations/one-minute-madness. [Accessed 26 June 2016]

65. MOOCs

MOOCs ARE 'MASSIVE open online courses', which are often (but not always) free and have no prerequisites for enrolment other than access to a computer. MOOCs are delivered by a number of universities and other organizations across the world. Defined as 'a course of study made available over the Internet without charge to a very large number of people', they involve collaboration, shared resources and often have limited tutor input. These courses can attract thousands of participants from all over the world and often act as a taster course for universities, who use them to showcase courses, extend their reach and identify new audiences.

The first UK MOOC was launched in 2012 , and there are now over 54 MOOCs in the UK and even more worldwide (Higher Education Academy, 2013). Library staff can be involved in MOOCs in two ways, as collaborators in the creation of a course, or as participants, as part of their ongoing learning and development. At Leeds University, LKS staff were involved in the creation of MOOCs developed by the University and hosted on the Future Learn platform (Green and Howard, 2014). The role of the librarian was multifaceted; advising on resources, copyright issues, accessibility, open access and digital literacy and creating links within the organization.

For the learner, MOOCs provide informal learning opportunities via courses which vary in length, from 2 to 12 weeks (Higher Education Academy,

2013). Generally, MOOCs have a defined start and end date, although some are flexible and can be accessed at any point in time. They differ from other forms of online learning in that they facilitate connections between other learners and tutors outside the 'classroom' rather than being a solitary process. Participants should expect a mixture of learning methods including videos, lectures, reading, assignments, evaluations and online discussions (MOOC News and Reviews, 2013).

Flexibility

There is some evidence that participants use MOOCs flexibly, without completing the assessed elements of the course, and completion rates can be particularly low, at around 10%. Matt Holland (2014a) suggests that completion rates may not be the most appropriate evaluation for MOOCs, as is traditionally the case for face-to-face courses. MOOCs provide opportunities for new ways of learning through traversing in social networks (connectivism) or with the learner setting their own goals and evaluating their progress (constructivism) (Duke, Harper and Johnston, 2013). In either case, traditional methods of evaluation may not apply. Participants who do complete courses may receive an honour certificate (often provided free of charge) and in some cases, where subscriptions are paid, verified certificates may be awarded.

Platforms

The following platforms partner with universities and companies to offer MOOCs on a range of topics:

- Future Learn: www.futurelearn.com
- Coursera: www.coursera.org
- EDX: www.edx.org
- Udacity: www.udacity.com.

MOOC list (www.mooc-list.com) pulls together lists of courses from various platforms.

Example from practice: Matt Holland – LKS manager (NHS)

MOOCs are a game changer. MOOCs at their best are engaging and encourage networking and participation with others, meeting, networking and learning from an international community of learners. They finally realize the potential of eLearning that is open and accessible.

For librarians, as with other professionals, they offer the opportunity for personal and professional development in a wide range of subjects that were previously hard to access. For those delivering professional development they are the solution to reaching professionals where they are and delivering content for them to use when they choose to access it. Librarians need to take this opportunity to broaden their horizons, to experience eLearning as many of their users will experience it.

Librarians will be asked to help source content for MOOCs and they may choose to use MOOCs as a means of delivering information skills to users. My advice to colleagues new to the profession or old hands is to take at least one MOOC and soon (Holland, 2014b).

There are many more MOOCs appearing on the market that are specifically aimed at LKS staff, or individuals can create their own personal course from a range of courses. Recently, a project in north-west England ran a successful course aimed at developing literature searching skills for health library staff and had over 600 participants (LIHNNMOOC, 2016). Claire Sewell (2014) has blogged about how she uses MOOCs for CPD and to fill gaps in her knowledge, creating her own 'MOOC Library Degree' to cover library skills, management and leadership, marketing, technological skills, teaching and job applications.

⌕ Best for

- Providing accessible and flexible learning opportunities which can be accessed from anywhere.
- Opportunities to network with other learners in online spaces and set their own learning goals.

► More

- Librarians may become involved in supporting colleagues who are developing MOOCs and may start to develop library-focused courses of their own, as MOOCs can reach a large number of people internationally.

▲ To think about

- As courses are free and learners are expected to monitor their own progress and workload, levels of completion and participation have been shown to be low.
- Not many library-specific courses, but lots of courses for related skills such as management, communication and technology which may be of use (Sewell, 2014).

References

Duke, B., Harper, G. and Johnston, M. (2013) *Connectivism as a Digital Age Learning*, www.hetl.org/wp-content/uploads/2013/09/HETLReview2013SpecialIssue Article1.pdf. [Accessed 11 January 2015]

Green, R. and Howard, H. (2014) Moocing the Most of Library Resources, *CILIP Update*, March, 38–9.

Higher Education Academy (2013) The *Pedagogy of the Massive Open Online Course: the UK view*, The Higher Education Academy, York.

Holland, M. (2014a) Five Rules for Participating in Moocs, *CILIP Update*, March, 40.

Holland, M. (2014b) *RE: 101 Tips for Developing Your Staff: MOOCs*, e-mail to T. Pratchett, 4 December 2014.

LIHNNMOOC (2016) *Post-MOOC Update*, https://lihnnmooc.wordpress.com/ 2016/03/17/post-mooc-update. [Accessed 2 May 2016]

MOOC list (2014) *MOOC list*, www.mooc-list.com. [Accessed 3 December 2014]

MOOC News and Reviews (2013) *What is a Massive Open Online Course Anyway? MN+R attempts a definition*, http://moocnewsandreviews.com/what-is-a-massive-open-online-course-anyway-attempting-definition. [Accessed 3 December 2014]

Sewell, C. (2014) *The MOOC Library Degree*, www.librarianintraining.com/2014/12/ the-mooc-library-degree.html. [Accessed 2 May 2016]

Further reading

Marques, J. (2013) *The MOOC experience: Moocs go mainstream*, http://themoocexperience.wordpress.com/category/about-moocs. [Accessed 3 December 2014]

Murray, J.-A. (2014) Participants' Perceptions of a MOOC, *Insights*, **27** (2), 154–9.

66. Networks

NETWORKS, **WHETHER FORMAL** or informal, are hugely beneficial for professional development at any stage in a career. If you think about it, your team members are probably already involved in a number of informal networks without even knowing it, e.g. course mates from a library course, work colleagues, former work colleagues or Twitter 'friends'. Informal networking is a great way to learn about what others are doing in their workplace and developments in other sectors/institutions (both positive and negative) which can inform the practice of individuals and bring new ideas to your team. These networks provide the opportunities for knowledge to be shared and gained from information on training courses, career opportunities, sharing best practice or learning from projects.

Networks are useful for making connections beyond the workplace and provide good opportunities for low-cost professional development. There are many networks for library and information professionals to join which cover the various sectors within the LKS, e.g. School Libraries Group, Health Libraries Group and many others. As our sector is very diverse it is not possible to have everything in one place, so a combination of networks will be needed.

Involvement

The amount of involvement an individual has within a network is personal and will depend upon other time commitments. The CILIP regional member network in England gives a broad view of the LKS sector and provides access to events, training, professional registration support, CPD opportunities and other networking opportunities nearer home or work.

The Annual General Meeting (AGM) of the regional branch is a good place for your team to gain an insight into the network and its work over the past year. AGMs are a good place to meet people within the region from a range of different LKS sectors and can be great for those in your team who are working towards professional registration and want to expand their wider knowledge of other sectors. You may even recommend that individuals join a committee and have an active role in how it operates, e.g. secretary, treasurer, events co-ordinator. Your CILIP regional member network can advise if there are any vacancies (CILIP, 2015).

If individuals do not have time to join these more formal networks, virtual networks provide opportunities to participate on their own terms. The value of participating in networks online means that individuals can share content, promote events, seek help or join conversations, all at a time and place which suits their individual needs. A recent blog post focused on how Twitter contributed to one individual's professional development by providing a forum to gain advice, guidance, help and understanding (Haigh, 2015).

To get the most out of networking opportunities, encourage the individual to:

- not be afraid and to join in
- take it seriously, as their career will benefit from an outstanding network
- start with something they are comfortable with so that they can engage at a level that suits them
- if they cannot find the network they want to join, have a go at creating it themselves.

Example from practice: Helen Monagle – LKS professional (academic) and co-founder of the NLPN (New Library Professionals Network)

As part of my role within NLPN (2015) I collaborated on a Twitter chat with #uklibchat (2014) focusing on the topic of networks and networking. This provided a lot of useful information, including what networks people belong to and tips for successfully participating in networks. A summary of this web chat can be found here: https://uklibchat.wordpress.com/2014/11/06/uklibchat-summary-building-your-own-network-november-2014.

👍 Best for

- Keeping up to date in the chosen field.
- Continuing professional development.
- Sharing knowledge and receiving guidance.

▶ More

- Encourage your team members to get involved! The vast majority of library and informational professionals are happy to help out by providing guidance and sharing knowledge.
- Support individuals to create their own network if it does not exist already, as most existing groups were set up in response to an identified need.

⚠ To think about

- Coach team members to ensure that they do not overcommit themselves and are aware of their time limitations.
- Have regular reviews of the networks that individuals are involved in. If they have signed up to a number of mailing lists which are no longer relevant to their interests, suggest a clear-out to avoid information overload.

References

CILIP (2015) *Regional Member Networks*, www.cilip.org.uk/cilip/about/regional-member-networks. [Accessed 20 April 2015]

Haigh, J. (2015) *How Twitter has Contributed to my Professional Development*, https://jessdoeschartership.wordpress.com/2015/04/17/how-twitter-has-contributed-to-my-professional-development. [Accessed 20 April 2015]

NLPN (2015) *A Network for New and Aspiring Library Professionals*, https://nlpn.wordpress.com. [Accessed 24 September 2016]

#uklibchat (2014) *#uklibchat Summary – building your own network – November 2014*, https://uklibchat.wordpress.com/2014/11/06/uklibchat-summary-building-your-own-network-november-2014. [Accessed 21 April 2015]

67. Networks – setting up

AS **MENTIONED IN** Tip 66 (p. 170), if a network which meets an identified need does not exist, either you or your team members can set one up. Many networks were created by groups who identified a gap and developed a network with the aim of addressing this. It is important that networks have a clear purpose, which can be derived from an ethos or a policy. It does not have to be static and may change over time but it is important that the purpose of the network remains clear, so that it remains organized. You may decide to set up a network with a view to developing yourself, your teams and others in the wider LKS with similar interests and ethos. Alternatively, you may be supporting individuals to set up their own networks. The following example from practice demonstrates some of the skills which setting up a network can develop.

Example from practice:
Catherine McManamon – LKS professional (academic) and co-founder of the NLPN (New Library Professionals Network)

The NLPN (2012) was initially created to help fill a training-needs gap in the potentially stressful period between completing the Masters-level library qualification and securing the first professional library post. I was one of four students from the MMU MA Library and Information Management course in 2011/12 who felt that developing a professional network for our peers would help to strengthen our CPD and provide support in the areas where there were gaps in our knowledge and experience.

Planning the network's events has enabled all four of the network's organizers to develop our communication skills, our organization skills and our team work. It has given practical experience that we had not had before in our roles: securing funding, managing budgets, developing a brand and a social media presence, promoting NLPN, liaising with speakers and the members of our network. It had significantly enhanced our ability to be advocates for our profession and to recognize the importance of a community of practice beyond qualification and even the first professional post.

The network can be whatever is needed at that time, formal or informal, face-to-face or virtual or a combination of these. Some networks only exist for a short time, others may continue for a long time, and this will depend on the purpose of the network. These factors should be considered prior to setting up and be discussed with the network's steering group. A network does not have to involve all informal or formal activities but will often include a mix, depending on their objectives and available resources.

Formal training events which facilitate CPD offer rich learning opportunities, but can be costly and time-consuming to organize. More informal events which can be either virtual or face-to-face provide opportunities for people to meet and share ideas and can be less resource-intensive. A mixture of both virtual and face-to-face interaction can be employed, depending on the need. For example, Twitter provides a platform to reach a wider audience and can combat distance limitations. Face-to-face events provide opportunities for interaction, with people working together to complete tasks or solve problems.

Networks can be created either by an individual working alone or by a team of individuals working together. There are advantages and disadvantages to each approach, and to some extent the choice will depend on individual preference. Working with others means that the workload is shared and a range of skill sets are brought to the network. However, it can be challenging if some individuals are more committed than others. Networks which are run by individuals mean that they have autonomy and can run the network at their own pace. However, they can become isolated without a support network for sharing workload and generating new ideas.

Tools

There is a range of tools which can be adopted to suit the needs of a network. We have already mentioned the benefit of Twitter to get messages out and to enable people to make connections. Blogs are widely available and can be used to create websites, providing detailed information about the network. Wikis are a great tool for collaborating online and planning projects or events. Online meeting tools and conference calls are great tools for managing meetings where organizers are working together over a distance. Have a look at some of the other Tips in this book to find out more about individual tools.

👍 Best for

- Developing leadership and organizational skills for the individuals involved.
- Influencing the wider LKS sector outside the immediate working environment.
- Keeping up to date, CPD, sharing knowledge and bringing new ideas into your LKS.

▶ More

- Get other LKS staff to contribute to the network. People are happy to help out by providing guidance and sharing knowledge.
- If resources are tight, explore using free tools and apply to special-interest groups and member networks for funding.

⚠ To think about

- Ensure that anyone involved in setting up a network considers their time limitations and does not take on too much work. As a manager or supervisor, you may need to work with the individual to see how this extra work fits in with their day to day commitments.

Further reading

NLPN (2012) *About*, https://nlpn.wordpress.com/about. [Accessed 24 September 2016]

68. Networks – running

ONCE THE NETWORK is set up, the operational aspects need to be considered. A structure should be established and adhered to from the outset and roles may need to be allocated to the network leads. It is important to ensure that ongoing tasks are shared and monitored to ensure that they are completed. Individuals also have a responsibility to be realistic about what they can and cannot do, which will ensure that relationships between team members are maintained. Communication is also integral to an effective network, both internally with the network leads and externally with the network members. There are many communication channels which can be used to promote the network, such as e-mail lists, existing contacts, library schools, special-interest groups, social media and face-to-face meetings.

Tools and platforms

There are many free tools available to facilitate the running of a network, including social media, self-service ticketing platforms, e-mail and wikis. Social media is a good way to promote networks and to keep participants/members aware of any developments. Many networks within the library sector use social media to provide a current awareness service, alerting their members to useful resources, training events and developments in the profession. However, there are positives and negatives to all platforms, so encourage experimentation to decide what works best for those involved.

There are many different platforms for different purposes, such as Vine, which is a creative way of sharing videos, Twitter for providing useful information and updates and LinkedIn to formally promote events. Any tool should be fit for the intended purpose and be evaluated to ensure it continues to be valid. A social media page or profile with no content gives the impression that the network is no longer running and will therefore lose out on potential members.

A self-service ticket platform is a really useful tool for managing sales for events where there are costs to the individual. For free events Eventbrite provides a free service which enables personalization of event pages to include pictures, maps and a structure for the day. It has a facility to manage bookings, create waiting lists or cancel tickets if necessary. Eventbrite also provides a service to send reminders to attendees and create a list of attendees, which can be used as the registration form on the day.

E-mail is a great way to maintain communication in order to keep any networks running either between the network leads or external contacts such as speakers, venues, funders or people interested in the network. The great thing about e-mail is that it provides a paper trail to refer back to if needed. Wikis are also good for facilitating group interaction, providing functionality to comment and collaborate on documents together, essential when network leads are far apart.

🖒 Best for

- Personal and professional skills development and expanding network of professional contacts.
- Using a range of online tools and techniques which will benefit the LKS. For example, Eventbrite could then be used locally to manage events in your LKS.

⚠ To think about

- There are many tools out there; don't try to use everything but select those which are more suited to the needs of the network leads.
- Accept that mistakes may happen along the way, as the network leads will include individuals with different levels of skill, knowledge and experience. Encourage people not to be disheartened when things go wrong, as this is part of the learning experience. Use these instances to plan for the future and make changes.

69. Personal development plans

THE PERSONAL DEVELOPMENT plan (PDP) is a short, clearly focused document outlining individual learning needs in terms of skills, knowledge and experience. It is usually an action plan for a specific time period (usually a year) documenting key goals and stating how they will be achieved within existing resources and with clear timescales. The PDP should help staff to fulfil the requirements of their jobs but may also include longer-term goals for career progression.

Whilst each PDP will be unique to the individual, it should also incorporate the aims of your library service and organization, especially when embedded within the appraisal. As well as a PDP prepared for an appraisal, individuals may also be expected to create a plan to underpin the Chartership process (CILIP, 2014a). The PDP should be balanced between individual aims and organizational goals to ensure commitment and engagement from all concerned. There are many formats for PDPs and it is likely that your organization will provide a standard template which you will be expected to use as part of the appraisal process. Generally, a usable PDP will outline key learning and development needs, SMART objectives against each area, clear timescales and how completion will be evidenced.

Identification of learning and development needs is the basis of a workable PDP and should be clearly defined at the start of the year. The PKSB (CILIP, 2014b) is a useful self-assessment tool (available to CILIP Members only) which covers a range of technical, professional and generic skills required by library, information and knowledge management staff. Alternatively, a standard set of questions may be used to identify individual requirements, such as these outlined by the CIPD (2014):

- How do you identify your learning and professional development needs?
- What are the three main areas or topics you wish to develop in the next 12 months and how will you achieve these?
- What are the key differences that you plan to make to your role/organization/clients/customers in the next 12 months?
- When will you next review your professional development needs?

These questions can help you to find out what your staff perceive as being their key learning needs, enabling you to review them alongside the library action plan, strategy and wider organizational requirements. This should ensure that individual needs are clearly aligned to employer and employee priorities.

SMART objectives

Once the individual has identified their learning needs, specific objectives and actions should be defined to fulfil these needs. Each learning need could have multiple actions which should be SMART – specific, measurable, agreed, realistic, time-bound (Chapman, 2014). If you're setting a standard, or an objective for yourself, or agreeing an objective with another person, the task or standard must meet these criteria to be effective. The objective could be completed through attending courses, but could also be achieved through shadowing, visits, report writing, article submission, training, course design, developing a product or reading/researching. Encourage staff to be creative about how they demonstrate success, especially where resources are limited.

The CIPD provides a range of templates which can be adapted for local use and an example based on the generalist template is included here in Table 69.1.

Table 69.1 *CPD record/plan – generalist example (CIPD, 2014)*

Learning and development need	How will I achieve this?	What resources or support will I need?	How will I demonstrate successful completion?	Target dates for review and completion
Create a project plan outlining different options for developing LKS social media presence	(a) Attend internal project management course. (b) Visit colleague at another LKS to discuss their approach and challenges. (c) Review other LKS approaches to social media.	Course if free. Time released for visit and travel costs. Time released from some duties to scope project.	Course attendance certificate and project management resources. Reflective piece for my portfolio on the visit. Project proposal and plan documentation.	Course Dec 2014. Arrange visit for Jan–Feb 2015. Complete proposal and plan by April 2015.

The plan should be monitored throughout the year to ensure that the individual is on target and to identify any issues which may arise. Encourage staff to complete a reflective piece if they attended a course and to document any research carried out, as this will be useful evidence for Chartership, or the appraisal meeting. This may be especially useful when learning/development needs are only partially fulfilled and will allow for discussion at the next appraisal.

🖒 Best for

■ Achieving agreement on priorities for the coming year and providing a documented and signed agreement which both parties can adhere to. The PDP will be a good monitoring tool and the clearer the objectives the easier they are to track.

▶ More

■ Try to ensure that you review the personal development plan with the individual to track progress and be prepared to make adjustments as required.

▲ To think about

- If you impose goals on individuals and they are not fully on board, they are unlikely to achieve their objectives. Employees who are involved in the process of setting their own objectives are more likely to be committed to their success.
- Ensure that goals are realistic, otherwise you could be setting your staff up to fail.

References

Chapman, A. (2014) *Acronyms and Abbreviations: SMART,* www.businessballs.com/acronyms.htm#SMART-acronym. [Accessed 8 November 2014]

CILIP (2014a) *Chartership: a guide for Members,* www.cilip.org.uk/sites/default/files/documents/Chartership%20Handbook%20070314.pdf. [Accessed 25 October 2015]

CILIP (2014b) *Professional and Knowledge Skills Base,* www.cilip.org.uk/cilip/jobs-and-careers/professional-knowledge-and-skills-base. [Accessed 8 November 2014]

CIPD (2014) *CPD Examples and Templates,* www.cipd.co.uk/cpd/guidance/examples-templates.aspx. [Accessed 8 November 2014]

70. Presentations – general tips

PRESENTING IS ONE of those things that people often say they do not like doing. Despite this, it is an important skill that all LKS staff should develop. Recruitment processes frequently require candidates to present, the success of teaching and training sessions is often reliant on the presenting skills of the person leading them and people will frequently learn of the existence of your service though a presentation, be it an induction, a talk at a meeting or some other event.

It is important to take every opportunity to practise and enhance the skills of your staff in this area. No one wants to be in the position where their dream job comes up or they have to put together a presentation to secure the future of their service and it is the first presentation they have done in years.

The key to a good presentation is preparation and lots of it. Some people can just stand up and deliver a brilliant presentation off the cuff but they are few and far between. The first steps in putting together a good presentation are for the individual delivering it to be clear about what the purpose of the presentation is and what they want the outcome to be.

Purpose and outcome

The purpose of the presentation can usually be classified into one of the following areas:

- informing
- persuading
- instructing
- entertaining.

The outcome is what you want to happen as a result of the presentation and will be closely linked to the purpose. For example, your staff member might be presenting to a group of students about how to use a database. The purpose of the presentation would be to instruct them in how to use the database and the outcome would be that they would be able to use the database to conduct searches on their own.

Planning

Once your staff member is clear about the purpose and the outcome they can start to plan their presentation. The flowchart in Figure 70.1 outlines a possible process for planning the content of a presentation which you could work through with the member of staff who is going to present. The important point to emphasize to the individual planning the presentation is not to include everything, as it is practically impossible to tell an audience every little detail about a topic without their losing interest. The final content should represent what the group needs to know to achieve the purpose, as opposed to everything the presenter knows about the topic.

Beginning, middle and end

As with most forms of written communication, presentations can be broken down into three main areas. Put simply these are the beginning, the middle and the end:

- **Beginning:** This is often the part of the presentation where the audience is at its most responsive and attentive. The opening remarks should be designed to capitalize on this. Make sure your staff member knows to introduce themselves, welcome the audience and explain the purpose of their presentation.
- **Middle:** The middle of the presentation has to meet the promise of the introduction, develop logically and lead to the conclusion. To achieve this make sure that the presentation flows in a logical manner, that the

member of staff understands their topic and that they support the message using both research and the knowledge of the audience.

- **End:** This is the part of the presentation that the audience will take away with them and should include a brief summary of the main points. Closing remarks should not be used to introduce new information. The individual

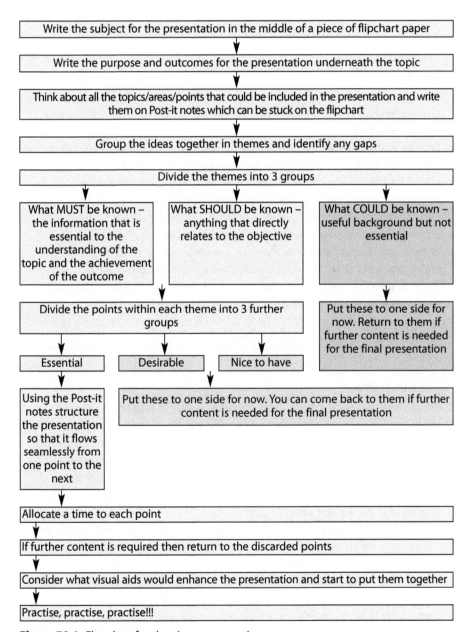

Figure 70.1 *Flowchart for planning a presentation*

delivering the presentation should aim to bring it to a close in a way which invites questions and, if necessary, makes clear to the audience what actions are now required of them.

👍 Best for

■ All types of presentation, regardless of length, venue or formality.

▶ More

■ Good-quality visual aids can enhance a presentation, making it appear more professional and memorable. These should be used to reinforce the message being conveyed.
■ Discuss with your staff members ways to stimulate the seven intelligences (Chapman, 2006) through the presentation and supporting materials.
■ It is important to engage with the audience from the beginning, by maintaining eye contact with the audience. Techniques to enhance engagement from the start include sharing a story, a case study or a quote, posing a question or using a relevant graphic or cartoon.
■ Presentations featuring more than one presenter can be very effective; encourage your team members to practise as much as they can in advance. The transition between presenters must be seamless and each individual must be clear about their role. If they want the presentation to be conversational, they must practise in advance before an audience to ensure it doesn't sound stilted and over-scripted.

⚠ To think about

■ Timing in a presentation is crucial; encourage staff to practise a number of times in advance with someone monitoring the time it takes. If the presenters try to cram too much in, they will speak too fast, weaken their message and could appear unsure of their topic. If they run over time at a conference or an interview they might be cut off before they reach their final, and lasting, message. It is important that the presentation is neither too long nor too short and must include time for questions.
■ Delivering presentations which others have prepared can be more difficult than preparing them from scratch. If your team members are put in this position then make sure that they are clear about the purpose of the presentation they are delivering, get in as much practice as possible and, if they can, customize the visual aids to suit their style.
■ Remember that visual aids are visual! Discourage individuals from putting information on slides unless you and they are sure that everyone in the room

can see the screen. Make sure that the messages conveyed by the aids are clear and simple; they are there to enhance the message not to distract from it or to confuse the audience. Avoid clip art, as it can look unprofessional and outdated.

■ Technology can and does fail. Make sure your team members can deliver their presentation without it if necessary. Handouts of slides can be useful if this happens.

References

Chapman, A. (2006) *Howard Gardner's Multiple Intelligences,* www.businessballs.com/howardgardnermultipleintelligences.htm. [Accessed 15 March 2015]

Further reading

Blanchett, H., Powis, C. and Webb J. (2012) Presenting and Performing. In *A Guide to Teaching Information Literacy: 101 practical tips,* Facet Publishing, London.

Acknowledgement

Many thanks to Deborah Dalley from Deborah Dalley and Associates – www.deborahdalley.com – for permission to base this Tip on her pre-course handbook *Presentation Skills Course for HLG Presenters – Preparing Your Presentation.*

71. Professional membership

JOINING A PROFESSIONAL association offers numerous opportunities for the personal and professional development of you and your team. Cherwin (2010) identified the following as the main benefits for individuals of joining an association:

- enhancing your network
- taking charge of your career
- broadening your knowledge.

Membership fees will vary from association to association, as will the opportunities on offer. Most associations provide a similar offer to their members to that of CILIP (The Chartered Institute of Library and Information Professionals). The current CILIP offer is outlined in Table 71.1.

Table 71.1 *Benefits of CILIP Membership (CILIP, 2014a)*

Professional development	In order to keep your skills, knowledge and education up to date, you have access to a range of services and products that will enhance your ability to carry out your role, as well as develop yourself professionally and further your career.
Grants and bursaries	CILIP Members have opportunities to apply for grants, bursaries and awards such as the IFLA (International Federation of Library Associations and Institutions) first timer grant and the Travelling Librarian Award. Visit the web pages of CILIP's Special Interest Groups and Regional Member Networks to find out about grants they offer.
Special deals and discounts	CILIP Members enjoy a wide range of exclusive discounts and special deals, including on books and journals, CILIP events, CPD eLearning modules and insurance. You can claim a free Facet book up to the value of £59.95 or a £20 National Book Token for each new member you recruit.
Information and support	As a Member you get access to a range of information and support to help manage and develop your career, including career coaching, expert advice on employment law, help getting your next job and bursaries to attend events.
Advocacy and campaigns	Through campaigning and public affairs, CILIP works with all levels of local and national government, the European Union, key external organizations and the general public to ensure the work and views of our Members are recognized and valued.
Monthly magazine, journals and e-bulletins	Stay up to date with the latest news, views and developments from the sector. CILIP Membership gives you access to news, in-depth features, interviews with thought-leaders, and articles from across the information profession. You will receive our regular *CILIP Update* magazine, weekly latest news bulletin and access to a wide range of professional journals.
Networking and community	Join CILIP now to put yourself at the heart of the library and information community. Share your ideas and expertise, develop your knowledge and contacts and broaden your horizons through our Member Networks. According to member surveys this is one of the most valuable benefits of CILIP Membership.
VLE (virtual learning environment)	CILIP's VLE allows all Members to: • access supporting resources for the Professional Knowledge and Skills Base (PKSB) • record the continuing professional development (CPD) they have completed in the past year • develop their portfolio for professional registration • access support materials, and submit their application online.

Networking and other opportunities

CILIP (2015) report that Members frequently cite the opportunities it provides to network as the most important benefit of Membership. In addition to the national opportunities on offer, including an annual conference, all CILIP Members automatically become Members of their local regional member network (CILIP, 2014b). Members are also entitled to join up to two Special Interest Groups (SIGs), which cover a wide range of LKS areas of interest. In addition to the opportunities that Membership of a SIG offers, including development events and networking within a defined area of professional interest, each group is run by a committee. Joining the committee can develop a number of skills which can be transferred back into the workplace, including organizing conferences and other development events, acting as a Chair, treasurer or secretary and editing newsletters. The current list of CILIP SIGs are shown in Table 71.2.

Table 71.2
CILIP Special Interest Groups (CILIP, 2014c)

- Academic and Research Libraries Group
- Cataloguing and Indexing Group
- Commercial, Legal and Scientific Information Group
- Community, Diversity and Equality Group
- Government Information Group
- Health Libraries Group
- Information Literacy Group
- Information Services Group
- International Library and Information Group
- Library and Information History Group
- Library and Information Research Group
- Local Studies Group
- Multimedia Information and Technology Group
- Patent and Trademark Group
- Prison Libraries Group
- Public and Mobile Libraries Group
- Publicity and Public Relations Group
- Rare Books and Special Collections Group
- Retired Members Guild
- School Libraries Group
- Student Committee
- UK eInformation Group
- Youth Libraries Group

Best for

- Creating a professional network and demonstrating ongoing professional commitment.

More

- Some associations offer organizational membership which can offer good value for money and can be an attractive benefit to both current and potential staff.
- This Tip focuses on CILIP, as it is the main professional body for library and information professionals in the UK. There are, however, a number of other bodies which might be of interest. There is a list on Wikipedia of UK professional bodies which covers most of them: https://en.wikipedia.org/wiki/List_of_professional_associations_in_the_United_Kingdom.
- If you are interested in bodies outside the UK then searching for professional associations on Google will throw up a number of lists.
- Wikipedia also has a list of international professional associations. See https://en.wikipedia.org/wiki/List_of_international_professional_associations.

References

Cherwin, K. A. (2010) *Why Join a Professional Association?*,
    www.higheredjobs.com/Articles/articleDisplay.cfm?ID=157. [Accessed 23
    February 2016]

CILIP (2014a) *Benefits of Membership*, www.cilip.org.uk/membership/benefits-
    membership. [Accessed 23 February 2016]

CILIP (2014b) *Regional Member Networks*, www.cilip.org.uk/about/regional-member-
    networks. [Accessed 23 February 2016]

CILIP (2014c) *Special Interest Groups*, www.cilip.org.uk/about/special-interest-
    groups. [Accessed 23 February 2016]

CILIP (2015) *Networking and Community*,
    www.cilip.org.uk/cilip/membership/membership-benefits/networking-and-
    community. [Accessed 23 February 2016]

Further reading

IFLA (2016) *International Federation of Library Associations and Institutions*,
    www.ifla.org. [Accessed 23 February 2016]

Acknowledgement

Many thanks to Matthew Wheeler, Development Officer (Member Support)
CILIP – www.cilip.org.uk/cilip/about/cilip-people/staff/member-services/
matthew-wheeler – for checking the information provided in this Tip.

72. Projects

YOUNG **(2013, 14)** defines projects as 'Temporary endeavours to achieve
some specific objectives in a defined time'. This means that projects are
not something which are part of the day-to-day operation of a service, or
business as usual. They are a one-off occurrence which is unique and will
ultimately result in a change to your service, whether by changing a process,
introducing a new product or creating an innovative service. Projects can vary
in size and scope, will be of different timescales and will require additional
resources, whether financial or human. Projects can range from large-scale
national programmes of interconnected projects, interdepartmental working
groups or smaller project groups.

   You and your teams will be involved in a number of projects, whether local,
for example to implement a new library management system, or a national
programme of work, such as the Knowledge for Healthcare Programme
(Health Education England, 2014) in the UK. This programme incorporates a
number of workstreams, each with a number of smaller task and finish

groups which are responsible for delivering specific outcomes. Each task and finish group comprises health library staff from different organizations across England, who are working together to deliver their smaller project outcomes. Your team members may be involved purely in library-based projects, but can also bring their unique specialist skills in knowledge management, evidence or information to interdepartmental organizational projects involving a number of staff from different teams.

Tools

Newton (2013) defines a project as having a number of stages, including defining the project, planning the project, identifying resource requirements, delivering the project, managing risks, evaluation and learning lessons. There are a number of tools which can be used to manage projects and whichever you choose is likely to depend on the complexity of the project and your requirements. Check out Tip 73 (p. 190) for more information about project management tools. Project definition and planning are central to ensuring that everyone understands what the project aims to deliver, the resources required and individual roles, and this is discussed in more detail in Tip 100 (p. 266).

The project team

The project team will be led by a project manager, who is responsible for the overall success of the project. Their role will be task delegation and tracking the progress of the project. The project manager will also be responsible for identifying and managing risk and reporting project progress to key stakeholders, those with an interest in the project, for example the sponsor and the senior manager who is accountable for the project (Newton, 2013).

The project team will involve central members who are involved in the project from beginning to end, but may also involve individuals who join the project to deliver a single task or objective at a given point in time. In order for the project team to work successfully, Young (2013) states that everyone needs to commit to the role, liaise with others, contribute to planning, risks and documentation, monitor their tasks, escalate issues to the project manager and support others. There are a number of opportunities for your team members to be involved in projects, either as managers, central team members or ad hoc team members.

Benefits

Some of the main benefits of being involved in projects for individuals, LKS and the organization are outlined in Table 72.1.

Table 72.1 *Benefits of being involved in projects*

Individuals	LKS	Organizations
Developing transferable skills	Transforming the way that services are delivered and solving problems	Utilizing LKS staff expertise in the areas of knowledge management, evidence and information
Delivering tasks on schedule and managing workload	Making your teams aware of the bigger picture	Learning from what happened before
Learning about new processes and project management tools	Introducing innovations to improve the user experience	Can save money and make business more efficient
Raising personal profile and making personal contacts	Developing relationships with non-library teams	Continual improvement processes embedded throughout the organization

Training opportunities

If you have individuals within your teams who are interested in developing their project management skills, there are a number of training opportunities that you can tap into. Professional library organizations such as CILIP (2015) or the Library Leadership and Management Association (LLAMA, 2016) provide one-off courses or programmes for individuals to sign up to. If your team members would like an accredited qualification, in the UK, PRINCE2 courses are recognized qualifications which are available both as classroom-based or online options (PRINCE2, 2016). Many of the available options will have significant costs attached, so look at your organizational in-house training programmes, as there may be some free generic training to help team members develop and improve their project management skills.

Approaches and methodologies

There are a number of project management approaches and methodologies which you could explore with your teams to get the right fit for you, such as Agile (Sprint projects), Lean and Six Sigma (Newton, 2013). Introducing a standard approach to managing projects will help you as a service manager to keep track of the status of all projects within your team. In addition, a standardized approach makes it easier for your team members to transfer between projects within your service or organization. This section of the book has only provided a brief introduction to projects and how they can benefit your service and teams. It is not intended to be an in-depth review of complex project management techniques and Further Reading is provided at the end of this Tip.

Example from practice:
Tracey Pratchett – LKS manager (NHS, FE and public)

I have always enjoyed working with other people, regardless of their role or the organization they work for, as I gain so much learning from others. I've been really lucky that my line managers have enabled me to collaborate on a range of projects both large and small. Since joining the NHS, I have been a member of the MAP Toolkit Steering Group (MAP, 2015), participated in a project to evaluate clinical librarian services in the NW (Brettle et al., 2010) and worked with procurement teams to integrate evidence into their decision-making projects (Pratchett, 2015).

Currently I am jointly leading a project to develop some national e-learning information literacy modules with Sarah Lewis (Pratchett and Lewis, 2016). This is one of the biggest projects I have been involved in, as it involves managing a budget, monitoring progress, reporting to stakeholders and working with a dispersed team. This project is answerable to the whole NHS library community and is part of the Knowledge for Healthcare strategy. Without my earlier experiences, I don't think I would have had the confidence to take on such a large task.

🖒 Best for

- Projects are good for making changes to services, introducing innovation and delivering efficiencies. A well designed project will be completed within agreed timescales and budgets.

▶ More

- Developing a clear process for managing your projects will take time and effort. You may be able to minimize this by getting expert help from project managers within the wider organization, or adopting the accepted process within your organization.

⚠ To think about

- Projects which are not clearly defined from the outset or controlled appropriately are more likely to fail. In order to ensure success, spend some time adopting a clear approach to project management which is consistent across the team.
- Without an agreed proposal and a clearly defined plan, projects are likely to fail completely or overrun. Spending time at the beginning of the project on defining what you want to achieve will pay dividends in the long term.

References

Brettle, A., Maden-Jenkins, M., Anderson, L., McNally, R., Pratchett, T., Tancock, J., Thornton, D. and Webb, A. (2010) Evaluating Clinical Librarian Services: a systematic review, *Health Information Libraries Journal*, **28** (1), 3–22.

CILIP (2015) *Practical Project Management for LIS Staff*, www.cilip.org.uk/cilip/products-and-services/onsite-training/onsite-training-courses/management-and-personal-2. [Accessed 16 April 2016]

Health Education England (2014) *Knowledge for Healthcare: a development framework*, https://hee.nhs.uk/sites/default/files/documents/Knowledge%20for%20healthcare%20-%20a%20development%20framework.pdf. [Accessed 16 April 2016]

LLAMA (2016) *Project Management: a skill set every leader needs*, www.ala.org/llama/%E2%80%9Cproject-management-skill-set-every-leader-needs%E2%80%9D. [Accessed 16 April 2016]

MAP (2015) *MAP Toolkit*, https://maptoolkit.wordpress.com. [Accessed 19 June 2016]

Newton, R. (2013) *The Project Management Book*, Pearson Education, Harlow.

Pratchett, T. (2015) *Providing Evidence for Supplies Group University Hospitals of Morecambe Bay NHS FT*, https://maptoolkit.wordpress.com/2015/08/06/providing-evidence-for-supplies-group-university-hospitals-of-morecambe-bay-nhs-ft. [Accessed 19 June 2016]

Pratchett, T. and Lewis, S. (2016) *STEP by STEP: the origins of the Service Transformation E-Learning Project (STEP)*, http://kfh.libraryservices.nhs.uk/step-by-step-the-origins-of-the-service-transformation-e-learning-project-step-by-tracey-pratchett-and-sarah-lewis. [Accessed 19 June 2016]

PRINCE2 (2016) *PRINCE2 Courses and Certification for Project Management*, www.prince2.com. [Accessed 16 April 2016]

Young, T. L. (2013) *Successful Project Management*, Kogan Page, London.

73. Project management tools

PROJECT MANAGEMENT TOOLS can help you and your teams to develop plans, identify resource requirements, keep tasks on track, mitigate risks and share the workload. Which tools you choose are likely to depend upon the size and complexity of your project. It is also worth contacting other departments within the organization, such as IT, research or commercial teams, as project management software may already be licensed for use, or there may be an established project management methodology within which you need to work, that would influence your selection of tool.

This Tip describes (Table 73.1) some of the tools which you can use with your teams to ensure that projects are delivered successfully. It is not intended to be an exhaustive list, as a quick search of the internet will uncover a mass of available resources, but we will consider a number of cloud-based tools which can be used collaboratively and are available for a variety of budgets.

Table 73.1 *Project management tools (Burger, 2015)*

Description	Costs
Microsoft Project Pro for Office 365 https://products.office.com/en-gb/project/project-and-portfolio-management-software	
Sophisticated tool designed to work with other Office systems, e.g. Word, Excel and SharePoint. Allows planning, task and resource management and collaboration online.	Fee charged per month per user, plus annual subscription.
Trello https://trello.com/	
Uses the Kanban project management method, creates a visual representation using cards to allocate tasks.	Free subscription with unlimited users and projects. 10MB storage. Additional features available for business and enterprise at an additional cost.
Zoho Projects www.zoho.com/projects/?gclid=CjwKEAjw86e4BRCnzuWGIpjLoUcSJACaHG55lz04jlTMzxphPvF2g25B2H15S6Ugq3LqkSnqtdB-HRoCZiXw_wcB	
Allows collaboration and includes a range of templates (e.g. Gantt charts), reporting features, feeds (likened to Facebook) and allows users to create complex task lists.	Free subscription, 1 project and 10MB storage. Express, Premium and Enterprise options available for an additional cost.
Producteev www.producteev.com	
Allocate tasks and share with your wider team. Provides updates and filters and enables project objectives to be organized by individual or time.	Free subscription, unlimited users and projects. Pro option available for an additional cost.
PBworks Project Hub www.pbworks.com/	
Provides a single-page overview of your project, e-mail updates and task lists. This can be shared with your team and gives them the opportunity to comment on the project.	Free subscription up to 15 users, 5 projects 50MB storage. Additional features available with an upgrade.

Whilst many of the options listed above offer a free subscription, it is worth checking out their limitations before you go ahead. For example, some tools provide limited space for document storage, which may be crucial for your project, and you may need to upgrade at a later date in order to continue use. If you decide that your team does not require a cloud-based tool to track the progress of projects, a range of templates provided by the Project Agency are shared on the BusinessBalls website (Chapman, 2016).

❌ Best for

- Keeping projects on track and ensuring that they are delivered on time.
- Sharing tasks and progress with the wider team. Cloud-based tools are great for collaboration.

▶ **More**

■ There are lots of tools available which can enhance your project, so review a
number of approaches to ensure that you pick the right fit for your teams.

⚠ **To think about**

■ Some project management tools can be complex and difficult to understand.
If you have a simple, small-scale project to complete, a simple action plan
with timescales will be sufficient.

References

Burger, R. (2015) *The Top 6 Free and Open Source Project Management Software for Your
Small Business*, http://blog.capterra.com/free-open-source-project-management-
software. [Accessed 10 April 2016].
Chapman, A. (2016) *Blank Project Management Templates: saving time! saving money!
saving stress!*, www.businessballs.com/project%20management%20templates.pdf.
[Accessed 10 April 2016]

74. Reflection – facilitating

STAFF WORKING TOWARDS CILIP qualifications will be expected to provide
evidence of their reflective practice, which should be linked to the
criteria and their personal development plans (CILIP, 2014a, b, c). Managers
and supervisors have a role to play in ensuring that reflective practice does
not become something which is merely done as a one-off to meet criteria
outlined in formal activities. You can also encourage staff to reflect in
appraisal and professional development meetings using a questioning
approach. In her blog, *Half Pint of Hard Earned Wisdom*, Donna Watt suggests
that the following questions can be used to lead people to a place where
they can transform their practice:

> What will you do differently?
> Did your learning question your practice, or reaffirm what you already do?
> What is your action plan and how will you measure the impact of any change?
> Have you started a journey of professional discovery as a result of new ideas?
> Do you have any new questions as a result of the experience?
>
> Watt, 2011

Some organizations include standard questions within their appraisal
documentation which can be used to encourage the appraisee to reflect on
their performance. It is also useful if you consider the same questions in

advance of the appraisal meeting to ensure that you can encourage your staff member towards deeper learning, outcomes of which can be fed into formal personal development plans. This questioning approach can also be used with project teams or individuals in order to examine projects, incidents and development activities.

By adopting a questioning approach to appraisal and development meetings, you can enable staff to reflect on their practice, leading them to analyse their role in situations, to understand how they could make changes and to help them resolve any issues. Through reflective practice you can also support staff members to extract positive results from their experiences which can impact on their future work. The next Tip (p. 194) provides practical examples for facilitating reflection and tips for reflective writing.

⬧ Best for

■ Encouraging and facilitating reflective discussion in appraisals and project meetings or following incidents to ensure that participants move towards deeper understanding.
■ Extracting positive experiences and lessons learned from mistakes or incidents.

► More

■ Try to make the process meaningful and ensure that lessons are learned and captured and fed into personal development plans or library strategy documents.
■ Use either predefined questions from your organization's documentation or established models such as Gibbs' (Tips 75, p. 194 and 76, p. 196) or write your own questions, which both you and the individual or team can consider before the discussion commences.

⚠ To think about

■ Be careful not to make reflection something which people 'just do', as it will be quickly perceived as a tick-box exercise and can create resentment for teams and individuals.

References

CILIP (2014a) *Certification: a guide for members*, www.cilip.org.uk/sites/default/files/documents/Certification%20Handbook%20070314.pdf. [Accessed 19 September 2015]

CILIP (2014b) *Chartership: a guide for members,* www.cilip.org.uk/sites/default/files/
documents/Chartership%20Handbook%20070314.pdf. [Accessed 25 October 2015]
CILIP (2014c) *Fellowship: a guide for members,*
www.cilip.org.uk/sites/default/files/documents/Fellowship%20Handbook%20070
314.pdf. [Accessed 30 October 2015]
Watt, D. (2011) *Reflective Practice – How Do We Model This for Library Professionals?,*
http://halfpintofwisdom.wordpress.com/2011/09/11/reflective-practice-how-do-
we-model-this-for-library-professionals. [Accessed 22 April 2016]

Further reading

Grant, M. (2007) The role of Reflection in the Library and Information Sector: a
systematic review, *Health Information and Libraries Journal,* **24** (3), 155–66.

75. Reflective practice

REFLECTIVE PRACTICE IS described as a process which can happen either during an event or after an event ; this section of the book will focus on the latter. The concept of reflective practice has been widely adopted in education, health, management and many other professions, so it is not surprising to see it integrated into LKS work.

So, what does it mean to be a reflective practitioner? Marks-Maran and Rose (cited in Forrest, 2002) define reflective practice as a process of redefining our understanding, with a view to improving self-awareness and evaluating our actions, whilst for Ghaye and Lillyman reflection 'acts as a bridge from tacit knowledge to considered action' increasing accountability, encouraging questioning and establishing professional wisdom (cited in Forrest, 2008, 229).

Gibbs' (1988) experiential learning cycle is an often adopted method to facilitate reflective practice with a systematic approach. The reflective cycle involves six stages of reflection, to lead the practitioner towards deeper learning and enable them to change their behaviours, as illustrated in Figure 75.1.

Being reflective does not come easily to everyone and some people are more predisposed to reflective learning than others. It is important to remember that staff may need more support from you in order to adopt this approach

Figure 75.1 *Gibbs' experiential learning cycle (Gibbs, 1988)*

towards enhancing their professional practice. Although CILIP includes criteria to ensure that professionals reflect on their practice, being reflective is not just about collecting evidence, or thinking about how to apply learning from a course. Reflective practice is a rich approach which provides a forum for challenging traditional views, which may be uncomfortable at times. As a leader you should not only facilitate others to be reflective but it is important that you also model reflective practice behaviours. Through a process of reflection, people can challenge themselves towards a deeper understanding of experiences, making rewarding changes for the future.

🖒 Best for

- Critically analysing events, incidents or personal development activities to change practice.
- Encouraging staff towards deeper learning in a systematic fashion.

▶ More

- Reflective practice provides opportunities to reflect on events and activities both during and after they have been completed.

▲ To think about

- If you are asking you staff to be reflective, ensure that you also model these behaviours.
- Not everyone feels comfortable reflecting on practice; they may not be predisposed to learning in this way, or may find the process challenging and uncomfortable.

References

Forrest, M. S. E. (2008) On Becoming a Critically Reflective Practitioner, *Health Information and Libraries Journal*, **25** (3), 229–31.
Gibbs, G. (1988) *Learning by Doing: a guide to teaching and learning methods*, www2.glos.ac.uk/gdn/gibbs. [Accessed 22 April 2016]

Further Reading

Grant, M. (2007) The Role of Reflection in the Library and Information Sector: a systematic review, *Health Information and Libraries Journal*, **24** (3), 155–66.
Schon, D. A. (1991) *The Reflective Practitioner: how professionals think in action*, Ashgate, Avebury.

76. Reflective writing

REFLECTIVE WRITING IS useful for those who are expected to demonstrate their ability to reflect. They may be expected to provide evidence of reflective practice during the organizational appraisal process, and it is built into the CILIP framework of Professional Registration (CILIP, 2014a, b, c). If you are supporting people within your team with CILIP qualifications, it is useful to provide them with tools to help them to write reflectively about their professional experiences. This writing may inform their evaluative statements or could be submitted as pieces of evidence in their own right. CILIP (2015) suggest that through reflective writing candidates can outline their personal responses, exploring learning and self-awareness and their understanding of the wider professional context. Through the process of challenging their assumptions and reactions, reflective writing demonstrates the ability to implement or recommend improvement and consider actual or desired outcomes.

You can encourage staff to write reflectively about any event, incident, project or personal development activity and there are many models which can be adapted to provide frameworks for reflection to support the writing process for those in your teams who are not familiar with this method of writing. Rolfe, Jasper and Freshwater (2011) provide a simple three-step framework with prompts to aid the writer (Table 76.1).

Table 76.1	*Three-step reflective framework adapted from Rolfe, Jasper and Freshwater (2011), reproduced with permission from Palgrave MacMillan*
What	. . . happened? . . . is being examined?
So what	. . . does this teach you about your attitude/approach/skill? . . . was going through your mind as you acted? . . . other knowledge can you bring to the situation? . . . went well? . . . could you have done to make it better? . . . is your new understanding of the situation? . . . broader issues arise from the situation?
Now what	. . . do you need to do to improve things/resolve the situation/feel better? . . . broader issues need to be considered if this action is to be successful?

Many people use blogs to reflect on their learning experiences, whilst others use diaries, journals or learning logs such as the CILIP VLE. All of these are useful tools to integrate reflective writing into practice. Reflective writing can be difficult to fully master if left too long after the event, and so it is best to encourage staff to make notes as soon as possible which can act as prompts when they have time to reflect in more depth. Often people find reflective writing time-consuming but, as with any skill, as it is practised it becomes easier. It is also worth reminding staff that reflective pieces do not need to be lengthy essays, just short personal pieces. Handy tips for reflection writing include:

- Use the first person . . . 'I'.
- Avoid being descriptive: 'So what?'
- Be honest and evaluative.
- Be selective, don't try to include everything.
- Make it an ongoing process (daily, weekly).
- Reflect on an incident and attach supporting evidence.
- Write soon after the event.
- Structured writing or 'free-style'? Adopt a style which suits.

Finally, for staff who feel that they require training in reflective writing, watch out for CILIP training courses, or locally provided training which is available for staff on the route to Chartership. These courses take place across the UK and you can direct staff to the CILIP events calendar, where they will find more details.

🖒 Best for

- Identifying learning needs to feed into staff personal development plans.
- Providing evidence of reflective practice which can be embedded into portfolios.

► More

- Give staff an existing framework with questions/prompts to make the process easier.
- Encourage staff to find a process that works for them then they are more likely to stick to it.
- Watch out for training courses available nationally and locally and flag these up to your staff.

⚠ To think about

- Don't let it become an arduous process; encourage it to be part of ongoing development.
- Try to encourage staff to really engage with the process in order to achieve a deeper understanding of their role and to implement real change.
- One or two key reflections of good quality are better than lots of descriptive pieces with no reflective elements.

References

CILIP (2014a) *Certification: a guide for members,*
    www.cilip.org.uk/sites/default/files/documents/Certification%20Handbook%2007
    0314.pdf. [Accessed 19 September 2015]
CILIP (2014b) *Chartership: a guide for members,*
    www.cilip.org.uk/sites/default/files/documents/Chartership%20Handbook%
    20070314.pdf. [Accessed 25 October 2015]
CILIP (2014c) *Fellowship: a guide for members,* www.cilip.org.uk/sites/default/files/
    documents/Fellowship%20Handbook%20070314.pdf. [Accessed 30 October 2015]
CILIP (2015) *What Level is Right for You?,* www.cilip.org.uk/cilip/jobs-careers/
    professional-registration/what-level-right-you. [Accessed 22 April 2016]
Rolfe, G., Jasper, M. and Freshwater, D. (2011) *Critical Reflection in Practice,* 2nd edn,
    Palgrave Macmillan, Basingstoke.

77. Research activities

> Research is a systematic method of studying a problem to discover and develop defensible solutions.
>
> Weiner, Weiner and Beile, 2012

GOOD RESEARCH EXPLORES an issue in depth and should create new knowledge which can be used by others to improve their practice and delivery of their services. To increase the impact of research outputs, it will be written up and shared widely via journals and conference presentations. Research which is not publicized is of little value to the wider profession, so dissemination is crucial. Carrying out research in your LKS can help you to evaluate performance, identify gaps, measure impact or effectiveness and identify good practice.

Miggie Pickton (2016) has outlined the benefits of LKS staff undertaking research for the individual, the service/organization and the wider profession (Table 77.1).

Table 77.1 *Benefits of research for individual, LKS and the profession (Pickton, 2016)*

For the individual	For the service/organization	For the profession
• Learn something new • Develop skills • Variety of work • Job satisfaction • Personal development • Reputation • Career prospects	• Demonstrate impact • Find out what users want • Same experience as research users • Decision making • Problem solving • Staff motivation • Recognition	• Professional excellence • New knowledge • Evidence base • Positive change • Vibrant library community • Reputation

Getting involved

Action research or practitioner research is a common research methodology used in the LKS field, where research is completed within daily practice. Common areas of action research are investigating the impact of information literacy or the adoption of emerging technologies. Wilson (2013) defines the role of the practitioner or action researcher as an LKS professional who explores their environment from within, asking questions and reflecting on their practice; one who is 'curious about practice in a formalized way, and wanting to know more about practice in order to make that practice better' (Wilson, 2013, 112).

For LKS staff carrying out research at work, their supervisor or line manager needs to provide an environment which is supportive to ensure success. Research can be time-consuming, so it cannot be bolted on to an already full-time post; time should be made available away from daily duties to enable the research to happen.

Alternatively, LKS staff can work collaboratively on research projects with non-LKS colleagues. This opportunity is more likely to occur within an academic or specialized environment such as health, where non-LKS colleagues are participating in their own research. This is the role of an embedded librarian (McCluskey, 2013), where the LKS professional is an active partner in the research process. In this model, the embedded librarian continues to provide traditional LKS support to the research group that they are part of, whilst actively participating in the research of the group.

LKS staff will often be expected to undertake research during postgraduate education and as a manager you can facilitate this process by providing opportunities for research to be undertaken within the LKS. Providing space and time for individuals to complete their research project also has the added benefit of providing insights into your service. If you are keen to create a research culture within your teams, not only do you need to provide time, but you must enable staff to attend relevant training to develop their skills and knowledge in analysis, statistics, research methods and project management, for example.

Getting involved in research can be challenging for the individual. Jane Secker and Emma Coonan (2013) presented their experiences of being involved in research as extremely rewarding and positive, but they also cited lack of time, limited budgets, research being viewed as a low priority and limited support from managers and colleagues as barriers to success. As a supervisor or manager, there are a number of practical solutions for you to support your team with their research projects and there are a range of funding opportunities which could be the enabler for research projects. Successful applications for bursaries or awards (Tip 55, p. 138) can cover the costs of allowing staff time to carry out and write up the research, conference attendance, training courses and the cost of specialized equipment or software. Finally, act as a mentor to support individuals through the process and provide protected time if possible, as this will improve their experience of the process.

👍 Best for

■ Demonstrating the impact of existing LKSs and identifying potential innovative projects and services from the existing evidence base.
■ Providing individuals with additional skills which can benefit your service. As LKS staff develop new skills and understanding of research techniques and approaches, they will be in a better position to support users who are also researchers.
■ Creating a culture where research and improving practice is the norm.

▶ More

■ Research does not always have to be a large-scale research project which takes up a lot of time.
■ Be innovative about finding opportunities for your team members to become involved in research. Expand an existing evaluation project to include research elements in it and encourage your staff to write up and publish. Alternatively, create opportunities for staff to work with research groups within the organization, thus sharing the workload and responsibility.

⚠ To think about

■ As a manager, you need to accept that research can be time-consuming and you may need to provide some protected time for individuals to work on the research project. If dedicated time is not provided the successful completion of the project will be jeopardized.

References

McCluskey, C. (2013) Being an Embedded Research Librarian: supporting research by being a researcher, *Journal of Information Literacy*, **7** (2), 4–14.
Pickton, M. (2016) Facilitating a Research Culture in an Academic Library: top down and bottom up approaches, *New Library World*, **117** (1/2), 105-27.
Secker, J. and Coonan, E. (2013) *The Librarian as Researcher*, https://cardiesandtweed.wordpress.com/2013/11/27/librarian-as-research-doing-research-in-your-day-job-by-emma-coonan-and-jane-secker-workshop-write-up. [Accessed 24 September 2016]

Weiner, S., Weiner, J. and Beile, P. (2012) *Practice into Research, Research into Practice*, www.lib.purdue.edu/sites/default/files/infolit/orientation.pdf. [Accessed 8 April 2016]

Wilson, V. (2013) Formalized Curiosity: reflecting on the librarian practitioner-researcher, *Evidence Based Library and Information Practice*, **8** (1), 111–17.

78. Secondments

A **SECONDMENT IS** a temporary transfer of an individual from one part of the organization to another for a short period of time, usually for up to a 12-month period (CIPD, 2014). On occasion, secondments can also be arranged between different organizations. A defining feature of the secondment is that the employee's substantive post will be held for them until the end of the temporary contract, but it can be filled on a temporary basis until the secondment ends and the employee returns to their original position. Arrangements such as this can be beneficial for the employee, the original employer and the new employer.

A secondment can provide a short-term opportunity for an individual to gain experience in a different role. In the case study below, both employees had worked in the same role for a number of years, but there were limited opportunities for promotion within the LKS. This short secondment enabled them to use their skills in a different way and to gain experience in a different role. Secondments can also provide opportunities to develop skills in new areas such as project management, leadership or web development which would enhance their future career prospects. Finally, the secondment offers security, enabling the employee to try out a different role for a short period of time, with the same terms and conditions and the knowledge that they will return to their original role at a later date.

In the current climate, there are fewer opportunities to promote existing employees, and a secondment arrangement can accommodate this to some extent. If the post which the seconded staff member leaves remains vacant, you may save money in the short term. However, careful consideration should be taken to ensure that remaining staff are not placed under additional pressure to cover the vacant post. In the case study below, the original secondment was for three months, but was extended, placing extra pressure on the remaining staff who covered the vacancy. Consider whether the temporary vacancy could be filled by other team members, providing development opportunities for other staff. Alternatively, the short-term post could be filled from someone outside the existing team, thus encouraging new ideas, approaches and perspectives. When the seconded employee returns to the library, they may also bring new skills, confidence, enthusiasm and ideas to transform the service.

For the employer, the secondment enables them to use existing experience within the organization. Transferring an employee between departments is quicker and means that the employee often knows how existing systems work. In the case study below, the LKS staff were able to commence work on the new role immediately and vital project time was saved. Recruiting staff in this way resulted in reduced costs for the organization by removing the need for costly external advertisements. Organizationally, there is an opportunity to grow leaders from within and provide unforeseen promotional opportunities.

Example from practice:
University Hospitals of Morecambe Bay NHS Foundation Trust

When the organization was subject to an investigation, an internal team was created from existing staff who were seconded to new roles on a temporary basis. The role of Information and Document Management Specialist was filled by two members of the library team who brought different skills. The library staff worked half the week for the investigation and continued in their substantive posts for the remainder of the week. The role involved organizing, cataloguing and submitting evidence to the external investigation. The secondment benefited the individuals in that it provided an opportunity for progression and to work with different staff groups within the organization. For the library service, this project raised the profile of the service and the skills and abilities that library staff can bring to projects. (Shawcross and Pratchett, 2014)

Secondments do require careful planning and consideration to ensure that existing services can continue and remaining staff are not placed under additional pressure while they pick up the work of their seconded colleagues. Secondments should be continually monitored and the employee should record and share how their learning and new skills can be applied on their return.

⍟ Best for

- Can provide individuals with opportunities for career, skills and knowledge development within their existing organization. Enables organizations to exploit the skills of existing staff and saves money on recruitment costs.
- Can also raise the profile of the library and the skills of the library team, by stealth.

► **More**

■ Organizations can use secondments as part of a programme of talent management, providing individuals with additional responsibility where opportunities for promotion are limited.

⚠ **To think about**

■ If one of your team goes to a secondment you may not be able to recruit to a short-time post. This means that the extra work needs to be divided between existing team members and could increase pressure on staff within the remaining team. This can also create resentment for those for whom secondments are not available.
■ The employee may not want to return to their former role and could be dissatisfied when they return. It may be difficult for them to settle back in (CIPD, 2014).

References

CIPD (2014) *Secondments: factsheet,* www.cipd.co.uk/hr-resources/factsheets/secondment.aspx. [Accessed 20 June 2015]

Shawcross, J. and Pratchett, T. (2014) *Managing Information Flows in Critical Times,* Health Libraries Group Conference, Oxford, 24–25 July, www.CILIP.org.uk/sites/default/files/documents/Joanne%20Shawcross%20%26%20Tracey%20Pratchett.pdf. [Accessed 20 June 2015]

Further reading

Cope, E. (2013) *Secondment from Cataloguing to Acquisitions,* https://pteg.wordpress.com/2013/02/08/secondment-from-cataloguing-to-acquisitions-elly-cope. [Accessed 24 June 2016]

Jordan, K. (2013) *Secondment from Faculty Librarian to Research Publications Librarian for 9 Months,* https://pteg.wordpress.com/2013/02/19/secondment-from-faculty-librarian-to-research-publications-librarian-for-9-months-katy-jordan. [Accessed 24 June 2016]

Stacey, D. (2013) *Secondment from Subject Librarian to Bibliographic Services Librarian,* https://pteg.wordpress.com/2013/01/23/secondment-from-subject-librarian-to-bibliographic-services-librarian-david-stacey. [Accessed 24 June 2016]

Staffshare (2011) *The Benefits of Secondment to Employees,* www.staffshare.co.uk/docs/StaffShare%20SECONDMENT%20BENEFITS.pdf. [Accessed 20 June 2015]

Stuart Edwards, E. (2013) *Secondment from Reader Services to Academic Services as an Information Librarian,* https://pteg.wordpress.com/2013/02/08/secondment-from-

reader-services-to-academic-services-as-an-information-librarian-emma-stuart-
edwards. [Accessed 24 June 2016]

79. Shadowing

JOB SHADOWING IS an informal process where one staff member works alongside
either a more experienced colleague or someone who is doing a different job.
Individuals can shadow colleagues within the organization, or arrangements
can be made to shadow in external organizations within either the same or
different sectors. The benefits of shadowing for the individual are that they gain
experience, make contacts, expand their knowledge and may develop a greater
understanding of a different area of work. Taylor (2013) writes about her
experience as a teacher librarian in an Australian school, about using job
shadowing to overcome isolation, share experience and network with others.

As a manager or supervisor of staff, you can use shadowing to keep existing
staff engaged, helping them to develop new skills or services. You could also
offer opportunities to students or staff from other organizations, inviting them
to shadow one of your team. This is a good way of contributing to the
profession, but also of scouting for new talent and growing your own team.
In larger organizations, you could make arrangements for LKS staff to
shadow other professionals to gain a greater understanding of user needs and
to spot opportunities to develop new services. For example, in a university
an LKS professional could shadow an academic member of staff or, in the
NHS, shadow a clinician.

Shadowing scenarios

Below are a number of scenarios where shadowing could be considered:

- A new staff member shadowing an existing staff member doing the
  same job is a good way to learn the ropes, understand organizational
  values and get them up to speed. Shadowing the person who is leaving
  the post can be an excellent way of keeping the organizational memory
  and maintaining former staff talent (About Money, 2015).
- A new or existing staff member could visit a different organization
  which is offering a similar service to learn about the role, develop new
  skills and implement revised processes. This could be a good way of
  building networks and finding a mentor.
- An existing staff member could shadow LKS staff from other
  departments. This would work really well in a large higher educational
  service, where staff could work with other teams to develop their own
  skills, bring in new methods of working and generate ideas (Foley,

Barbrow and Hartline, 2015).

- An existing staff member could shadow someone from another department. This would work well if the staff member/LKS wanted to introduce a new service which involved learning a new skill, e.g. IT. This could also be useful to gain a greater understanding of the needs of service users, e.g. shadowing a clinical staff member in a health organization or a teacher in a school.
- Students and staff from other organizations shadowing your staff could provide opportunities for new information professionals who are not currently working and help them to gain skills and experience. This is a great way to give back to the profession and can be a useful way of finding new talent and introducing new ideas into your service.

If you arrange a shadowing opportunity for one of your staff, you should ask a number of questions at the outset (Taylor, 2013 and MMU, 2014):

- Will the person shadowing follow a person for a whole day, to get a real feel for the job, or will they just observe for a short period of time?
- Are there any specific objectives or outcomes that you and the 'shadower' want to achieve?
- How will the 'shadower' record what they have learned so that this can be shared within the team, or contribute to their portfolio?
- When is a good time/ date to undertake shadowing? It shouldn't cause extra work for the person being shadowed.

It is important to ensure that the purpose and expected outcomes are discussed and documented with the 'shadower' and person being shadowed at the outset to ensure that expectations for all concerned are managed. If one of your team is the 'shadower' you should ensure that they write up their learning and share their findings with the team (London School of Economics, 2014).

🖒 Best for

- ■ Keeping existing staff motivated and providing opportunities to learn new skills or ways of doing things which will benefit both their personal development and the library service as a whole.
- ■ Maintaining organizational memory by connecting new staff with the outgoing post holder, or alternative staff within the team. Job shadowing can be an integral part of succession planning and providing a smooth handover.
- ■ Providing opportunities for students and upcoming professionals is a great way to strengthen the profession as a whole and can also be a great way of identifying upcoming talent for your service.

► **More**

- Ensure that the visit is well planned with both the person shadowing and the person being shadowed. This means ensuring that expectations are clearly managed, timings are agreed and that both participants are happy with the proposal.

⚠ **To think about**

- Shadowing should be a realistic experience for the person shadowing. A day watching someone respond to e-mails, however, would not be a good use of anyone's time. Ensure that the visit is planned around a specific activity e.g. meeting, teaching session.
- Provide simple documentation to capture and share the learning, otherwise the visit will not be valuable to the service or the individual.

References

About Money (2015) *Why Do Organizations Need to Provide Job Shadowing for On-the-Job Training?*, http://humanresources.about.com/od/On-The-Job-Training/f/Why-Organizations-Need-To-Provide-Job-Shadowing.htm. [Accessed 13 June 2015]

Foley, D., Barbrow, S. and Hartline, M. (2015) Staffshare: creating cross-departmental connection in the library, *College and Research Libraries News*, **76** (1), 26–9.

London School of Economics (2014) *Job Shadowing*, www.lse.ac.uk/intranet/staff/humanResources/learningAndDevelopment/Managing-Your-Career/Job-Shadowing.aspx. [Accessed 13 June 2015]

MMU (2014) *Job Shadowing Guidelines*, www2.mmu.ac.uk/media/mmuacuk/content/documents/human-resources/a-z/guidance-procedures-and-handbooks/Job_Shadowing_Guidelines.pdf. [Accessed 7 April 2015]

Taylor, S. (2013) *Job Shadowing for Librarians: librarians are go*, http://librariansarego.blogspot.co.uk/2013/05/job-shadowing-for-librarians.html#!/2013/05/job-shadowing-for-librarians.html. [Accessed 7 April 2015]

80. Social media

> Social media allows people to create, share or exchange information, ideas, and pictures/videos in virtual communities and networks.
>
> Wikipedia, 2015

SOCIAL MEDIA CHANNELS and tools such as Twitter, Facebook, blogs, YouTube, Flickr and Slideshare allow you to discover, disseminate, organize, collaborate and even curate information. It provides news from around the world at a speed that is incomparable with news dissemination 20 years ago. It empowers, democratizes and has even brought about regime change. LKS staff can use it to promote their services, engage with their customers, stream content (Taylor & Francis, 2014), create professional networks and update current awareness.

Social media is included in CILIP's PKSB (2013) section 'IT and Communication' (Sections 12.4–12.7). The PKSB describes an information professional who understands social media tools in a variety of ways – not just for communication and networking but also using them to create user-generated content, and as part of media and PR skills.

It is important that managers help staff to foster an awareness of social media in this information age. Staff need to know how their users are discovering and using information, so they can answer questions about it and exploit tools to promote their service. Here are a few handy tips for using social media:

- Starting out? Try a Twitter account first – it's very quick and easy to create. It also will help with you and your staff's current awareness.
- Finding out about new stuff? Have development meetings. Get each member of staff to research a new and different social media channel and bring it to present at the meeting.
- Librarians involved with children and young people should explore Snapchat, Instagram and the latest craze for following vlogging and vloggers.

Being open to social media in the first place is important, so if you want to develop this in your staff, have your own accounts in at least a couple of tools. You can then encourage staff to do the same. Even if you are only using a couple of social media channels, an awareness of functionality will make it easier for you and your staff to learn how to use new tools. Leading by example in this way shows staff how important social media is to you, and having a Twitter account will help you to find out about new social media tools. Table 80.1 lists some useful social media sites.

You can introduce LKS accounts to answer customer service enquiries and engage with your users. Staff who are answering queries in this way will be able to practise their skills. By having an organizational social media presence, you are sending a message to your staff that you are committed to using social media within your service.

The following example from practice is adapted from an article written by two library assistants as they reflect upon the possible uses of social media in promoting their service before and after a half-day training event (Perestrelo and Roylance, 2013).

Table 80.1 *Useful sites to get you started*

Social media resource	Suggestions for using the resource
Flickr www.flickr.com	Use Flickr to share and store photos. You could add images about local or special collections to promote them.
Facebook https://www.facebook.com	Use Facebook to chat to and engage with your users. You can promote your service, events and collections using text, links, photos and video.
Instagram https://www.instagram.com	Instagram is for sharing photos. Use it to raise awareness of your service by using hashtags, and sharing photos of your collections and resources. Show behind the scenes 'shots' so that users get a glimpse of what goes on in the library.
LinkedIn https://uk.linkedin.com	LinkedIn is a great way for librarians to link with other professionals. You can add CVs, get people to write testimonials for you, post comments and link to your blog posts, articles etc. LinkedIn Groups are also great for networking and sharing information.
Slideshare www.slideshare.net	Slideshare can be searched for useful presentations on 100s of different topics. You can also use it to disseminate your own presentations, training and workshops. Lots of presenters give their audience the Slideshare URL so that slides can be used at a later date.
Snapchat www.snapchat.com	Engage with users in a similar way to Twitter or Facebook but instead of text you send photos and videos (or stories) to your friends and followers.
Storify https://storify.com	Use Storify to curate social media posts with a particular hashtag, keyword or account. You could do this to promote events or a particular subject, adding your own narrative to the post timelines. Lots of information professionals use Storify to curate tweets from conferences to create a record of the event.
Twitter https://twitter.com	Use Twitter to chat to and engage with your users. Twitter has limited space but you can write short posts that promote your service, events and collections. You can link to a variety of content, e.g. text, links, photos and video.
WordPress https://wordpress.com	WordPress is blogging software. It is easy to create an attractive blog without knowing lots of html. You can blog about your own interests or create a blog to promote the LIS. Lots of people are now using WordPress to create simple websites.
YouTube https://www.youtube.com	Use YouTube to find information, or to promote your service. You can create videos to showcase your library, your collections and even your staff. You can have your own YouTube channel and create video 'how-tos' for your users.

Example from practice:
Jennifer Perestrelo and Rebecca Roylance – LKS assistants (NHS)

Our thoughts before training:
JP: When I was asked if I wanted to attend a training session on social media my

immediate response was a resounding 'no'. As far as social media goes, I have never really been interested and can't see how it would be of any use to me. The whole Facebook thing and tweeting seems like a complete waste of time and I don't really want to be 'LinkedIn' to anything.

RR: Well, I, on the other hand, am a great fan of Facebook but that's as far as my social media interest goes. I haven't got a clue about tweeting and blogging but I'm dying to know more.

JP: Tweeting is something that birds do isn't it? I think so. We'll see . . .

What happened next:

JP: Well that was good wasn't it?

RR: It was more than good, I learnt so much. I think we should definitely set up a Facebook page for the library and I'm dying to PIN something and I even know what one of these '#' is and how to use it. I am impressed.

JP: Yes, it wasn't what I was expecting but I enjoyed it. We laughed a lot (mainly at my lack of knowledge and misconceptions of social media). When we discussed YouTube as a form of social media I was thrilled – I hadn't realized I was already taking part in this global phenomenon. I also realized that I do have some experience in blogging.

RR: Well, we know that Twitter is great for sending short messages but isn't very visual so it would be a better idea to go with Facebook if we were to set something up for the library, as it has more options like linking to other information and being able to add video and pictorial help guides.

JP: I learnt that people are quite curious and naturally interested in what other people are doing so they might, in fact, want to listen to what I have to say. Or not.

RR: I feel that it would be useful for the library to have a Facebook page. It would allow us to keep our users updated with things in the library, and promote our services. We also include pictures and 'how-to' videos. We could link to our events and it would reach out to so many more of our users than we are currently doing.

JP: I have come around to the idea of social media as a communication tool and am quite excited about setting something up to engage with our users.

RR: People access social media every day. What better way of reaching out and engaging with our users than by entering their social networks with our very own Facebook page.

JP: Absolutely, if we are going to keep up with our library users, we need to engage with them on their terms.

🖒 Best for

- Keeping up to date? – Twitter and blogs.
- Catching up with friends? – Facebook.
- Publishing your own photos and to find great images to work with? – Flickr.
- Finding 'how to' videos and publishing your own library videos for your users to watch? – YouTube.
- Discovering trends in presentations styles or finding slides from conferences? – Slideshare.
- Engaging with your customers. Use social media when teaching information literacy to get users to engage with their learning.
- Raising your profile and awareness of your library service.

⚠ To think about

- Make sure staff understand the 'dos and don'ts' of social media and how you want them to behave whilst they are using organizational accounts.
- Don't jump on every new channel that arrives. You might end up with a very disparate set of tools but only a few followers on each.
- Keep an eye on the trends – see what really takes off and looks like it's sticking around.
- If you aren't sure then ask your users what they want to use and how they want to communicate with you using social media.

References

CILIP (2013) *Your Professional Knowledge and Skills Base: identify gaps and maximise opportunities along your career path*, CILIP, London.

Perestrelo, J. and Roylance, R. (2013) Searching and Social Media: to tweet or not to tweet, *LHINKK Up*, **43**, 10–22, www.lihnn.nhs.uk/images/Documents/LIHNN/LIHNNK-Up/LU_43_Summer_2013.pdf. [Accessed 16 June 2016]

Taylor & Francis. (2014) *Use of Social Media by the Library: current practices and future opportunities: a white paper*, www.tandf.co.uk/libsite/whitePapers/socialMedia. [Accessed 2 March 2015]

Wikipedia (2015) *Social Media*, http://en.wikipedia.org/wiki/Social_media. [Accessed 22 April 2016]

Further reading

Bozarth, J. (2016) *Bozarthzone*, http://bozarthzone.blogspot.co.uk. [Accessed 22 April 2016]

81. SWOT analysis

SWOT **IS AN** acronym which stands for strengths, weaknesses, opportunities and threats (Chapman, 2015). 'SWOT analyses are commonly used in business and are an effort to aid with organizational evaluation when strategizing' (Feldmann, Level and Liu, 2013, 100). As a manager, you can use this simple tool to assess both internal factors (strengths and weaknesses) and external factors (opportunities and threats) within your service or organization. You can also use the SWOT analysis framework to assess specific aspects of your service such as promotion and marketing and use your findings to shape future strategies and action plans.

This framework is largely subjective and subsequently has been adapted by new professionals to plan their approaches to personal development (Woods, 2011) and to address specific challenging situations (Ruddock, 2010). It is a really simple framework, which can help an individual to capture some ideas quickly and easily, using this as a basis to develop a more detailed action plan.

The completed SWOT analysis can be discussed with the individual at appraisal and can also be included in any personal portfolios either within the organization, or for professional registrations such as Chartership (CILIP, 2014). It could also be used to problem-solve a single issue, or to plan for a specific project.

The Table 81.1 demonstrates how the SWOT framework can be used to

Table 81.1 *Personal SWOT Analysis by Tracey Pratchett*

STRENGTHS	WEAKNESSES
(Internal factors – skills, knowledge and attributes which I can draw upon to improve success) • Ability to build and maintain strong working relationships (LIHNN, Neonatal Outreach service). • Quick to learn new resources (Dialog databases). • Innovative approach to work and keen to improve services (Clinical Librarian Systematic Review, MAP Toolkit).	(Internal factors – attributes which can hinder my career success if unchecked) • Tendency to take on too much work due to over-enthusiasm. Must learn how to say no! • Find it difficult to delegate due to perfectionism. • Limited understanding of critical appraisal and statistics. • Limited experience of carrying out complex searches.
OPPORTUNITIES	**THREATS**
(External factors – things outside my personal sphere which I can use to achieve my goals) • LIHNN and HCLU networks provide a range of opportunities to learn from others and become involved in regional projects. • Opportunities within the organization to collaborate with clinical and non-clinical staff (Neonatal Outreach, Commercial and Service Development).	(External factors – things outside my personal sphere which could be a barrier to my success) • Cutbacks in NHS may result in reduced resources, which could reduce the opportunities available for professional development. • Increasing workload due to staff leaving and not being replaced makes it difficult to extend outreach service.

gather content for a more detailed personal development plan. The author was a new clinical librarian preparing her route to Chartership (CILIP, 2014). The Mind Tools website (Mind Tools, 2015) provides some useful advice about how a SWOT analysis can help individuals to analyse their current situation and plan their personal development. It describes SWOT as a powerful tool which 'can help you uncover opportunities that you would not otherwise have spotted . . . by understanding your weaknesses, you can manage and eliminate threats that might otherwise hurt your ability to move forward' (Mind Tools, 2015). It can focus the individual's mind and help them to take action, using strengths to their advantage, action planning to improve weaker areas, identifying new opportunities and bringing an awareness of threats to their current status.

The Mind Tools website also provides an extensive list of questions that can be used to focus the individual's mind on each area of the framework. The tool can work well for some individuals to assess internal and external factors, but due to human nature, it can be difficult to reflect openly and fully. Some individuals find it difficult to identify their strengths, but will have no problem developing a huge list of weaknesses, which could undermine morale. Alternatively, it can be difficult to identify potential threats as these are often external factors which may not only be outside our control, but also outside our sphere of awareness.

As a manager or peer, you could work with individuals using coaching techniques and your skills to help them to be honest and balanced when identifying their strengths and weaknesses, opportunities and threats. This involves being honest and sensitive to ensure that the answers come from the individual, not you, as this approach is largely subjective. It is worth bearing in mind that the SWOT analysis is just one tool and whilst being a simple approach, it could be over-simplistic for some situations which may need more detailed and ongoing coaching.

🖒 Best for

- Providing an honest assessment of an individual's current situation to identify where they can make changes for the future. The next stage should be to complete a personal action plan to address some of their weaknesses and harness strengths.
- Identifying personal strengths which can be used to create new opportunities.
- Developing strategies to improve upon weaker areas.
- Identifying opportunities which can be exploited to improve career prospects.
- Reducing the impact of threats on career and personal development.

▶ **More**

■ Work with individuals to help them to become more aware of their situation and personal traits. Use your coaching skills to encourage deeper reflection.

⚠ **To think about**

■ Advise staff not to generalize, and adopt the SMART (Tip 25, p. 59) approach. The more specific each point is, the easier it will be to improve upon weaker areas and reduce the risk of threats.

■ Don't take over! This is not about you telling individuals what they must do, but encouraging them to be subjective and find their own way. You don't want to demolish their morale.

References

Chapman, A. (2015) SWOT Analysis, www.businessballs.com/swotanalysisfreetemplate.htm. [Accessed 17 October 2016]

CILIP (2014) *Chartership: a guide for Members*, www.cilip.org.uk/sites/default/files/document/Chartership%20Handbook20070314.pdf [Accessed 6 April 2015].

Feldmann, L. M., Level, A. V. and Liu, S. (2013) Leadership Training and Development: an academic library's findings. *Library Management*, **34** (1/2), 96–104.

Mind Tools (2015) *Personal SWOT Analysis: making the most of your talents and opportunities*, www.mindtools.com/pages/article/newTMC_05_1.htm. [Accessed 6 April 2015]

Ruddock, B. (2010) *CILIP Chartership Portfolio*, https://bethaninfoprof.wordpress.com/CILIP-chartership-portfolio. [Accessed 6 April 2015]

Woods, L. (2011) *Personal SWOT Analysis*, https://darkarchive.wordpress.com/2011/05/24/personal-swot-analysis. [Accessed 6 April 2015]

Further reading

Team FME (2013) *SWOT Analysis: strategy skills*, www.free-management-ebooks.com/dldebk-pdf/fme-swot-analysis.pdf. [Accessed 6 April 2015]

82. Time management

MIND TOOLS **(2016A)** define time management as 'the way that you organize and plan how long you spend on specific activities'. Bartlett (2012) suggests that it is not that we don't have enough time, we just need to make the most of it and her article reviews a number of key books and journals available to help LKS staff adopt good techniques. Improving the way that you and your teams manage your workloads will increase productivity, enable you to deliver a more effective service and will remove stressors from within the team.

Feeling overworked is one of the key reasons that people feel stressed in the workplace and helping your team members to adopt good practice when it comes to managing their workload within the time available can help to alleviate this. You may identify that a member of your team is struggling via regular one-to-ones or during appraisal when they have dedicated time to speak to you about their workload and the difficulties that they face. Alternatively, other members of the team may tell you if a colleague is regularly missing deadlines or appears to be struggling to keep on top of their work. Monitoring feedback from customers can also highlight if there are issues with meeting deadlines within the team.

Improving an individual's time management skills

So what can you do to help an individual to improve their approach to time management? As with any issue, the first step is to talk to the team member in order to find out what the problem is and listen to their response. Use your coaching skills to help them to pinpoint the problem and to explore options with a view to finding a solution. It is important that you do not make assumptions about what is happening and also avoid taking on their workload yourself, as this will transfer the problem to you; it will not empower the individual or help them to be accountable for their own work.

Your role as a manager or supervisor is to listen to the individual and support them. You may find out that they feel overwhelmed by the amount of work they have to complete, or that they are setting unrealistic deadlines. Or there may be issues outside work which are impacting on their ability to focus and manage their workload. Mind Tools (2016b) highlight the following common time management mistakes:

- not keeping a to-do-list
- not setting SMART goals
- not prioritizing
- failing to manage distractions
- procrastinating
- taking on too much
- addicted to being busy
- multitasking

- not taking breaks
- ineffectively scheduling tasks.

A good start to helping the individual manage their workload more effectively is to get them to write a list of everything that they need to complete and to allocate deadlines to each piece of work using SMART goal setting techniques (see Tip 25, p. 59, for more information). Ensure that they take ownership of the plan and feel that the schedule is achievable and realistic within the timescales provided. Hopefully, developing a calendar of activities for the coming weeks will enable the individual to become more effective, improve their motivation levels and make them more focused (Mind Tools, 2016b).

It is important that you arrange a follow-up meeting with the employee to assess whether they managed to meet their self-imposed deadlines and to highlight any issues which may have impacted on their ability to fulfil their commitments. Initially, you may need to have regular weekly meetings to support the individual and help them to identify and address any problem areas; then you can monitor progress in your regular one-to-one meetings.

Finally, as with any skill, it is essential that as a manager, supervisor or colleague you also model the behaviours that you expect from your teams, in this instance good time management techniques. If you do not manage your workload effectively and regularly expect staff to deliver work to short and unrealistic deadlines, you will lose credibility by contributing to their inability to manage their own work. It is essential that you review your own practice and see if there is any way that you can improve the way that you manage your time and individual tasks. If you adopt some of the approaches and use some of the techniques and tools outlined in the next Tip (p. 216), you will be able to make the most of your time, but most importantly the most of your staff.

⚐ Best for

■ Ensuring that you and your teams make the most of the time that you have available to you and also to relieve stress and anxiety linked to the challenges of increasing workloads. As staff numbers are reduced and library budgets are shrinking, library teams are pressured to 'do more for less' and a good service wide approach to time management will support this.

▶ More

■ Review Tip 83 on time management (p. 216) for practical tools and techniques that you can implement with your teams to improve productivity.

⚠ To think about

- If there are people in your team who do not manage their time effectively, and this includes you as the manager or supervisor, it will impact negatively on the reputation of both the individuals within your service and the library service as a whole.

References

Bartlett, J. A. (2012) New and Noteworthy: making every hour count: librarians and time management, *Library Leadership and Management*, **26** (3/4), 1–4.

Mind Tools (2016a) *What is Time Management?*, www.mindtools.com/pages/article/newHTE_00.htm. [Accessed 3 January 2016]

Mind Tools (2016b) *10 Common Time Management Mistakes*, www.mindtools.com/pages/article/time-management-mistakes.htm. [Accessed 3 January 2016]

83. Time management tools

THERE ARE A wide range of tools and techniques that are referenced both on the internet and in the literature which you can use with your teams and individuals to make the best use of time and improve productivity. This Tip cannot cover everything – there are 61 tools listed on the Mind Tools (2016a) website alone – but it will introduce some key techniques and resources to suit a range of needs, circumstances and preferences. This will help you and your teams become more organized, remove stressors and improve productivity.

If you have an individual who is struggling with managing their workload, feels overwhelmed and misses deadlines, you should help them to identify the work that they have to do before they can start the task of getting organized. It is worth bearing in mind that this preparation phase can be time-consuming, so you will need to make sure that the individual has some time put aside to get to grips with what needs to be done. A number of techniques and templates are listed on the Mind Tools (2016a) and BusinessBalls (Chapman, 2016) websites, which you can use with team members to help them to identify their pressure points.

The Eisenhower principle

The Eisenhower principle (Mind Tools, 2016b) is useful to help identify and prioritize all tasks. The name originates from President Eisenhower's approach to task management. In his 1954 speech Second Assembly of the World Council of Churches he quoted Dr J Roscoe Miller 'I have two kinds of problems: the urgent and the important. The urgent are not important, and the important are never urgent' (Mind Tools, 2016b). This simple technique can be really useful for those who feel overwhelmed with the amount of work that they have to do which may impact on their productivity. Initially, create a full list of all tasks activities and then place each task into one of the four categories shown in Figure 83.1.

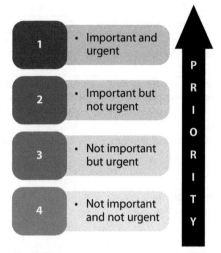

Once the most important and urgent tasks have been identified, these can be added to the to-do list and scheduled in order of importance. Other tasks can be scheduled for a later date, delegated to others or

Figure 83.1
The Eisenhower principle (Mind Tools, 2016b)

removed from the list altogether. A good tip is to encourage similar tasks to be grouped together and scheduled to be dealt with at the same time, thus making the most of the time available.

Activity logs

Activity logs are also a useful tool to identify where time is spent and, more crucially, to identify where time is wasted (Mind Tools, 2016c). Every single task or activity should be logged on a table using the following headings:

- date and time
- description
- feelings (e.g. energetic, tired)
- duration and value (high, medium, low or none).

This should be done for at least a week and should include everything from checking e-mails, chatting with colleagues, dealing with customers or carrying out project work. At the end of the week, when the data is analysed, it should highlight trends such as how much time is spent on low-value activities and also help the individual identify the times of day when they feel the most energetic or focused, so that more challenging activities can be scheduled accordingly. This learning can be used to help organize to-do lists and work schedules and can highlight low-value tasks which could be delegated or eliminated completely.

Table 83.1 *Examples of online time management tools*

Tool name and web link	Description	Costs
Evernote https://evernote.com	You can take notes, track tasks, and save things you find online.	Basic free version. Subscription Plus, Premium or Business.
Remember the Milk www.rememberthemilk.com	App which can create simple to-do lists. Can link to Evernote account and Google Calendar.	Basic free version. Subscription to Pro account.
Todoist https://en.todoist.com	App enables you to access tasks from anywhere and collaborate on shared tasks with others. Simple, clear to-do lists.	Basic free version. Subscription to Business and Premium accounts.
Toodledo www.toodledo.com	Powerful task manager which enables you to create simple or complex to-do lists.	Basic free version. Subscription to Silver, Gold and Platinum accounts.
Wunderlist www.wunderlist.com	Create to do lists, set regular alarms and share tasks with others.	Basic free version. Subscription to Pro and Business accounts.

Tools

There are loads of paper-based tools such as diaries, calendars and wall-planners which can help to schedule work more effectively. Online calendars can also be shared across your service and can be useful to share information about training courses, annual leave and team projects, often providing the functionality to share tasks, set reminders and allocate workload. Creating a weekly action plan with timescales, or a weekly activity schedule (Chapman, 2016) for individuals and teams, can be useful to ensure that work is completed on time and progress can be monitored via team and one-to-one meetings.

In addition to some of the more traditional methods for organizing work listed above, there are increasing numbers of online task management tools (see Table 83.1), also available as apps that can be downloaded to mobile phones and shared across other devices such as tablets, iPhones, iPads and laptops. These tools can be really useful to help keep a range of activities on track, and can also enable tasks to be shared with other people. Many of the tools identified offer basic free versions in addition to advanced features which can be subscribed to. Whichever tool is used, this will be influenced by individual preference, so we would suggest that you signpost them to your teams and encourage them to explore those available so that they can choose the best fit for them.

🖒 Best for

- Staying organized and keeping on track of the workloads of you and your teams.
- Prioritizing work to ensure that the most urgent tasks are scheduled appropriately.

▶ More

- There is no 'one size fits all' and different approaches will work for different team members, so allow each individual to find an approach which suits their preferences.
- In order to try some of these approaches, valuable time needs to be spent in the preparation phase, so it is important that this is taken into consideration.

⚠ To think about

- Some online tools may not be accessible at work, so it is important to check this out with local IT teams. If apps are blocked on work devices some of the online apps listed will not work effectively for your teams.

References

Chapman, A. (2016) *Time Management,* www.businessballs.com/time.htm. [Accessed 3 April 2016]

Mind Tools (2016a) *Time Management,* www.mindtools.com/pages/main/newMN_HTE.htm. [Accessed 3 April 2016]

Mind Tools (2016b) *Eisenhower's Urgent/Important Principle,* www.mindtools.com/pages/article/newHTE_91.htm. [Accessed 3 April 2016]

Mind Tools (2016c) *Activity Logs,* www.mindtools.com/pages/article/newHTE_03.htm. [Accessed 3 April 2016]

Further reading

Allen, D. (2001) *Getting Things Done,* Piatkus, London.

Acknowledgements

Thank you to Lisa Jeskins Training (www.lisajeskinstraining.com) for sharing time management training materials to assist with this section.

84. Training courses – attending

TRADITIONALLY **DEVELOPMENT OF** staff was associated with attendance at a formally taught training course. Hopefully this book will have demonstrated that there are many other ways of developing staff, but formal training courses still have their place.

Monster (2016), the employment website, identifies formal training as bringing the following four main benefits to individuals, teams and organizations:

- improved productivity and adherence to quality standards
- employees develop skill sets that allow them to undertake a greater variety of work
- improved ability to implement and realize specific goals outlined in a company's business plan
- increased ability to respond effectively to change.

Broadly speaking, this type of training can be divided into internally and externally delivered courses. Some of the internally delivered courses may be mandatory and staff will have no choice as to whether or not to attend them. It is still important to discuss mandatory training with your staff to ensure that they have learned what they were supposed to learn and to feed back to the training providers any issues or unmet needs. With other types of internal training individuals will have the option to attend or not.

For both external and self-selecting internal courses, a discussion will need to take place between the staff member and you as the line manager to agree why the individual wants to attend the training. This discussion should include the benefits that the training will bring to the individual, the team and the organization. It is important to be clear about the time commitment required and how the learning will be applied after the course is completed. Some courses will require pre- or post-course work and arrangements will need to be made to accommodate this as appropriate.

There are often cost implications associated with this type of training. Some internal courses might be charged back to your training budget, depending on the system in operation at your organization. For many external courses, though not all, there will be a fee and there could also be associated travel and accommodation requirements, depending on the location and duration of the course. Training budgets in many organizations have been cut in recent years. If you are in a position to access money for training for your staff you will need to be clear that this type of course is the best way of spending the money and that opportunities are fairly shared across the team. This is where having a development plan for your team can come in handy, as you will be clear about how important the proposed training will be in meeting the strategic aims of the individual, the team and the wider organization.

If you agree that it is appropriate for the individual to attend the course then you will need to set a time and date to speak with them on their return. This is to check their learning and ensure that it can be put in place and/or shared with others, depending on what was agreed.

Attending formal training events does not just develop staff in the skills, knowledge and behaviours outlined in the course aims and objectives. Staff will perceive that by investing in their development in this way the organization values them. This will strengthen their feelings of engagement with the organization and can enhance the organization's reputation, which will be beneficial in terms of recruitment and retention.

Attendance at internal courses can be a good way of getting to know people working in other teams and enhance an individual's understanding of the way their organization works. Both internal and external courses will have benefits in terms of improving communication and networking skills. Sharing the learning with other team members will develop the individual's own training skills. The benefit of attending a course could be further enhanced by asking the individual to write an article for a blog or newsletter about the training experience and the difference it has made to them in the workplace.

Example from practice: Sarah Cross – LKS assistant (NHS)

I wanted to improve the inductions I deliver to Trust staff so I attended a two-day course on how to deliver meaningful inductions. Day One of the training was about what we (the participants) thought made a good induction – and what didn't! As well as this, there was a lot of discussion about how different inductions were, despite the fact that we were all talking about very similar subjects. Two of the first and important ideas that we focused on were:

- What do we want people to remember/know from our induction?
- How do we want them to feel?

This brought home to me the fact that induction really isn't about trying to tell people everything that you do and shove it into the allotted time you have. In fact, sometimes less can be more, if you give your audience clear, concise and relevant information.

Our task after the first day was to prepare an induction session that we would share on Day Two, to be reviewed by the rest of the group. I'll admit I was nervous at the thought, but also enthused by all of the new ideas that had come to mind. When Day Two came and it was time to actually present the inductions I was still enthused about something which can, if we're not careful, become routine and rote. On the day, watching other people's presentations, it was great to see how different they were, even with a similar subject matter and a similar audience in mind in some cases. No two presentations were anything like the same.

When it came to my turn, I didn't feel like I would be doing the same thing as others, which I did find a little surprising. We had all managed to utilize what we'd learnt from the first day in different ways. The comments from the group were positive, thank goodness (!), and really supportive and helpful.

The course wasn't just full of lots of ideas and tips but also it was a friendly and good place to try out new ideas and get constructive and useful feedback about changes you'd made and things you might not even notice, going over and over something yourself. At the end of the two days I had not one but three new inductions that I can go forward and use with confidence thanks to the trainer and everyone else who attended!

👍 Best for

■ Time away from the day-to-day work environment to develop skills, knowledge and behaviours within a structured environment which can then be shared and implemented in the workplace.

▶ More

■ If a requirement for a particular training course has been identified in a significant number of individuals then commissioning your own event could be the most cost-effective way of meeting this need. See Tip 85 below for further information.

References

Monster (2016) *How Can Training Courses be Used as a Company Benefit?*, http://hiring.monster.co.uk/hr/hr-best-practices/workforce-management/ employee-pay-benefits/how-can-training-courses-be-used-as-a-company-benefit.aspx. [Accessed 9 April 2016]

Further reading

CIPD (2015) *Learning Transfer*, www.cipd.co.uk/toolclicks/learning/training-tools/learning-transfer/default.aspx. [Accessed 9 April 2016]

85. Training courses – commissioning

IF THERE IS a development need which is common to a significant number of staff then it might be more time- and cost-effective to commission an event.

This could be with an internal trainer or an externally sourced provider. Commissioning training can result in a very high standard of development for staff but can be expensive and time-consuming to plan.

Planning

If you decide to go down the route of commissioning training there are a number of things you will need to consider, the first of which is to clearly identify the training need and how you feel it can best be addressed. Only go down the training course route if you are sure this is the best way to proceed.

Secondly, you need to decide who will deliver the training. Do you need someone who understands your organization and/or sector or is specialist knowledge of the topic more important? For example, if you are looking to commission training on marketing do you want someone with a marketing background or someone with a LKS background who has done marketing as part of their role? If you are commissioning someone you have not used before then you will need to get references from people who have used their services in the past and follow these up.

Once you have identified your trainer you will need to work with them to agree the aims, objectives and content for the course. This can take time, as you need to be absolutely clear about what it is you want individuals to take away from the training and what changes you want to witness in terms of knowledge, skills and behaviours.

Cost

If you are using an external trainer there will be a cost involved. It is good practice and helps avoid any misunderstanding if you ask the trainer for a full quote which includes a breakdown of planning and delivery costs, travel and other expenses, plus the costs of any supporting material. Some trainers will be VAT registered and some will not, and this needs to be made clear in the quote. In some organizations you may need to source a number of quotes from different trainers to meet your procurement requirements. If you want to use a particular trainer but find they are too expensive do not be afraid to negotiate. Be honest with the trainer about why you are asking for the reduction. It is then up to the trainer to decide whether this is still a viable project for them if they reduce their costs.

Practical considerations

In addition to agreeing the course outcomes with the trainer there will be a number of practical considerations to take into account. These include:

- When the training will take place. It needs to occur as close to when the learning can be put into practice as possible and give participants enough time to absorb the changes they will need to implement.
- Where the training will take place. If you decide to use an external venue then you will need to visit it before the event to check if it is suitable for your requirements.
- The layout of the room. This will need to be agreed with the trainer and will depend on the type of course.
- What refreshments will be required and when they will be served.
- Any equipment requirements of the trainer. If you are using an external venue you might be charged extra for laptops or other electrical equipment, so it is important to check these in advance.

Prior to the course taking place you will need to work with the trainer to finalize all arrangements. If any pre-course work is needed you need to ensure that attendees have time to complete it and that they are clear about why they are being asked to do this preparatory work. You will need to agree with the trainer how the course will be evaluated and at what point this will take place. On the day of the course it is a good idea for the trainer to have a named contact. If you are not attending the course yourself, this person can troubleshoot any issues and assist with some of the practicalities such as registration.

Evaluation

Once the course has taken place you will need to evaluate it in terms of whether or not the trainer delivered what you asked for and if the training has resulted in the desired changes to skills, knowledge and behaviour. This will probably mean undertaking two different evaluations. One can take place as soon as the course has finished and can follow the standard 'happy sheet' evaluation which checks that participants were satisfied that the course met the advertised aims and objectives, felt the teaching style was suitable and that the venue was appropriate. The findings from this initial evaluation should be fed back to the trainer as soon as possible and any issues addressed.

The second piece of evaluation relates to the workplace and should focus on what is being done differently as a result of the training and what benefits this has bought to the individual, team and organization. There are a number of different ways of addressing this (see References and Further Reading below and Tip 10, p. 23, about Kirkpatrick's evaluation model), but the easiest within a team is generally through observation and one-to-ones. To ensure that change does occur and becomes embedded within working practices the team needs to get together as soon as possible after the training has taken place. They should agree how they will put the learning into action and how they will monitor the impact of the changes on their day-to-day service delivery.

👍 Best for

■ Standardizing training across a group so you know they have all been told the same things in the same way.

▶ More

■ If you have identified a need which applies to other LKSs, consider buddying up with others to put on the training together. This could cut costs for individual organizations and enhance the learning experience for individuals by exposing them to working practices and experiences from other services.
■ Alternatively, think about charging individuals from external institutions as a means of covering costs. You need to consider this carefully, as there are issues around what to charge and the amount of work involved in collecting payment. You need to be sure that following this route will generate income and not just create extra work.
■ If you don't have the time or resources to commission an event then talk to local or specialist networks, such as CILIP's regional Member networks (2014a) and Special Interest Groups (2014b), to see if they can assist in any way.

⚠ To think about

■ Proceed with caution when commissioning courses to solve problems. You need to be absolutely sure about where the issue lies before going down this route. A common example is commissioning a customer care course to improve relations between staff and users when the actual problem lies in the framework or system the staff are being asked to work within. In such cases training the staff in how to deal with people will not solve the problem unless changes are made to the system itself.

References

CILIP (2014a) *Regional Member Networks*, http://cilip.org.uk/about/regional-member-networks. [Accessed 9 April 2016]
CILIP (2014b) *Special Interest Groups*, http://cilip.org.uk/about/special-interest-groups. [Accessed 9 April 2016]

Further reading

CIPD (2015) *Evaluating Training*, www.cipd.co.uk/toolclicks/learning/training-tools/evaluating-training/default.aspx. [Accessed 9 April 2016]

CIPD (2015) *Planning and Designing Training*,
www.cipd.co.uk/toolclicks/learning/training-tools/planning-designing-
training/default.aspx. [Accessed 9 April 2016]

86. Training courses – planning, delivering and evaluating

RUNNING INTERNAL TRAINING courses is a means of developing the skills of those delivering them and sharing their knowledge across the team and organization to develop others. This Tip provides a brief overview of planning, delivering and evaluating training courses. See Further Reading below (p. 231) for references to more detailed information on this topic.

Planning

The first step in running a training course is to plan it. The basic steps required to plan an effective course are outlined in Figure 86.1.

Having an understanding of how people learn and the different training methods available are crucial when planning training courses. The first section of this book outlines a number of different theories as to how people like to learn and the factors which can influence their behaviour. Discuss with your staff member their preferred style of learning and what impact this could have on the way they are likely to deliver the training. For example, if they lean towards a theorist approach they will be naturally inclined to

Figure 86.1 *Steps to planning a training course*

include exercises that would appeal to theorists. For a well balanced session they need to include exercises and activities that will appeal to all learning styles (see Tips 2–4, pp 4–12).

The staff member planning a training course needs to be clear when setting the aims and objectives about what it is they want the individuals attending the course to learn and do differently as a result of participating in the training. As always, objectives should be SMART (see Tip 25, p. 59). If the training is for a specific department or team then encourage your staff member to collaborate with these individuals or their managers in advance, to agree the objectives and begin to build engagement prior to the taught session.

When the staff member starts to plan exercises, emphasize the importance of incorporating a variety of different types of activities which will encourage

Table 86.1 *Howard Gardner's multiple intelligence theory, adapted from Chapman (2016)*

Intelligence type	Description	Related tasks, activities or tests	Preferred learning style clues
Linguistic	**Words and language**, written and spoken; retention, interpretation and explanation of ideas and information via language, understands relationship between communication and meaning.	Write a set of instructions; speak on a subject; edit a written piece or work; write a speech; commentate on an event; apply positive or negative 'spin' to a story.	Words and language
Logical-mathematical	**Logical thinking**, detecting patterns, scientific reasoning and deduction; analyses problems, performs mathematical calculations, understands relationship between cause and effect towards a tangible outcome or result.	Perform a mental arithmetic calculation; create a process to measure something difficult; analyse how a machine works; create a process; devise a strategy to achieve an aim; assess the value of a business or a proposition.	Numbers and logic
Musical	**Musical ability**, awareness, appreciation and use of sound; recognition of tonal and rhythmic patterns, understands relationship between sound and feeling.	Perform a musical piece; sing a song; review a musical work; coach someone to play a musical instrument; specify mood music for telephone systems and receptions.	Music, sounds, rhythm
Bodily-kinaesthetic	**Body movement control**, manual dexterity, physical agility and balance; eye and body co-ordination.	Juggle; demonstrate a sports technique; flip a beer-mat; create a mime to explain something; toss a pancake; fly a kite; coach workplace posture, assess work-station ergonomics.	Physical experience and movement, touch and feel
Spatial-visual	**Visual and spatial perception**; interpretation and creation of visual images; pictorial imagination and expression; understands relationship between images and meanings, and between space and effect.	Design a costume; interpret a painting; create a room layout; create a corporate logo; design a building; pack a suitcase or the boot of a car.	Pictures, shapes, images, 3D space
Interpersonal	**Perception of other people's feelings**; ability to relate to others; interpretation of behaviour and communications; understands the relationships between people and their situations, including other people.	Interpret moods from facial expressions; demonstrate feelings through body language; affect the feelings of others in a planned way; coach or counsel another person.	Human contact, communications, co-operation, teamwork
Intrapersonal	Self-awareness, personal cognisance, personal objectivity, the capability to understand oneself, one's relationship to others and the world, and one's own need for, and reaction to, change.	Consider and decide one's own aims and personal changes required to achieve them (not necessarily reveal this to others); consider one's own 'Johari Window' (see References and Further Reading below, p. 231), and decide options for development; consider and decide one's own position in relation to the Emotional Intelligence model.	Self-reflection, self-discovery

all those present to participate in and engage with the training. Howard Gardner's multiple intelligence theory (Chapman, 2016) identifies seven different intelligence types; thinking about these when developing exercises can be a good starting point. Not every part of the session needs to cover all of the intelligences, but using Table 86.1 to look at the planned session with your staff member will ensure that they have not focused on one or two intelligence types at the expense of the others.

Recommend to your staff member that they draw up a training plan in advance of a session. This should include timings, planned activities and resources. They should produce a plan regardless of how big or small the training group will be. One-to-one sessions often require as much planning as larger sessions, depending on the topic. It is a good idea to include additional exercises in the plan in case something takes less time than they think it might or they need to try a different method of getting their point

Table 86.2 *Training plan, adapted from Bradshaw and Jeskins*

Training Plan for Surviving and Thriving During Change
Objectives: At the end of the workshop you will be able to:
- recognize your personal change style type and how that impacts on the way you react to change
- identify the key elements of resilience and explore ways to build your personal resources to cope during times of change
- recognize signs of stress in yourself and others and how to use a range of coping mechanisms to deal with it
- reflect on what elements of the changes are within your control, explore the options to manage them and develop a plan of action.

Time	Title	To Cover	Resources	Who
09.30–10.00	Welcome and icebreaker	• Welcome and introductions • Housekeeping • Outline of the workshop		Lisa and Claire
		• Complete the Change Styles questionnaire • Ask delegates to stand in a line depending on the result • Brief discussion about the differences	Change Styles questionnaire	Claire
10.30–11.15	Developing our resources (filling up the reservoir)	• Briefly talk through the four key resource areas – financial, social support, skills and experience, health • Individually rate each area out of 10 for how well developed that resource area is for you • In groups, brainstorm ways the area could be developed (be as creative as possible!) and write them on a flipchart	Strengthening Our Personal Resources handout	Claire to introduce Lisa and Claire to facilitate groups Lisa to get them to stick on wall and look round
11.30–12.00	Next steps	• Brief input on the circles of control and influence and on the power of choice • Go back to your concern chart and decide which circle each of those issues is in • Look at all the things in your control and influence and decide the first step to move each one forward		Claire to introduce Lisa and Claire to help with individual action planning Lisa to close

across. The example plan in Table 86.2 shows the opening and closing sessions, plus an example of how to plan an exercise for a half-day session delivered by two trainers on 'Surviving and Thriving During Change'.

When it comes to delivering a course there are a number of factors to take into consideration. In addition to the practical considerations outlined in the previous Tip (p. 222) on commissioning training, your staff member will need to take into account the size of the group. Delivering one-to-one training can be very different to training a group. If they are training a colleague in how to do an aspect of their role then it is important that they give this the same consideration that they would when training someone external to the team.

Group size

If your team member(s) are working with a group then the way they structure their session will depend on the size of the group. They should aim to make the session as interactive as they can, as there seems to be evidence that interaction results in learners retaining up to 80% of the information delivered as opposed to 15% retention in a purely taught session. With smaller groups this might involve moving people around to ensure they work with as many different people as possible and building in opportunities which will enable everyone to contribute and feed back on exercises. Interaction can be harder to achieve with large groups, particularly if the session takes place in a lecture theatre-style environment. Ways of introducing interaction with big groups include using polls or votes, asking people to talk to the people sitting nearest and providing plenty of opportunities for asking questions.

Evaluation

The final step is to evaluate the training. As outlined in the previous Tip (p. 222), this should ideally consist of more than one activity. It is important to get immediate feedback to enable your staff to check that participants were satisfied that the course met their requirements. They should use this feedback to review their training and implement any required changes in future sessions.

The skills developed by attendees will vary, depending on the training delivered. At a later date you will need to check what is being done differently as a result of the training delivered by your staff and what benefits this has brought to the individual, team and organization. There are a number of different ways of addressing this (see References and Further Reading, p. 231 below and Tip 10, p. 23, on Kirkpatrick's evaluation model).

The skills developed by those delivering the training will include planning, time management, presentation, evaluation and communication skills. As their line manager it is good practice to talk to the person delivering the training about any particular skills they are aiming to develop and how they will demonstrate progress. For example if they are aiming to improve their presentation skills then you might suggest asking a colleague to sit in on the session to give them feedback or to incorporate a session on delivery into the feedback form. You will need to follow this up with them after the training has taken place.

🖒 Best for

■ Running internal training courses enables the individuals delivering them to develop their skills and to share their specialist knowledge with other individuals and teams. This will deliver benefits across the wider organization and enhance the reputation of you and your team.

▶ More

■ It is important to think about how the training will be promoted as part of the planning activity. Consider how the individuals the training is aimed at are communicated with across the organization and feed into those channels. Make use of newsletters, organizational social media channels and any other form of communication available to your team. Put promotional flyers in communal areas such as coffee shops or canteens. If the training is targeting a particular group or team, then ask the trainer to visit a team meeting or suggest they talk to the people who have influence over that group, such as a line manager or a lecturer. When writing promotional material remind individuals to sell the benefits of attending the training as opposed to simply listing what they are planning to deliver.

■ Discuss with your team ways of embedding their training in other sessions. This might include delivering training as part of a team meeting or away day or negotiating a slot on a formally taught course.

⚠ To think about

■ Ensure your team members regularly review their training sessions to keep them fresh and relevant. Use the feedback from the evaluation forms to analyse what changes former participants would suggest. As trainers it is important that they participate in training themselves to get ideas for different exercises and methods of delivery. Encourage the trainers on your team to find opportunities to talk with colleagues, both internal and external, about how to make training sessions engaging and a valuable use of the attendees' time.

References

Chapman, A. (2016) *Howard Gardner's Multiple Intelligences*,
www.businessballs.com/howardgardnermultipleintelligences.htm. [Accessed 10 April 2016]

Further reading

Blanchett, H., Powis, C. and Webb, J. (2011) *A Guide to Teaching Information Literacy: 101 tips*, Facet Publishing, London.
Chapman, A. (2016) *Johari Window*,
www.businessballs.com/johariwindowmodel.htm. [Accessed 20 April 2016]
CIPD (2015) *Evaluating Training*, www.cipd.co.uk/toolclicks/learning/
training-tools/evaluating-training/default.aspx. [Accessed 9 April 2016]
CIPD (2015) *Planning and Designing Training*,
www.cipd.co.uk/toolclicks/learning/training-tools/planning-designing-training/default.aspx. [Accessed 9 April 2016]

Acknowledgements

Many thanks to Deborah Dalley, from Deborah Dalley and Associates – www.deborahdalley.com – for permission to base this Tip on her 'Training the Trainer' course.

Thanks are also due to Lisa Jeskins (www.lisajeskinstraining.com) and Claire Bradshaw (https://clairembradshaw.wordpress.com) for permission to reproduce part of the training plan from their 'Surviving and Thriving During Change' course.

87. Twitter

TWITTER IS A microblogging service that was launched in 2006. In January 2014 it was reported that 80% of world leaders are using Twitter (Scherr, 2014) and according to Taylor & Francis (2014) it is the second most popular social media tool used by LKS.

Twitter is a communication channel; it allows you to write short 140-character-long messages for the people who are following you to read. Being able to use Twitter will enable staff to develop skills and knowledge in areas of the PKSB that cover communication, networking and media and PR skills (CILIP, 2014. Sections 12.5, 12.6 and 12.7).

Many people believe that Twitter is all about what people had for lunch, pictures of cats or finding out 'who did what to whom' at a celebrity shindig. However, there is a large and enthusiastic community of LKS professionals out there who are sharing their knowledge, best practice, interesting articles and useful tools with each other. They are hosting library chats and journal groups, or they are helping each other to become Chartered. A number of useful hashtags are listed below. There is a lot of great (but informal) CPD out there that staff can get involved in. Encouraging your staff to use Twitter means they will be able to access all sorts of information useful for their professional development, including sector knowledge and informal learning. If you can't afford to send staff to key conferences, they can follow what is happening from the office for free!

Networking

Twitter is a great tool for networking. There are all sorts of librarians on Twitter and if you and your staff follow them, you can join in any conversation that interests you. You can ask questions or organize meetings with people who might be involved in similar projects. A librarian on Twitter starts to develop a wider knowledge of their profession as they start to connect with a broader range of people. Staff will get to know LKS professionals from other sectors, which is fantastic for cross-pollination of ideas. Twitter is gaining in popularity and lots of people are using it. Ensuring that your staff know how their LKS users are accessing information is key.

Table 87.1 *Useful LKS Twitter accounts and hashtags*

Twitter accounts you and your staff can follow	
• @CILIPinfo • @ALALibrary • @BritishLibrary	• @BL_Ref_Services • @librarycongress • @slaeurope or @SLAhq
• Look for your regional and special-interest groups too: @uksla, @infolitgroup, @CILIPPMLG, @CILIPldn, @CILIPnw etc.	
Hashtags to investigate	
• #savelibraries • #infolit • #uklibchat	• #chartership • #llrg (LKS leadership reading group)
• List of US LKS chats: https://magic.piktochart.com/output/2617218-library-twitter-chats-2	

Table 87.1 shows a number of useful Twitter accounts and hashtags. The @ symbol which you see before the usernames below enables users to direct a tweet or response to a specific person. The # symbol is used to categorize a tweet and allocate a subject. The latter is useful if staff want to browse conversations on a specific topic or issue, as by clicking on it they will see all related tweets.

Handy tips for using Twitter
• Add a profile picture rather than keeping the default image of an egg.

Some people use an avatar or a cartoon as representation of themselves if they don't want to use a photo, but the default image will put people off following the account.

- Write an informative bio which outlines who you are and what you do; it will also make it easier for people to search for you.
- Make it part of a routine. 'I will look at Twitter every day, Monday to Friday at 8.45 a.m. for 15 minutes'.
- Use the search function (although it is quite basic) to search for a subject or look for people to follow.
- Find someone who is the expert in their field and look at who they are following. You can 'steal' their list of followers.
- Follow conferences that cover subjects you are interested in. Find out what the hashtag is, as people will tweet their conference notes.
- Follow people and organizations similar to yourself and with similar interests.
- If you are thinking of tweeting for your organization, follow similar institutions and see how they do it. Choose your favourite and emulate them.

Example from practice:
Bethan Ruddock – LKS professional (adapted from Ruddock, 2010)

I first joined Twitter in March 2008, when I was a library student at MMU. I realized no one I knew was on it, and did nothing with it for about 6 months, when it started being talked about in the media. So, I started following my friend Kendra, and Stephen Fry, who at that point had a mere 50,000 followers or so, and followed everyone back. Well, I was so overwhelmed that Stephen Fry was following me on Twitter that I promptly ran away again, and didn't dare tweet for months.

I started using Twitter as an information professional in February 2009. Looking at my followers list, it starts off slowly, with colleagues, and then a few external contacts, and then gradually my followers build up and up and up – and most of them are people I've never met. My very first tweet – which said 'Bethan is discovering that no one she knows is on Twitter, which makes it kind of pointless' couldn't have been more wrong. I now rely on Twitter for a large amount of my professional interaction and networking, and I have to admit that I can't really remember the early days!

In 2010 I was named as a Rising Star of SLA. When the announcement of the Rising Stars came through, I didn't tweet about it. I didn't need to – my peers did it for me. I find my Twitter group wonderfully encouraging and supportive – always ready to tout any triumphs that peers and friends have had. So, my Twitter group tweeted it, and SLA and SLA Europe blogged it, and soon I got a message on Twitter from Debby Raven, editor of *Gazette*, saying 'congratulations', and asking if I'd like to be interviewed for *Gazette* about the award. I said 'yes', told her my e-mail address, and it went on from there. I'd never met Debby, and our original point of contact was purely social media-based. Of course, once the article was published I didn't need to promote it either – again, my Twitter group promoted it for me, and I gained loads of exposure – and a reputation for modesty!

In 2010 I did some research on the value of peer networks in preparation for a talk I delivered at the CDG New Professionals conference and the responses echoed my own experiences of using Twitter. Respondents said that they had been invited to speak at events, become involved in committees, written articles, given presentations and become involved in projects – directly through their use of Twitter. Other advantages of using Twitter included keeping people up to date; providing quick and easily accessible sources of good information; providing a wider perspective on the profession; being great places to make friends and meet like-minded info profs; helping with CILIP Chartership and Fellowship; and finding out about resources, projects and events.

Funnily enough I 'know' more new professionals this way than I do in 'real life' in my own region. So I find a sense of community in this online network and that helps me to feel motivated and engaged with professional issues; to feel that I am a librarian rather than someone who just happens to work in a library. I've become more reflective about my professional activities and I think I've also become more ambitious because I am tapped into the interesting things my peers are doing.

👍 Best for

- ■ Informal learning:
    - — learning about new technologies/software
    - — finding useful articles and blog posts
    - — following conferences.
- ■ Networking and promoting your LKS.

▶ More

- ■ Give staff time and permission to use Twitter at work.
- ■ If you have a Twitter account, lead by example and make sure staff know you think it is an important tool.
- ■ Create your own Twitter chat with staff, so that they know what to do if they want to join a more global chat. It would also help staff to practise using Twitter. (You could post a link to a topical journal article and discuss it).
- ■ Becoming confident in using Twitter for CPD will mean that if you decide that

you want to use Twitter for marketing your service or engaging with customers, your staff will already know how to use Twitter and may even have some creative ideas for the service.

A To think about

- The quality of your timeline (the stuff you read) is only as good as the accounts you have chosen to follow. If you are not getting useful information, unfollow accounts and try someone new.
- It can take time to see the benefit of being on Twitter. It doesn't work if you go in once for 5 minutes and then try again 6 weeks later. Encourage people to go in to their account every day for at least 2 weeks.

References

CILIP (2014) *PKSB*, www.cilip.org.uk/sites/default/files/Professional% 20Knowledge%20and%20Skills%20Base.pdf. [Accessed 2 March 2015]

Ruddock, B. (2010) *Growing up in Public: social media for professional development*, https://bethaninfoprof.wordpress.com/2010/08/05/growing-up-in-public-social-media-for-professional-development. [Accessed 16 June 2016]

Scherr, R. (2014) *Report: 80% of World Leaders Now Using Twitter*, www.dmwmedia.com/news/2014/01/03/report-80-of-world-leaders-now-using-twitter. [Accessed 22 April 2016]

Taylor & Francis (2014) *Use of Social Media by the Library: current practices and future opportunities: a white paper*, www.tandf.co.uk/libsite/whitePapers/socialMedia. [Accessed 2 March 2015].

Further reading

Haigh, J. (2014) *How Twitter has Contributed to my Professional Development*, https://jessdoeschartership.wordpress.com/2015/04/17/how-twitter-has-contributed-to-my-professional-development. [Accessed 22 April 2016]

88. Twitter chats

GETTING INVOLVED IN Twitter chats is a great way to learn and a good way to encourage reflection on learning. They are also a great way of building personal networks. You could set up your own Twitter chat to provide a learning opportunity for yourself, your team members and other LKS staff in the wider network. To do this you need to create a hashtag, tell people about it, tell them what you are going to talk about and set up a time for you all to 'meet'. Then you would all tweet using the chat hashtag.

People are using Twitter chats to discuss topical news or subjects in the profession but also as book clubs and journal clubs. Public and school libraries have even organized author chats with children's and young adult's authors. There are several established Twitter chats that you and your staff can get involved in and they will often set an agenda, a number of questions or a topic for people to prepare for:

- #uklibchat @uklibchat
- #chartership chat
- #edchatuk
- #ukmedlibs @UKMedLibs.

Staff who are undergoing Chartership find the Chartership chat very useful, as they can ask questions and get support from other Chartership candidates.

In addition to participating in LKS Twitter chats, you can encourage staff within your teams to join conversations that your users are involved in. In the health sector, for example, health professionals may participate in journal club discussions such as #TwitJC or join conversations facilitated by #Wenurses or #WeAHPs. LKS staff can join or observe these discussions to develop their skills in critical appraisal, get ideas for delivery and develop their understanding of LKS users.

Example from practice: Tom Roper – LKS professional (NHS)

Inspired by the US #medlibs chat, and by ones like the British #uklibchat and #chartership chats, three of us set up #ukmedlibs, meeting monthly. Participants say they value the informality – 'you don't have to worry about talking with your mouth full', said one – and between April 2015 and June 2016 302 people have participated, easily the number that might attend a good-sized professional conference. Following a fast-paced chat can be challenging, so good facilitation is important, and compressing thoughts and communicating clearly within the discipline of 140 characters is a skill that needs to be mastered. Practice makes perfect.

We gather statistics on the chats which show we have had, as at June 2016, 2.3 million tweet impressions. Participants value the ability to discuss professional issues in a new and informal way. Some have cited participation in chats in portfolios for professional accreditation and revalidation. Indeed, participation in every chat over a year would give at least 12 hours towards CILIP's required 20 hours a year of CPD activity.

👍 Best for

- Sharing your learning and experiences with peers in other organizations.
- Useful for networking with other LKS staff and your users.

⚠ To think about

- Remember, if you are creating a hashtag, to search for it first before announcing it to everyone. Check it's not a real word that people would add to any tweet and run it by someone else to make sure it can't be misconstrued. A football team started doing a Friday 'ask a footballer a question' slot and they used the tag – #ask*footballersname*, which was fine when it was #askStephen or #askJohan. On the day it was #askJesus, the tag was hijacked and used for hundreds of Jesus and Bible-related puns.

Further reading

Sewell, C. (2015) #*Chartership Chat – 30/3/15*, www.librarianintraining.com/
2015/03/chartership-chat-30315.html. [Accessed 22 April 2016]

89. VLEs

A Virtual Learning Environment (VLE) is a collection of integrated tools enabling the management of online learning, providing a delivery mechanism, student tracking, assessment and access to resources.

Jisc, 2006, 5

Table 89.1 *Advantages of using a VLE (Jisc, 2006, 8–9 and 30–1)*

For tutors	For learners
• Enhanced collaboration and communication. • Active engagement with learners. • Building a community of learners. • Specific signposting to a wide variety of resources. • Administrative tools which allow tutors to see how often learners have accessed the VLE and what material they have engaged with. • Can save time.	• Enables better time management. • Accommodates different learning styles. • Access to a wide range of learning and development materials. • Immediate feedback through the use of multimedia such as quizzes and simulations. • Can allow increased and faster learning. • Can enhance the face-to-face experience.

VLEs ARE MOST commonly used in education but do have applications in other sectors. As with many of the tools and activities in this section, using a VLE provides opportunities for individuals as a learner and in developing materials and/or courses for delivery through the VLE. VLEs have been identified as bringing a number of advantages to the learning process for both tutors and learners, as shown in Table 89.1.

In recent years a wide range of learning opportunities have become available through the introduction of VLEs and their associated platforms. MOOCs (Massive Online Open Courses) are frequently delivered using this type of technology and can offer development opportunities for individuals which they would not have previously been able to access.

If you are managing individuals who are undertaking work-related training accessed via a VLE then you do need to ensure that they have protected time to undertake the training and any related activity. The same procedures need to be in place as those you would follow

Step 1	• Analyse requirements
Step 2	• Define learning objectives
Step 3	• Decide on approaches
Step 4	• Write content outline
Step 5	• Write story board
Step 6	• Develop
Step 7	• Quality assurance review
Step 8	• Launch

Figure 89.1
Process for developing e-learning materials (Kelsall, 2015)

for more traditional training activities, including monitoring the learning which is taking place and discussing ways it can be applied in the workplace and how it is to be shared with others.

Developing materials and resources for VLEs will develop a wide range of skills for individuals. In addition to the technical skills required, individuals have the opportunity to develop the skills required to make online learning a viable and credible option for learners. Kelsall (2015) outlines the process shown in Figure 89.1 in developing e-learning materials.

Skills and knowledge developed through following that process will include, but are not limited to:

• analytical skills
• knowledge of learning and development theories

- knowledge of the different approaches you could take and how to deliver these; possibilities include using quizzes, videos, case studies, etc.
- understanding how to structure content so it makes sense to the learner
- designing learning activities
- writing skills
- marketing and promotional skills.

A further development opportunity for LKS staff in organizations which use a VLE is to embed LKS resources within courses developed by other teams and departments. Types of resources could include links to 'the online catalogue, electronic resources, information literacy resources and online articles' (Jisc, 2006, 37). Working in partnership in this way will enhance individuals' networking and team-working skills, in addition to demonstrating the added value that LKS staff can bring to the learning experience.

🖒 Best for

- Providing an enhanced learning experience through the 'delivery of learning materials, on-line assessment, [and] communication and collaboration tools' (Moffat, 2004).

▶ More

- It is not always necessary to develop materials and resources from scratch. In recent years a wide range of Open Education Resources (OERs) which 'range from one-page Word documents to complex interactive online tutorials' (CILIP Information Literacy Group, 2015) have been made freely available. These can be used off the shelf or adapted to make them fit for purpose.
- As part of their Member offer CILIP (2016) provide a VLE which allows all Members to:
  — access supporting resources for the Professional Knowledge and Skills Base (PKSB)
  — record the continuing professional development (CPD) they have completed in the past year
  — access online training
  — access the impact toolkit (CILIP, 2015)
  — develop their portfolio for professional registration, access support materials and submit their application online.

⚠ To think about

- VLEs will only provide the advantages listed above if a lot of thought and planning goes into their development and maintenance. They are an enhancement of the learning experience and require as much commitment as standard face-to-face delivery, if not more.

References

CILIP (2015) *Impact Toolkit*, http://cilip.org.uk/membership/benefits/virtual-learning-environment-vle/impact-toolkit. [Accessed 13 March 2016]

CILIP (2016) *Virtual Learning Environment (VLE)*, http://cilip.org.uk/cilip/virtual-learning-environment-vle. [Accessed 13 March 2016]

Jisc (2006) *Effective Use of VLEs: Introduction to VLEs*, http://tools.jiscinfonet.ac.uk/downloads/vle/what-is-vle.pdf. [Accessed 13 March 2016]

Kelsall, J. (2015) *e-Learning Development*, #BlendToLearn, August, https://prezi.com/-ysqqfw9bkku/e-learning-development-blendtolearn-august-2015. [Accessed 16 March 2016]

Moffat, M. (2004) *EEVL News: EEVL, VLEs, institutional and library portals*, www.ariadne.ac.uk/issue39/eevl. [Accessed 16 March 2016]

Further reading

CILIP Information Literacy Group (2015) *Open Educational Resources (OERs)*, www.informationliteracy.org.uk/teaching/oers. [Accessed 16 March 2016]

CILIP Information Literacy Group (2015) *Finding OERs*, www.informationliteracy.org.uk/teaching/oers/finding-oers/. [Accessed 16 March 2016]

CILIP Information Literacy Group (2015) *Using OERs*, www.informationliteracy.org.uk/teaching/oers/using-oers/. [Accessed 17 March 2016]

90. Visits

UNDERTAKING AND HOSTING visits with other LKSs in either the same sector in which you and your team are employed or a different one are a good means of learning about how each other's services operate. Visits can be a cheap and easily organized development activity. Their value can be enhanced by offering attendees the opportunity, if possible, of meeting with their opposite number for an informal chat.

Visits can be used for numerous purposes, including:

- to discover how a service similar to the one you and your team work within is run
- to view a new build or a remodelling of an LKS space
- to see how another LKS runs a service or manages a resource which your service is thinking of introducing
- to learn about the experiences and roles of LKS staff working in other sectors
- as a means of developing wider professional knowledge.

Organizing a visit offers a number of development opportunities for an individual or a small team. Factors to take into account when organizing or hosting a visit include:

- the purpose of the visit
- the number of people participating in the visit
- the date, time and location
- the name of the visit organizer and the contact at the LKS to be visited
- how long the visit will last and what will be included. The itinerary could include a demonstration of a resource or service, an individual meeting with their opposite number and/or a tour of one or more sites.
- transport and refreshment requirements.

Once a visit has taken place it is important that the visiting participants contact the host service to thank the staff for their time. If there was a specific purpose to the visit, such as fact-finding before introducing a new service, then it is good practice to let the LKS visited know what actions were taken as a result.

Asking one of the participants in the visit to write up the experience for a blog or newsletter provides a further development opportunity. This could be further enhanced by asking an individual from the visiting group and one from the host service to work together to produce something which could be shared across both services.

🖒 Best for:

- ■ Gaining an understanding of how other LKS departments operate both within and external to the sector in which you and your team are based.

▶ More:

- ■ Visits do not have to take place in isolation. Working with other services to plan a programme of visits to each other's services can strengthen ties

between services and provide excellent networking opportunities.
- Twinning a visit with other activities such as a meeting can enhance the value of both activities.
- Study tours can offer excellent opportunities to visit a number of different services often, but not always, in a different country. These can be organized on an individual level or there are more formal group opportunities available. CILIP, in partnership with the English Speaking Union (ESU), offers an annual bursary under the title of The Travelling Librarian (2015) which is an 'opportunity for a CILIP Member to build professional relationships between library and information professionals in the UK and their counterparts on a study tour in the United States or a Commonwealth country' (CILIP, 2016).

References

CILIP (2016) *Travelling Librarian Award*,
    www.cilip.org.uk/cilip/membership/membership-benefits/careers-advice-and-support/grants-and-bursaries/travelling. [Accessed 6 March 2016]

Further reading

CILIP (2015) *Travelling Librarian Award Reports*,
    www.cilip.org.uk/cilip/membership/membership-benefits/careers-advice-and-support/grants-and-bursaries/travelling-0. [Accessed 6 March 2016]

91. Volunteering

VOLUNTEERS HAVE CONTRIBUTED successfully to the work of LKS since time immemorial (Forrest, 2012). Volunteering is a good way for your staff to gain skills that they would not necessarily gain in their current role or workplace. This experience can lead to the individual discovering hidden benefits for their own organization and contributes to their own continuing professional development. Volunteering can occur either within working hours by volunteering to help in other areas/departments within the workplace or externally, e.g. job shadowing in another organization or being involved in a committee. These roles can be either long-term or short-term, depending on what the project entails.

Volunteering is an excellent way to fill gaps in skills needed for promotions or new roles (UKLIBCHAT, 2012) and provides volunteers with an opportunity to gain an insight into different sectors. Taking advantage of volunteering opportunities is a great way for individuals to improve their CVs, make professional connections and find out more about working in the

LKS community (CILIP, 2013).

However, it is important that the volunteer does not over commit themselves. Volunteers need to be clear on how much commitment is required from them and how this can be factored into their existing workload.

🖒 Best for

- Gaining skills that wouldn't otherwise be available in the workplace.
- Ongoing professional development.
- Gaining an insight into different sectors.

▶ More

- Helps gain skills needed for career progression.
- Good for networking and making professional connections.

⚠ To think about

- Individuals taking on too much.
- Time management issues.

References

CILIP (2013) *Volunteering,* www.cilip.org.uk/cilip/jobs-and-careers/starting-library-and-information-career/how-become-librarian/getting-2. [Accessed 22 October 2015]

Forrest, M. (2012) Student Volunteers in Academic Libraries, *New Review of Academic Librarianship,* **18** (1), 1–6.

UKLIBCHAT (2012) *Chat Summary – Job Hunting,* https://uklibchat.wordpress.com/2012/06/18/chat-summary-job-hunting. [Accessed 22 October 2015]

92. Webinars

A **WEBINAR IS** defined as a talk on a subject which takes place online, allowing a group of people in different places to watch, listen and sometimes respond simultaneously (Macmillan Dictionary, 2015). Webinars are an economical and efficient way to provide staff education (AWHONN News and Views, 2010), offering a great alternative to traditional courses, which usually involve taking time out of work (including preparation, travel time and overnight stays) and often require funding. Attendance at all-day workshops can leave staff thinly stretched, thus creating hardship for those left staffing the building in their absence.

Webinars (especially archival webinars, which allow staff to watch them at their convenience) address this problem, as they are often not very long and mean that staff do not have to leave their desks or the physical building in order to participate in the learning (Matteson, Schlueter and Hidy, 2013). Furthermore, with ever-decreasing staff development budgets, webinars provide an excellent way to keep up to date with developments without the expense or time commitment required from a course or conference.

There are many webinars covering a multitude of topics, including copyright, MOOCs, discovery services amongst many others. The very nature of the internet means that it is not location-driven, therefore you can take part in webinars broadcast from other parts of the world. However, it is important to be aware of the time zone that it is occurring in so that you do not miss it. It is also important to be aware of any cost implications and to advise staff to check these with their line managers. They may be able to arrange funding as part of personal development and it is worth checking whether the organization is affiliated with the provider, as this can entitle participants to free access.

Webinar providers

Examples of webinar providers include organizations such as the National Information Standards Organization (NISO, 2016) which tend to cover topics such as responsive web design, MOOCs or text mining. Membership is needed to join these webinars, so check whether your organization is a member. Other providers include associations such as the United Kingdom Serial Group (UKSG), which focuses on developments in the serials world such as altmetrics or Creative Commons, and publishers, which focus their webinars on providing training or information about their products, such as ProQuest (see Further Reading).

The profession has a robust range of short-term continuing education offerings, exemplified in webinars, conference sessions and workshops, but programmes of that length do not always contribute to in-depth learning (Matteson, Musser and Allen, 2015); therefore it is important not to rely on them as the sole form of your development but rather as an aid.

⚬ Best for

■ Keeping up to date in your chosen field.
■ Continuous professional development.

▶ **More**

■ You can get answers to specific questions about your particular situation.

■ If the webinar has been recorded you can watch it at your own leisure, thus enabling you to balance your workload.

⚠ **To think about**

■ Ensure that you are aware of the timing of the webinar you have signed up to, especially if it is being broadcast outside your own country.

■ Most webinars are free but some may require membership, so check if this is something your organization subscribes to or if your registration can be paid for if the session is relevant to your work.

References

AWHONN News and Views (2010) Webinars, *Nursing for Women's Health*, **14** (5), 419–21.

Macmillan Dictionary (2015) *Webinar – definition of webinar in English from the Oxford Dictionary*, www.macmillandictionary.com/dictionary/british/webinar. [Accessed 27 July 2015]

Matteson, M. L., Musser, S. and Allen, E. (2015) From Good to Great Managers, *Library Management*, **36** (1/2), 127–41.

Matteson, M. L., Schlueter E. and Hidy, M. (2013) Continuing Education in Library Management: challenges and opportunities, *Library Management*, **34** (3), 219–35.

NISO (2016) *NISO – National Information Standards Organization*, www.niso.org/home. [Accessed 22 April 2016]

Further reading

ProQuest (2016) *NISO ProQuest – Training Webinars*, www.proquest.com/customer-care/training-webinars. [Accessed on 22 April 2016]

UKSG (2016) *UKSG Webinars*, www.uksg.org/webinars. [Accessed on 22 April 2016]

93. Writing blog posts

SETTING UP A personal blog is a great way for your staff to raise their individual profiles, and can be particularly beneficial for continuing professional development activities such as Chartership. Blogs can be used to start discussions and raise awareness on topical issues, can act as a reflection tool to help with learning or will help to develop personal learning networks. Many LKSs now have their own blogs to promote and discuss their service and collections, so any skills in blogging that your staff develop can be used to develop your LKS content. It is an easy way to create original content which can be shared on other social media channels such as Twitter and Facebook.

Content

Ensure that the writer is interested in the content; if they are bored writing about something this will be clear to the audience. For your LKS blog, you can make it more engaging by having different individuals within the team write contributions, although you may need to set some ground rules to ensure that the 'voice' used doesn't differ too widely and there is some consistency. You need to be aware that everything which is posted on your LKS blog is visible to a wider audience, so it is worth deciding on a style and sticking to it.

For personal blogs, advise your staff or colleagues to reflect on something that they have learned. This could be a review of some training they've attended or a conference, but most importantly they must tell their readers how they will apply the learning to practice. It can also be good to reflect on mistakes or failures, particularly if a mistake enabled them to learn something, and this would also be useful evidence for a professional portfolio if individuals are considering Chartership, for example. Readers like to know about the time something went wrong and what individuals will do differently next time or any changes which were made and their impact.

Any blog should be regularly updated with new posts, as this will keep it dynamic and engage the audience. It is also essential that individuals are writing about something they are passionate about, as this will come through to the reader of the post. Remember that a blog doesn't have to be perfect; encourage your writers to have confidence in their early drafts, otherwise there is a danger that they will never end up posting anything. Whilst spelling and grammar should enable easy comprehension, it is best not to be too much of a perfectionist, as blogs are supposed to be quite informal. You can always encourage team members to read and comment on each other's posts before they are published.

Appearance

Blog posts should have attractive headlines, as these will reel their readers in, and the blog should look visually attractive. Including lots of videos and images is a really good way of improving the look of a blog. Ensure that posts are not too text-heavy or overly long, as people will switch off. We live in a world of scanning, so make it easier for people to do so by encouraging individuals to chunk text up and use white space, headings, bullet points, quotes and links to make it easier for people to scan through easily. It can be tempting to try to include every single widget that blogging software provides, but try to discourage this: pages which look overwhelming will lose readers. Thinking about the look of blogs and 'designing' in this way will make them interesting to look at and mean that people are more likely to read what your writers have to say.

Example from practice: Matt Holland – LKS manager (NHS)

I am a regular contributor to the LIHNN Clinical Librarians Blog. Part of the motivation is vanity. As a one-person service I have something to say but no audience to present to. Blogs provide the platform and I provide the ideas. It's a good medium to work with. Short, somewhere between 800 and 1000 words. Lots of structure to get ideas across simply. Brief, clear and straightforward are the watchwords. Read our 16-page library strategy . . . no one ever will. Blogging does improve your writing skills and will help get that strategy down to two sides of high-impact A4.

I blog about things that interest me. Typically, they reflect everyday library activity with a focus on technology. I believe you learn a lot about something when you write about it. For me blogging is a personal and professional development activity. There is real value, too, in sharing and talking about the details of work life and professional practice. How else can we learn or know about what others are doing?

👍 Best for

- Use a personal blog to reflect on your work or your learning and promote your work to your peers.
- Use an LKS blog to write about events and activities and to share thoughts or information which are of interest to your users.

⚠ To think about

- Try and post regularly to engage and sustain your audience.

Further reading

Holland, M. (2016) *Need a New Year's Resolution – Contribute to the Clinical Librarians Blog in 2016,* https://lihnnclinicallibs.wordpress.com/2016/01/05/need-a-new-years-resolutions-contribute-to-the-clinical-librarians-blog-in-2016-by-matt-holland.

94. Writing business cases

IT IS A very challenging time for LKSs and staff at all levels will find themselves increasingly required to make business cases to develop, strengthen and secure LKSs as budgets are being reduced and services cut. A good, clear and well structured business case can make all the difference to the success of a project, or make a compelling case for securing LKS funds for the coming year.

Skills

Developing skills in writing business cases is essential for LKS staff aiming to progress to management level but it is also essential for everyone in the team to be involved in developing a business case. By involving all members of your team, you will ensure that they are aware of organizational priorities and challenges such as funding cuts which may impact on the delivery of library services in the future.

Purpose

Business cases are usually needed for large-scale projects, restructure of services or redesign proposals, especially when justification for large amounts of money is needed. A good business case is vital to the successful implementation of a project. Robinson (2005) suggests that business cases tend to fall into one of two categories:

- Reactive business cases are written to address a situation which is thrust upon you, for example a freeze in recruitment or a reduction in your yearly budget. Your case would demonstrate an understanding of the organizational context, but would be used to outline the implications of such a reduction on service delivery.
- Proactive business cases are written when you want to introduce a new service, for example to purchase a new library management system or to make a case to employ new staff to support research activity within an academic LKS.

Robinson (2005) also states that a business case can be used as a tool to make daily business decisions which involve pricing, capital investment, product development, project implementation and contracts. Robinson discusses the questions which you should consider when developing a business case, particularly in light of senior position holders and organizational context. She suggests that you consider what questions the Chief Executive might ask (Table 94.1). By addressing these questions in detail, you will demonstrate your awareness of organizational context, priorities and challenges by speaking the language understood by senior managers in the organization.

Consultation

It is essential to involve all relevant parties and stakeholders in a consultation process prior to writing the business case. This results in wider ownership and also ensures that all options and issues are identified at the outset. Consultation with the LKS team is essential, as some members may be wary of the implications of the proposal, or could potentially see it as a threat to the status quo. This general fear of change could impact negatively on the long-term application of the new project (CILIP, 2015). It is also vital to consult a range of organizational stakeholders from the very beginning. This provides an opportunity for you to identify organizational priorities, challenges and the political context, whilst ensuring that your proposal is written in a language and style which takes these into consideration. A wider consultation at the outset will enable you to identify alternative approaches or options which you may not have considered. You could write a short options appraisal for each possible solution, evaluating its impact and include a SWOT analysis for each, and this should be embedded within the final business case to demonstrate analysis of alternative approaches.

Table 94.1 *Writing a business case (Robinson, 2005)*

Why?	How?
• Why do you want to be involved? • Why is this important? • Why now? • Why make this a priority?	• How can this help us achieve our goals? • How do we start this? • How will people find time to contribute? • How can we measure our success?
What?	**When?**
• What are the benefits to the organization? • What resources will we need? • What makes you qualified for this role? • What is the consequence of taking no action?	• When can I expect results? • When will you need my help? • When will I see the impact of this approach? • When should I free up resources?

Structure

A good business case should include (Robinson, 2005 and Platt, 2007):

• executive summary
• description of the current situation and/or problem
• discussion of the various options and alternatives which may solve the

problem or improve the situation
— including a SWOT analysis for each option
- analysis of the benefits of preferred option and rationale for selection
- resources required and costings for preferred option (short and longer term)
— including potential return on investment
- action plan for implementation
- risk assessment
- evaluation methods and measures of success
- recommendations.

👍 Best for

■ Providing a good strong case which is aligned to organizational requirements. It considers alternative approaches and provides a detailed analysis of the benefits and costs associated with the project, which will make it more likely to be accepted by senior managers.

▶ More

■ Business cases tend to be large documents, but you can use these principles for both large and smaller-scale projects.

⚠ To think about

■ Ensure that your business case is closely aligned to organizational priorities and also is realistic and achievable within the existing climate. Consultation with a range of stakeholders and a wide range of team members is key – if you have written the business case in isolation, you are less likely to achieve the funding you need, or get the backing required for success.

References

CILIP (2015) *5 Tips for Making a Successful Business Case*, www.CILIP.org.uk/blog/5-tips-making-successful-business-case-library-access-management. [Accessed 2 January 2016]

Platt, N. (2007) *Writing a Business Case*, http://strategiclibrarian.com/2007/08/08/developing-the-library-business-plan. [Accessed 2 January 2016]

Robinson, L. (2005) Writing a Business Case to Improve Organisational Impact, *Legal Information Management*, **5** (1), 30–3.

95. Writing case studies

ROBERT K. YIN defines a case study as

> a story about something unique, special, or interesting – stories can be about
> individuals, organizations, processes, programs, neighbourhoods, institutions,
> and even events
>
> Yin (2003), cited in Neale, Thapa and Boyce, 2006, 3

There are many definitions of case studies for research, but this quote shows
how diverse the case study can be, which is also true of their application in
LKS. They can be used to provide detailed information about a single case or
can be used across a sector, e.g. public libraries, to describe and compare
events or services in a number of settings.

Approaches

In research, Davey (1991) describes a number of approaches to designing
case studies which include illustrative (a description of events), exploratory
(an investigation of events), cumulative (an ongoing collection of data to
make comparisons and draw conclusions) or critical (designed to examine
a particular cause and effect). Case studies designed for research purposes
are often localized and are developed to learn about a situation by
collecting and evaluating data with a view to making recommendations
and drawing conclusions. Davey (1991) highlights a number of challenges
with the case study as research methodology, as they can be selective in
their use of data, less analytical than other forms of research, lacking in
rigour, difficult to generalize and difficult to control variables when
comparisons are being made.

Uses

Despite these pitfalls, case studies provide an opportunity for LKS staff to
become involved in research and to develop their writing skills. Although
much of what is written about the case study design and process comes from
the research perspective, because they can be descriptive and less analytical
they enable staff to present information in a simple and easy-to-read format.
Case studies can also be used to view a project retrospectively based on an
evaluation of the literature and analysis of the data. This may not be a highly
rigorous approach to research *per se*, but can be useful to identify challenges
or mistakes, to highlight lessons learned and make recommendations for
future change and service development.

As the case study is often less analytical than many other forms of research, it can be a good introduction and less daunting for the novice who wants to develop their writing skills. Short case studies are often written by LKS staff and are shared within the organization to promote services and raise awareness of LKS projects.

Getting published

It can be difficult to get case studies published in scholarly journals, so recommend that your staff do some research into the best place to publish their piece. It is worth reviewing previous editions of a journal to see whether case studies are accepted and what the format is like, and most journals provide authors' notes which give clear information about the types of articles that are accepted and provide a clear layout. However, although some scholarly journals may not accept case studies, there are numerous opportunities to publish in a number of less formal places, whether it be on websites, in blogs or within reports to showcase best practice and share learning across sectors.

Use of case studies in LKS

- The Designing Libraries website includes a number of short case studies from academic libraries, public libraries and school libraries to showcase transformational design in the UK.
- The Arts Council (2013) published a report which includes 10 research case studies of community libraries based on document reviews and interviews with relevant participants.
- Wakeham et al. (2012) published a case study to demonstrate how they developed subject guides based on interviews with users, LKS staff and other LKSs.
- The MAP Toolkit (2015) provides a forum for library staff in the NHS to share projects and demonstrate how they are aligned to key drivers in the organization.
- Fouracre (2015) published a descriptive piece about reviewing collections at the Royal College of Surgeons of England.

Figure 95.1 shows an example structure for a case study from the *Health Information and Libraries Journal* which provides a useful guide of what to include for those who don't know where to start. Advise individuals that if they are submitting a case study to a specific journal, they will always be bound by their specific requirements and should check the authors' notes accordingly.

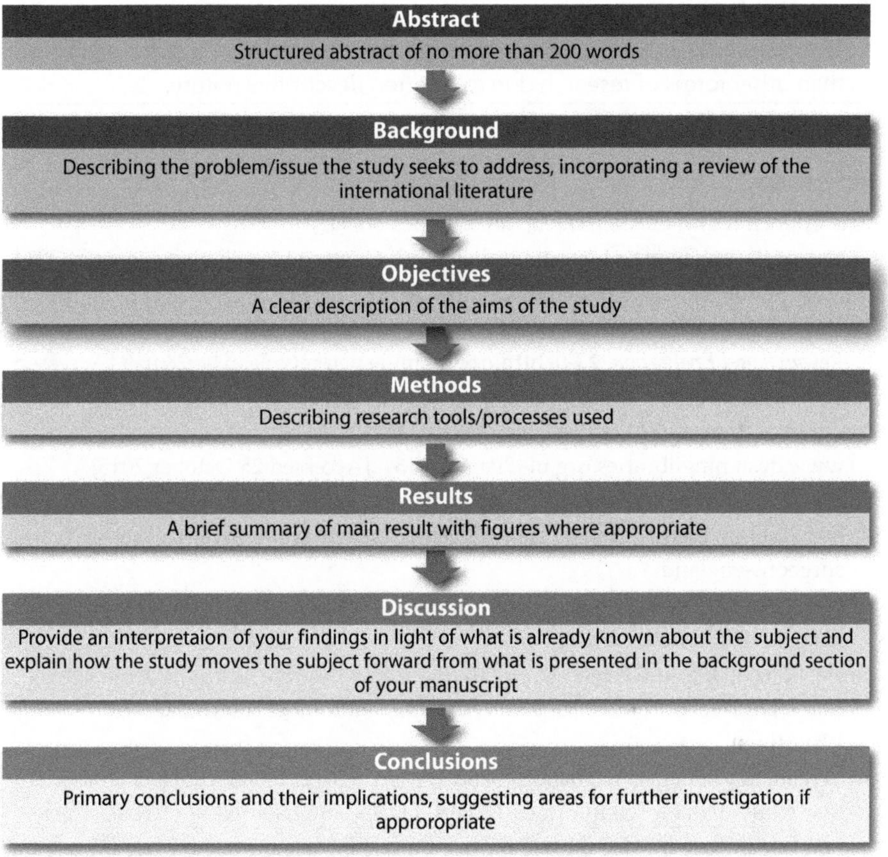

Figure 95.1 *Example structure of case study for the* Health Information and Libraries Journal *(Wiley, 2016, http://onlinelibrary.wiley.com/journal/10.1111/ (ISSN)1471-1842/homepage/ForAuthors.html)*

👍 Best for

- Case studies can be a good introduction to the research process for the individual. They can provide an informal approach to writing and there is scope for publication outside scholarly publications.
- They are good for sharing best practice and raising the profile of the LKS within the organization or the wider LKS community.

▶ More

- Sometimes case studies can be easier and quicker to get published if the author approaches blogs, trade journals or organizational newsletters.

⚠ To think about

■ The case study as a piece of research may be criticized as being less rigorous than other forms of research due to its often descriptive nature.

References

Arts Council (2013) *Community Libraries: 10 case studies,* www.artscouncil.org.uk/media/uploads/pdf/Community_libaries_research_2013 _case_studies.pdf. [Accessed 25 October 2015]

Davey, L. (1991) The Application of Case Study Evaluations, *Practical Assessment, Research and Evaluation,* **2** (9), http://pareonline.net/getvn.asp?v=2&n=9 [Accessed 12 August 2016].

Designing Libraries (2012) *Case Studies,* www.designinglibraries.org.uk/?PageID=134. [Accessed 25 October 2015]

Fouracre, D. (2015) Digitisation at the Royal College of Surgeons England, http://blog.wellcomelibrary.org/2015/06/digitsation-at-the-royal-college-of-surgeons-england.

MAP Toolkit (2015) *Case Studies,* https://maptoolkit.wordpress.com/case-studies. [Accessed 25 October 2015]

Neale, P., Thapa, S. and Boyce, C. (2006) *Preparing a Case Study: a guide for designing and conducting a case study for evaluation input,* Pathfinder International, Watertown.

Wakeham, M., Roberts, A., Shelley, J. and Wells, P. (2012) Library Subject Guides: a case study of evidence-informed library development, *Journal of Librarianship and Information Science,* **44** (3), 199–207.

Wiley (2016) *Author Guidelines for the Health Information and Libraries Journal,* http://onlinelibrary.wiley.com/journal/10.1111/(ISSN)1471-1842/homepage/ ForAuthors.html. [Accessed 23 April 2016]

Yin, R. K. (2003) *Case Study Research: design and methods,* Thousand Oaks. Sage Publications.

Further reading

Sadeh, T. (2008) User Experience in the Library: a case study, *New Library World,* **109** (1/2), 7–24.

96. Writing e-mails

THE USE OF e-mail is central to most business operations and LKSs are no exception. It is one of the quickest and easiest methods of communicating with colleagues and users. The language used and the way that e-mails are written and managed can have a huge impact on the recipient. Many organizations have an e-mail acceptable use policy, which is likely to outline how e-mail should be used and whether there are any restrictions on employees, for example, whether they can use work e-mail for personal use. As a supervisor or manager, you need to have a good understanding of your organization's e-mail policy so that you can direct your staff to these documents if there are any issues with the way they use it. However, a policy will not outline how you use e-mail within your LKS and, to a large extent, how *you* use it to communicate with your employees and direct reports will set the tone for your service.

Your employees will use e-mail to communicate with each other, colleagues throughout the organization, LKS staff outside your service and crucially with your users; it will be an integral part of their working lives. E-mail may be used in one-to-one conversations, including a select group of people or on a distribution list where many of the recipients are not known to the sender.

Issues

However, just because e-mail is quick and easy to use, Morgan (2013) states that it can become a source of misery for staff. We are all too familiar with the overloaded inbox or wading our way through a long thread within a forwarded message to try and find the crux of the conversation. Also, the immediacy of e-mail has changed our expectations about turnaround and the e-mail inbox can soon become a pressured environment. Morgan (2013) suggests that we are prone to overuse e-mail, which can have a negative impact on the way our employees see us and the way we see them. Sometimes we should just talk to each other rather than e-mailing colleagues sitting two feet away from us.

Creating a good impression

A well structured e-mail creates a positive impression, whilst a poorly constructed e-mail will create a negative one. As a communication tool e-mail is very quick, but can be the cause of misunderstandings, as it is one-dimensional and open to misinterpretation, since the recipient cannot see other communication cues such as body language. For conflict resolution, the phone or a face-to-face meeting are preferable approaches, as an e-mail exchange can exacerbate an already difficult situation (Romkema, 2012). E-mail is a skill that we all need to hone, particularly at work, where we need to find the balance between a friendly and a professional tone.

Potter (2012) considers how we can use e-mail as a promotional or marketing tool; when done well it can create traffic to a website or resources, but when used poorly it can alienate users. Send an e-mail newsletter and with a single click users are directed to an online resource in a way that is not possible with the printed medium, but be careful to avoid information overload. Make every contact count!

Below are some useful tips to ensure that you and your staff use e-mail to create the right impression (Mind Tools, 2015; Romkema, 2012; Morgan, 2013):

- Have a clear subject, which outlines the purpose for the reader, particularly if you are using e-mail for promotional activities. The subject line should grab the attention and draw the reader in, as you need them to open it.
- Think about your audience; you may use different tones for colleagues, managers and users. It's okay to be less formal than a letter, but it may not be okay to use emoticons such as :-), slang, jargon or acronyms.
- Ensure that each e-mail covers only one topic, has a clear structure and clearly outlines expected actions. Short sections and bullet points can help give clarity; remember that people often skim-read e-mails and so could miss important points.
- Don't send large attachments, as these may not arrive, due to e-mail inbox limits.
- Don't e-mail when angry! Write a draft, save it, take some time then rewrite it when you are calmer.
- E-mail is a permanent record. You don't know where it will be used and who will see it, so always write an e-mail as if everyone will see it.
- Set standards about how quickly you will respond to an e-mail. Agree that you and your team will respond in three days and stick to this. If you can't deal with the query immediately, acknowledge receipt and state when you will be in touch.
- Ensure that every e-mail is signed off with name, job title and contact details. Some libraries use e-mail signatures to promote resources, so standardize these across your team.
- Ensure that you protect the e-mail addresses of the recipients if you are sending to a group. If you use bcc rather than cc, the group members will not be able to see the e-mail addresses of the other recipients.
- Manage your inbox, using folders, colours, and flags to ensure that issues are identifiable and dealt with.

👍 Best for

- Communicating quickly and efficiently with users, colleagues and friends. Can be a useful marketing and promotional tool to direct users to online resources.
- Can be used by employees to develop their profile and connect with librarians and potential employers via mailing lists, for example.

► **More**

■ If you make your team adhere to e-mail rules, ensure that you do the same. Lead by example and demonstrate what good e-mail use looks like.

⚠ **To think about**

■ Don't overuse e-mail, and think about your tone. E-mail is not a good way to reprimand your staff or have those difficult conversations. Make time to speak to your teams face to face and use e-mail effectively to share information.

References

Mind Tools (2015) *Writing Effective Emails*, www.mindtools.com/CommSkll/ EmailCommunication.htm. [Accessed 26 October 2015]

Morgan, J. (2013) *5 Ways Email Makes Your Employees Miserable*, www.forbes.com/sites/jacobmorgan/2013/10/15/5-ways-email-makes-your-employees-miserable. [Accessed 26 October 2015]

Potter, N. (2012) *The Library Marketing Toolkit*, Facet Publishing, London.

Romkema, J. (2012) *10 Tips for Effective Email Communication*, www.globallearningpartners.com/blog/10-tips-for-effective-email-communication. [Accessed 26 October 2015]

97. Writing journal articles

GETTING WORK PUBLISHED in scholarly academic or professional trade journals is a great way of raising the profile both of individuals within the team and your service as a whole. Journal articles can reach a wide national and international audience and can open many doors, including invitations to speak at national conferences, or provide opportunities for individuals to become involved in LKS projects with a wider reach. Not only are they a great way of disseminating research or your LKS's work, they can also be a good way of sharing individual learning from undergraduate or postgraduate studies, as a good dissertation can be converted into a journal article with a little formatting. Whilst this Tip focuses on writing for academic or professional journal articles, it should be read alongside other sections of this book which consider the process of writing newsletters, case studies or blog posts.

Opportunities

When reviewing the literature, there are lots of opportunities for budding writers to tackle a range of subjects, including larger research projects, smaller local projects, reflective articles or literature reviews. This is not an exhaustive list, but gives an indication of some article types which have been published successfully. Journal articles are an excellent method of sharing learning from internal projects or activities, such as adopting a new teaching method or designing a new website.

Ultimately, anything which would be of interest to your peers can be written about and submitted to a journal for publication.

Topics

When it comes to choosing the topic for a writing project, there are no limitations and Fallon (2009) suggests that a good place to start is by jotting down some ideas that interest the writer. Whilst as a LKS manager or supervisor you may have specific ideas of the projects that you would like your staff to write about, they are the ones doing the writing and therefore they need to be enthused by their topic. Writing an article can be a long and difficult journey, and so it is important that the writer is fully engaged and supported by you to ensure a successful outcome.

Choosing the right journal

Once the author has decided on the topic, choosing the right journal is the next step. This will occur before much of the writing takes place, as the choice of journal will impact upon the article type and define the structure and format to be adhered to during the writing process. Scholarly academic journals such as the *Health Information Libraries Journal* are usually subject to peer review. This means that articles are read by library professionals prior to publication, without disclosing the author's name to them, to remove bias. Peer reviewers read and comment upon the article content and make suggestions for improvement before it is accepted for publication. Being published in academic journals is a rewarding process but it can be challenging and competition can be fierce.

Professional or trade journals, such as *CILIP Update* magazine, tend to be published more frequently than academic journals and often have a wider readership (Fallon, 2009). Whilst academic journals are likely to be more theoretical or research-based, Fallon indicates that articles published in professional journals are usually focused on the practical application of a project or experience. Wherever the author chooses to publish, the article can be submitted to only one journal at a time, so doing some research to find the right place is essential to ensuring a successful outcome. It may be useful to contact the editor of the journal informally, prior to submission, to ask whether they would be interested in publishing something on the proposed topic.

Abstracts

Usually prior to article submission, a short abstract of approximately 200 words (depending on the requirements of the specific journal) will need to be submitted. Abstracts can be structured or unstructured and again this will be outlined in the journal's author guidelines. Fallon (2015) indicates that a good abstract is not an introduction to the article, but should guide the reader through its key points, summarizing all relevant content; she suggests that the draft be completed before the article is begun and be revisited once completed. If the author is unsure about how to approach abstract writing, advise them to read abstracts for articles on similar topics which have already been published in their journal of choice.

Streamlining the process

Here are some additional tips which will help to streamline the process for individuals who are hoping to publish journal articles:

- Review the literature – this will indicate whether the proposed article is unique and will help the author to select the most appropriate journal for submission. If a journal has recently published an article on a similar topic, another article is less likely to be accepted, so it may be worth considering alternative options.
- Consider priorities – think about what the author wants to achieve by publishing the piece. Is it important that the article is published in a peer-reviewed journal? Do they want to reach a particular audience? Does the time to publication matter? Have they considered publishing in open access journals versus traditional journals?
- Notes for authors – these provide crucial guidance for authors and should always be checked at the beginning of the writing process. They will advise the types of article which are accepted by the journal and provide guidance on the required structure or headings to be used. These notes will also outline formatting requirements such as referencing, structure, font size, images and numbering. Ensuring that the article is produced in the preferred style of the journal will improve the chance of its being successful and save precious editing time for the author.
- Writing style – everyone has their personal writing style, but academic journals may prefer a more formal tone than professional or trade journals. Articles which have already been published can provide some useful guidance on writing style. As a general rule, it is good practice to ensure clarity of writing, to avoid jargon and to minimize complex language which can result in confusing messages. Suggest that any article is proofread by someone who does not understand the topic,

maybe a friend or family member, asking them to highlight any parts that are difficult to understand.

- Editing and revising – ensure that the author is prepared to revise and edit the article both prior to and after submission. Sometimes it can be disheartening if they feel that they will never complete the final article. It is rare for an article to be accepted without recommended changes or revision and the author should also be prepared to understand that an article may not be accepted by the editor of the journal. It is always worth considering alternative journals for submission and revising the article accordingly.

Example from practice: Amy Finnegan – LKS professional (NICE)

In 2016 I co-authored an article that was accepted for publication in a library journal. I would definitely recommend co-authoring an article with a friend or trusted colleague, as I found writing an article requires motivation and honesty; I appreciated having someone to discuss ideas, issues and the submission process with.

We selected a journal that we knew to be supportive. This was important to us, as it was the first article that we had written and we were unfamiliar with the process. During the process of creating and submitting an article for publication, I have learnt a lot of lessons that I will be aware of when writing another article in the future. I'd definitely recommend writing an article, particularly if you want to gain an insight into the world of an academic/researcher.

🖒 Best for

- Sharing information about your service and projects with a wider audience, which is great for building the reputation of both your LKS as a whole and individuals working within the team.

▶ More

- You can help your staff to improve their writing and develop their confidence by regularly asking them to submit written pieces to smaller publications and also to encourage wider reading of articles within the profession to encourage thought and broaden experience. Fallon (2009) suggests that the best way of improving writing skills is to write regularly.

⚠ To think about

- Writing can be a time-consuming process, especially when it takes place

outside day-to-day work. If possible, make time for staff to write at work.
- Once the article has been drafted and submitted for publication, it can take months before it is actually published. This is particularly true for submissions to academic, peer-reviewed journals, where rewrites and amendments are common. Writers also need to be prepared to accept and act upon constructive feedback.

References

Fallon, H. (2009) The Academic Writing Toolkit: writing for professional and peer reviewed journals, *SCONUL Focus*, **45**, 66–71.
Fallon, H. (2015) *Writing Abstracts for Peer-Reviewed Journals*, http://academicwritinglibrarian.blogspot.co.uk/2015/07/writing-abstracts-for-peer-reviewed.html#.Vxikg_krJdg. [Accessed 21 April 2016]

98. Writing newsletters

NEWSLETTERS ARE ISSUED periodically, and can be powerful advocacy tools for connecting with LKS users, promoting new services or marketing activities. It is also worthwhile exploring whether any internal newsletters are published within your organization and submitting articles about your service to these. Organizational newsletters or bulletins often have a wider reach than the traditional LKS newsletter and can be useful to get your messages out; the communications or media teams will be able to advise you about the internal publication routes available and the processes involved.

For staff who want to develop their experience of writing for an LKS audience, recommend that they look at special-interest groups, as these often provide opportunities to submit short articles. It could be just the opportunity that your team member is looking for! The CILIP *Health Libraries Group Newsletter* (CILIP, 2016) is one such newsletter, which encourages health librarians to submit article and book reviews, or share reports from meetings with its readership. There may be other opportunities for staff to submit articles to LKS professional newsletters, where they can report on conference attendance or share their work-based experience with their peers.

Target audience

Whichever type of newsletter your staff are writing for, it is important that articles consider the target audience. To some extent, the structure, format and style of the article will be dictated by the editor, so for external newsletters it is worth getting in touch prior to submitting your content. Articles within your LKS newsletter should be linked to your marketing plan as an extension of your promotional activity and be written in an engaging and less formal style than a journal article, for example. Spend some time thinking of catchy titles for newsletter articles to draw the reader in and ensure that articles are short, clear, informal and accompanied by images or photographs.

This approach will make content more engaging and keep your audience interested. A range of articles on different topics by different authors will serve a wider audience. With publishing tools being widely accessible, and including a range of pre-set templates, the e-mail newsletter has taken over from the printed version to some extent. Electronic newsletters are easy to create as a simple pdf file and disseminate to a wide range of users; archives can simply be stored on the library website or VLE.

Example from practice: Anne Weaver – Head of Library and Information Services (school library)

In her article about school libraries and advocacy, Anne Weaver (2010) discusses how the newsletter is a key method of communicating with the whole school community. It provides a crucial role in informing stakeholders about the activities of the service, with a long-term view of establishing value, securing budgets and maintaining staff.

Anne discusses the transition from creating a printed newsletter, which is valuable to the service, but the production of which is time-consuming and expensive. The introduction of e-mail newsletters has meant that they can be easily distributed at limited cost, enabling the school library service to communicate directly with students, parents, teachers and governors.

⸂ Best for

- Newsletters can be an excellent marketing or promotional tool for your service. You can use them to share your news stories within both the organization and the wider profession.
- Writing for a newsletter can be a good introduction to writing for individuals within the team. It can help them to build confidence in their writing ability and provide a foundation for writing for wider publication.

▶ More

- Blogs provide an alternative to the printed newsletter and can be more flexible, updated regularly and can also provide statistical information about readership and reach. Read Tip 93 (p. 245) on blog posts for more information.

▲ To think about

- ■ Printing a glossy newsletter can be a costly and time-consuming process, and printed newsletters can also be viewed as old-fashioned. It is also difficult to assess the impact of a printed newsletter and know whether it is being read by the target audience without undertaking extensive research. Explore the potential for developing an electronic newsletter which can be e-mailed to your target audience or creating an electronic newsletter using MailChimp (2016) or blogging software, as these often provide some statistical information about impact and readership.

References

CILIP (2016) *Health Libraries Group Newsletter*, www.cilip.org.uk/health-libraries-group/newsletter. [Accessed 21 April 2016]

MailChimp (2016) *MailChimp*, http://mailchimp.com. [Accessed 23 April 2016]

Weaver, A. (2010) Library Trailers – Using E-Mail, E-Mail Newsletters and Annual Reports for Advocacy, *Access*, **24** (3), 20–3.

Further reading

LIHNN (2016) *LIHNNK UP: read the newsletter*, www.lihnn.nhs.uk/index.php/lihnnhome/lihnnk-up/read-the-newsletter. [Accessed 21 April 2016]

99. Writing procedures

PROCEDURES PROVIDE DETAIL about established processes which are clearly presented and adopt a step-by-step approach. They are crucial documents which outline exactly what needs to happen and how this will be done, thus ensuring that tasks are carried out in a consistent fashion and in a predefined order (Oxford Dictionaries, 2016). Most LKSs will have a range of procedures governing their work. These are essential documents which ensure that business can continue in an uninterrupted fashion, enabling any team member to pick up a task at any given time. Procedures are useful for complex tasks that include a lot of stages, activities which are integral to the effective running of the service and occasional (e.g. annual) tasks which are not part of the day-to-day routine.

Well written and easy to follow procedures are essential for streamlining processes, ensuring that services run efficiently and sharing information with the wider team. Therefore, having staff who are able to write well and develop clear guidance documents is vital. Team members who are good at writing procedures can also use this skill to create user-focused documents, such as guides and instructions, which enable library members to get the most out of your service.

Templates

A standardized template will ensure that all documents are produced in a consistent format and will help you to control the quality of your documentation. This will be really helpful for team members who are new to the process of writing procedures. There is no single format for a procedure, so it is important that whatever you choose works for your service; typically, a template will include some or all of the following:

- title
- author name
- date approved
- approving group or person
- review date
- version
- introduction
- purpose of the document
- roles and responsibilities
- glossary of terms
- the content – step-by-step procedure
- references
- appendices
- changes or amendments.

To ensure good governance practices are adhered to, procedures will also include page numbers and a footer which includes the document title, date approved and version. Figure 99.1 presents a flowchart for the process of writing procedures.

Tips for writing procedures

The following tips are adapted from Mind Tools (2016):

- Keep language simple and clear.
- Consider the use of documents.
- Consider whether overlong procedures can be broken down into smaller documents.
- Avoid ambiguous terms, e.g. 'may' or 'should', for clarity of focus.
- Use headings and bullet points.
- Ensure the procedure is tested by someone who is not familiar with the process.
- Include only relevant information.
- Include images, graphs, tables to present information simply.

- Develop a simple flowchart to represent the procedure.
- Write for the appropriate audience; you can check literacy levels using the SMOG calculator at the National Literacy Trust (2016) website.
- Always proofread.
- Get someone from another team who is not familiar with the procedure to test it. If they can't follow it, then it needs changing.

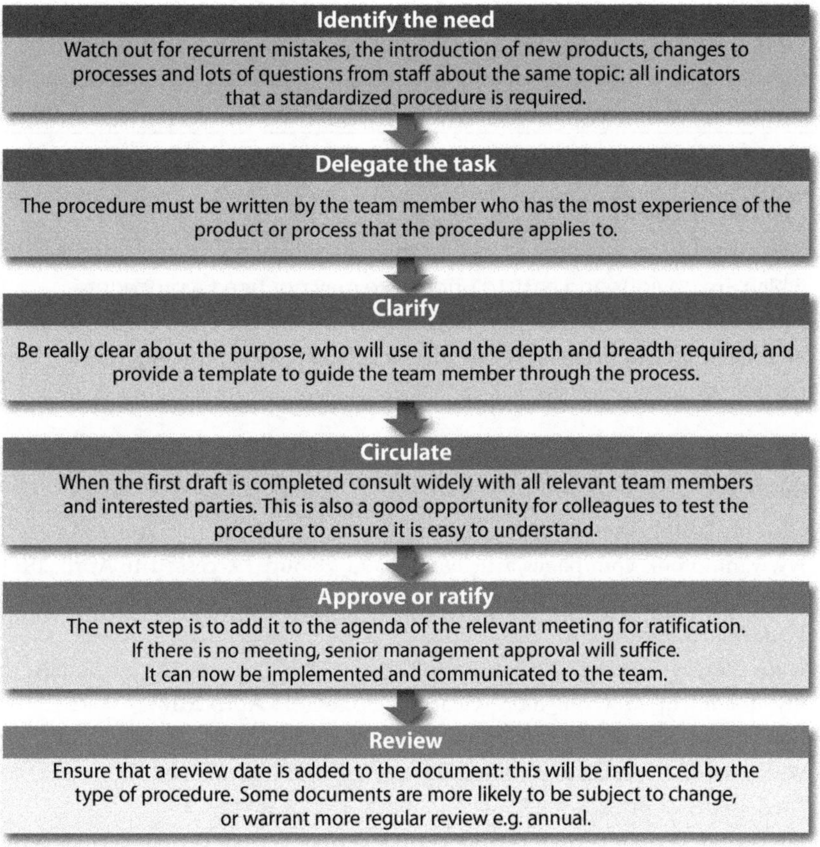

Identify the need
Watch out for recurrent mistakes, the introduction of new products, changes to processes and lots of questions from staff about the same topic: all indicators that a standardized procedure is required.

Delegate the task
The procedure must be written by the team member who has the most experience of the product or process that the procedure applies to.

Clarify
Be really clear about the purpose, who will use it and the depth and breadth required, and provide a template to guide the team member through the process.

Circulate
When the first draft is completed consult widely with all relevant team members and interested parties. This is also a good opportunity for colleagues to test the procedure to ensure it is easy to understand.

Approve or ratify
The next step is to add it to the agenda of the relevant meeting for ratification. If there is no meeting, senior management approval will suffice. It can now be implemented and communicated to the team.

Review
Ensure that a review date is added to the document: this will be influenced by the type of procedure. Some documents are more likely to be subject to change, or warrant more regular review e.g. annual.

Figure 99.1 *Flowchart for writing procedures*

One final note: whilst this Tip focuses on LKS procedures, many of the suggestions can also be applied to user guides, instructions and policy documents. Whilst the templates will be different, the processes will be the same.

👍 Best for

- Sharing knowledge within the team and ensuring that vital information is not kept within an individual's head. This is essential to maintain business continuity when individuals leave or are on sick leave.
- Ensuring that good governance practice is adhered to and that documents are controlled is good for maintaining a high-quality and effective service.

▶ More

- Writing procedures which are clear and easy to follow is a skill which can be transferred to other areas of your service, such as writing guidance and user manuals which LKS members can understand.

⚠ To think about

- Don't introduce new procedures for the sake of having procedures. Tasks which are obvious and easy to undertake may not need a procedure. Procedures should be used for tasks which are complex and crucial to the effective running of the service, otherwise you are introducing bureaucracy for the sake of it.

References

Mind Tools (2016) *Writing a Procedure*, www.mindtools.com/pages/article/newTMC_78.htm. [Accessed 16 April 2016]

National Literacy Trust (2016) *How Can I Assess the Readability of my Document or Write More Clearly?*, www.literacytrust.org.uk/about/faqs/710_how_can_i_assess_the_readability_of_my_document_or_write_more_clearly. [Accessed 16 April 2016]

Oxford Dictionaries (2016) Definition of 'procedure' in English, www.oxforddictionaries.com/definition/english/procedure. [Accessed 15 April 2016]

100. Writing project plans

THE PLANNING PROCESS is a crucial activity for any project to be successful and developing your staff in this area is vital to ensuring that your service grows and adapts to change. Effective project planning ensures that outcomes are delivered on schedule and within budget and that everyone involved knows what is expected of them. In this Tip we will discuss developing the initial project brief and the creation of project plans, which should be monitored throughout the lifetime of the project.

The brief

The project brief or specification is sometimes called a project implementation document (PID) or a project charter, and this will be informed by the project management approach that is used (Mind Tools, 2016). Whatever you call this document, it will clearly define the project proposal and intended outcomes, including as much detail as possible. If the parameters of the project are not clearly outlined from the outset, this will contribute to the project's not being completed or failure to achieve the intended outcomes (Young, 2013). It is therefore essential that all resource requirements, timescales, team roles and limitations are described in detail from the beginning. The entire project team and all relevant stakeholders must be involved in developing the brief, to mitigate misunderstandings and to manage expectations. Involving the entire project team in the planning process and securing agreement about their roles and the project outcomes means that the project is more likely to succeed and individuals are more likely to commit to fulfilling their responsibilities.

There is no single approach to presenting a project brief, and to some extent this will be dictated by your organization, the methodology you use and the size of the project. As a minimum, your project brief should answer the following questions (Young, 2013; Mind Tools, 2016):

- Why is the project needed?
- What is the scope of the project?
- What are the boundaries of the project?
- What are the principal objectives?
- Who are the key stakeholders?
- What resources are needed?
- How much will it cost?
- Who needs to be involved and what are their roles?
- What risks have been identified?
- What is the expected output or outcome?
- How long will the project take?

The plan

Another vital component of delivering a successful project is to produce a realistic and achievable (Carroll, 2009) plan which will guide the whole team throughout the process. Newton (2013, 40) defines a project plan simply as 'a set of structured information that defines the what, the when and the who'. This document will translate the broader objectives outlined in the project brief into a detailed and time-bound action plan which everyone understands (Young, 2013). It will break down each of the main project aims into a series of smaller SMART objectives (see Tip 25, p. 59), each of which is then allocated to a member of the team. The size and complexity of the project plan will be dependent upon the scale of the project and the number of aims or milestones. Newton (2013) highlights that there are many different types of plans, which include work schedules, resource plans, risk logs, Gantt charts and communication plans, so it is worth spending time identifying those that you want your staff to use.

Monitoring

Once the project brief is signed off and the project plan is in place, the project can begin. For success to be achieved, it is essential that the project plans are monitored regularly via meetings and that as key milestones are completed this is communicated to all stakeholders, even those who are not actively involved in delivering the project. Regular meetings, project update reports and a good communication plan are all ways of keeping projects on track and communicating progress and will help you to identify any risks which could threaten the success of the project. As the line manager or supervisor, you may not be directly involved in the project deliverables, but you will play an essential part in supporting your team members to deliver the project, by helping them to solve problems, dealing with resourcing issues and holding them to account, thus ensuring that the project is delivered on time and within budget.

Templates

There is no single template for initiating and planning projects, so check with your organization's project management team to identify accepted practice and documentation which you can use or adapt to meet your needs. Alternatively, there are a number of templates available on the internet or in project management books, for example those provided by the Project Agency, which you can find on the BusinessBalls website (Chapman, 2016).

🖒 Best for

- Encouraging your team members to adopt a standardized approach to managing projects and by developing their skills in this area, ensuring that any projects which are instigated within your LKS have a good chance of success.
- Good planning skills are also transferable to other areas of professional development, such as developing personal development plans at an individual level, as they involve similar skills.

► **More**

■ For team members who need additional support in this area, suggest that they attend a project management course; some suggestions are provided in Tip 72 (p. 186).

⚠ To think about

■ Projects which are not well planned will be disorganized, have unclear outcomes, be likely to run over budget, take longer to complete or fail completely.

■ Good planning from idea to implementation ensures that the project matches organizational priorities and will manage the expectations of individuals within the team and key stakeholders. Failure to involve everyone and communicate effectively can result in internal politics and misunderstandings which will challenge the project's success.

References

Carroll, J. (2009) *Project Management for Effective Business Change,* Easy Steps, Southam.

Chapman, A. (2016) *Blank Project Management Templates: saving time! saving money! saving stress!,* www.businessballs.com/project%20management%20templates.pdf. [Accessed 10 April 2016]

Mind Tools (2016) *Project Initiation Documents,* www.mindtools.com/pages/article/newPPM_85.htm. [Accessed 16 April 2016]

Newton, R. (2013) *The Project Management Book,* Pearson Education, Harlow.

Young, T. L. (2013) *Successful Project Management,* Kogan Page, London.

101. Writing reports

REPORT WRITING SKILLS are essential in the workplace and you and your teams will be expected to write reports to share information about your service with others, or to provide a record of activities or projects that you have completed (Greenhall, 2010). Some examples of routine reports that you may need to write are annual reports summarizing performance, reports outlining progress and completion of LKS projects and incident reports, all of which may vary in length, breadth and scope but will also have a number of similarities.

Purpose

When asking your team members to write a report for you, ensure that you provide clear and detailed guidance outlining the exact purpose of the report, as this will inform the approach to planning and structure used. Greenhall (2010) suggests that the following eight questions should be answered before embarking on a report to ensure that the objectives are clearly defined from the outset:

1 Why is the report being written?
2 Who will read it?
3 Who else will read it?
4 Why do they need it?
5 What do they already know?
6 What do they need to know?
7 What don't they need to know?
8 What will they use the information for?

Once the purpose of the report is understood, encourage your staff to gather together all relevant information which they feel should be included in the report, considering the audience that the report is aimed at. Greenhall (2010) suggests that mind mapping is a great technique that can be used to brain-dump all information which you think should be included in the report and a subsequent mind map can then be created to group similar items together, creating a clear and logical structure.

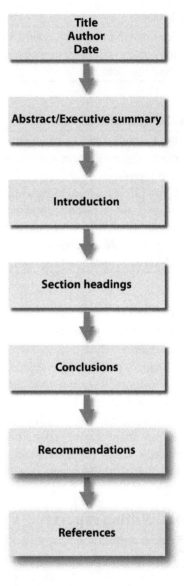

Figure 101.1 *Report structure*

Structure

Whilst the structure of a report may vary, generally most examples will follow some version of the structure shown in Figure 101.1.

All reports should be clear, concise and to the point and it is good practice to include headings and subheadings to enable the reader to go to relevant information quickly and easily. It is also good practice to include charts, images, tables and graphs, which are useful tools for providing data and information clearly and succinctly. Using a good clear font such as Arial 12 point, short paragraphs and sentences, emboldened headings and bullet points are all great ways of making the content of a report accessible.

Proofreading

Finally, offer to proofread the report for your team member before publishing it, to ensure that the language used is clear and that the finished product is easy to understand. The Open University (2015) offer a free 15-hour online course which is designed to help students write effective essays and reports, and would be a useful basis for those in your team who need to develop these skills. In addition, Greenhall's (2010) book includes a number of activities and checklists to enhance the report writing process.

🖒 Best for

■ Reports are great for presenting information for a specific purpose and for a specific audience in a clear style using a formal structure which makes it easy to navigate.

▶ More

■ Staff will be expected to write reports for a number of purposes in the workplace and will need to write reports as part of their study or continuing professional development.

▲ To think about

■ Overlong, rambling discussions without headings or bullet points are essays not reports.

References

Greenhall, M. (2010) *Report Writing: skills training course*, Universe of Learning, Bury.
Open University (2015) *Essay and Report Writing Skills*, www.open.edu/openlearn/education/essay-and-report-writing-skills/content-section-3. [Accessed 29 December 2015]

Index